VOICES FROM THE REAR

VOICES FROM THE

REAR

Vietnam 1969-1970

George M. Watson, Jr.

Copyright © 2001 by George M. Watson, Jr.

Library of Congress Number:		2001116399
ISBN #:	Hardcover	0-7388-6314-9
	Softcover	0-7388-6315-7

All rights reserved. No part of this book may be reproduced or transmitted in any form or by any means, electronic or mechanical, including photocopying, recording, or by any information storage and retrieval system, without permission in writing from the copyright owner.

This book was printed in the United States of America.

To order additional copies of this book, contact:
Xlibris Corporation
1-888-7-XLIBRIS
www.Xlibris.com
Orders@Xlibris.com

Contents

ACKNOWLEDGMENTS 9
PREFACE 11
CHAPTER 1—BASIC 15
CHAPTER 2—ADVANCED INDIVIDUAL TRAINING 52
CHAPTER 3—CHERRY 83
CHAPTER 4—THE BEST OF BIEN HOA 127
CHAPTER 5—PHU BAI 171
CHAPTER 6—REST AND RECUPERATION 220
CHAPTER 7—GOODBYE, VIETNAM 235
CHAPTER 8—THE FINAL CHALLENGE 279
EPILOGUE 313
GLOSSARY 317

Dedicated to
my compassionate wife Nancy Louise Watson
whose constant letters made my ordeal survivable
and this account possible

Acknowledgments

While the bulk of this book was accomplished from my memory and photographs and collection of letters to my wife Nancy, I am thankful for the support and time of several of my professional coworkers. I appreciate the careful reads and suggestions provided by Dr. Perry Jamieson, Dr. Wayne W. Thompson, Dr. Daniel R. Mortensen, Dr. Mark Grandstaff, Dr. Michael Gorn and Bernard C. Nalty. Barbara Wittig and Dr. Priscilla D. Jones provided superb editorial assistance and suggestions, as did retired Air Force historian, Dr. Fred Beck. David R. Chenoweth made excellent suggestions for photographs, and Dr. Richard I. Wolf provided tremendous help in formatting the work for publication. Dan Cragg and Walter J. Boyne, both accomplished authors, read the piece and provided encouragement. To the above and to any I might not have mentioned I am eternally grateful.

PREFACE

The late 1960s and early 1970s was a difficult time for American society. The Vietnam war had a tremendous impact on several generations of Americans. At the same time attitudes towards that war radically changed. The axiom that a democracy could not long sustain a protracted conflict became a reality. By 1969 and certainly by 1970 the counterculture's stance against the war was gaining strength, penetrating the souls and minds of that ever evasive silent majority. It is within this time frame that my story is set.

Highly emotional experiences are difficult to forget. They are imprinted for life. Fear, frustration, hatred, physical pain, helplessness, loneliness, sadness, and humor had never been as sharply concentrated before. I wrote this book because I wanted to share them. I wanted to reveal my ordeal to show others what it was like serving in the U.S. Army and in Vietnam during the period January 1969 to January 1971. Although this was my experience, these feelings and views were felt and expressed by many who endured a similar fate. Indeed, my Vietnam ordeal was representative of what the majority of the 2.6 million young men who served in that unpopular war observed. The whole experience conjured up an awareness that I had never sensed before.

When I returned from Vietnam I shared stories. I found that I could entertain a friend who was a known talker and possessed a fine sense of humor. He called my anecdotes "great" and said that they would soon become his yarns. I felt I had a story to tell. Soon after at graduate school a fellow student commented that my GI Bill, which didn't even cover the annual tuition, was worth more than her National Defense Fellowship. It was as if the veterans didn't deserve the GI Bill. My blood boiled and I quickly snapped back, saying that the GI Bill ought to be worth five times as much as her stipend, especially since she didn't have to give up two years of her life for it.

When I finished school in 1974 I was looking for permanent employment and working as a temporary employee for Manpower Inc. I occasionally confronted an employer who blamed the plight of the economy and the reason that I couldn't find a full time job on all those hippies like me who protested the war. These people did not know that I served in the war or anything about my background. All they knew was that I didn't have a job. I wanted to make it known to these Archie Bunker types that a lot of decent hard working students, many with college degrees with career goals, had served their time in Vietnam. Many came back to a tighter job market and could not find regular employment. There were many men who worked their way through school and did not have the wherewithal—time and money—to attend every protest movement. Nor did they have the influence to avoid the draft or join the crowded National Guard rosters. They were faced with a dilemma. Despite their animosity towards the war many were eventually caught up in the war. This paradox confronted many soldiers. I thought that this was a point to be set straight.

During the late 1970s and early 1980s I talked to contemporaries who had not served in the military or in Vietnam. I mentioned the sheer trauma and pain of being drafted, emphasizing that the draftees really and truly fought that war. I received remarks such as "Well, that is the way it is in all wars and we can't change that." A jolt of pain passed through my stomach. It was as if I was being dismissed and my service invalidated. It was as if that whole generation of Vietnam veterans was responsible for some sort of negative aberration on the hitherto winning march of American History. Other draftees had fought and won in other wars; it was only the

VOICES FROM THE REAR

Vietnam draftees who had put a blot on that otherwise spotless record. And worse yet was that I was being slighted by individuals who had not served a single day in the military.

At the end of the 1980s I would meet younger people in their twenties who had no idea what the Vietnam war was all about or what it was like having lived through those times. It was then that I started to put down my ideas on paper.

I guess both consciously and subconsciously I had intended to write something about this experience. My memories did not wither with age. Yet, I needed time to digest the thoughts that would not fade. I remember telling guys in Vietnam that I would someday have to write about this ordeal. Some responded "Put me in the book." In Vietnam I wrote religiously to my girlfriend Nancy whom I later married, about my experiences in Basic Training, AIT, and Vietnam. I asked her to preserve the two hundred and twenty-five letters that I sent. While stationed at Ft. Dix following Vietnam I worked for several evenings during the fall of 1970 pulling out the letters and placing them in chronological order, awaiting some proper time to piece the story together. These letters remained with me as I moved and were stored in a box marked "Vietnam Letters." These letters and my personal recollections became the framework upon which this book is based. Only on those rare occasions where something derogatory or negative has been stated about an individual's actions have I substituted an alias. Otherwise I have used the names of persons as I remember them.

CHAPTER 1

BASIC

It was cold, about 10 degrees above zero and snowing. Winters in Maine never seemed as bad. The memory of a Christmas dawn in the late 1950s returned briefly. Long johns, sweaters, an overcoat, and a Navy watch cap tied down with a scarf held off a sub-zero chill as I waded through five-foot snowdrifts with a happy dog darting around my legs. Quiet white peace, and warmth, prevailed eons ago. I knew I was wiser on that Christmas morning than now, a huddled twenty-four-year-old outside a dim barracks at Ft. Dix, New Jersey, on January 7, 1969. In shared misery, nearly 75 of us stood shifting from one foot to the other, our entire collective humanity sunk within ourselves.

A voice of authority rang out from the head of the line. "You'll be out of here within an hour and you will receive a good night's sleep."

Oh, bullshit! It was already 2:30 in the morning. Two hours later, the shivering mass of us took our Army-issue blankets and stumbled into wooden buildings to find bunks. The earlier arrivals were already snoring in every rack available. We sank to the floor, but the wooden planks looked as good as any mattress.

Lying there with now-familiar anxiety rolling around the pit of my stomach, I ran over the events of the last twenty-four hours, and the twenty-four years before that. Most of my fellow-sufferers were then in a group entering the United States Army Recruiting Station and Induction Center on Forest Avenue in Portland, Maine. After wading through a ream of paperwork that made me government-issue, I had three hours to kill while waiting for an assembly in which we would swear the standard oath of allegiance. A familiar face among the enlisted men in the station turned out to be a friend from the local campus of the University of Maine. What a break for Ed Millett! The sole son of an infirm mother, he got a compassionate assignment in his hometown. He had eight-hour days and a warm place to sleep, something that concerned me greatly now.

My healthy parents were part of that good, law-abiding "silent majority" that voiced no dissent against the war. They were like millions of Americans still trying to understand it. As young adults during World War II, they believed in the just and good war that had characterized their generation. My father tried to enlist three times, but with only 10 percent of his hearing, he stayed home. My staunch Roman Catholic family believed at once all the teachings of Church and U.S. Government about the treacherous nature of godless Communism. During the early 1950s, all of us, including Grandma and Gramps, were on our knees with the radio version of the family rosary, beseeching God to stop the spread of World Communism. I once asked my grandmother: "If a communist came to our door why could we not just shoot him?" It could not be done, she said solemnly. I conjured up a ten-foot-tall bulletproof giant who always got his way. There were more than one of them, and they were active all over the world. Communists were in Korea, and Drew Pearson would talk about them every evening on Grandma's radio. During the Army-McCarthy hearings, the communists became invisible and penetrated almost every branch of our government. For an eight-year-old, the rosary could easily seem like the only logical hope. Nearly eighteen years later I would prove Grandma wrong. I was on the verge of learning how to shoot communists.

VOICES FROM THE REAR

Ours was a Down East stoicism in everything. We repressed physical and emotional aches and pains with a quiet prayer to some saint. A lot went unsaid in this kind of triangular relationship, where two people talked around issues and the silent saint listened in as a third party. Life communicated itself in the local sense of humor. Crowded dinner tables on Sundays and holidays were always stages for laughter, cutting up, and funny stories. Dry wit cut through the reserve and put poignancy to the sufferings of everyday life. Anyone caught taking himself seriously was dead. Without my realizing it, the Army was to hone all this to a flinty cynical edge.

Getting along in a crowd seemed normal. Besides my parents and my father's parents, the family had six kids, of which I was second in line: my older brother Ronnie, a sister Estelle, ten months younger than I, a seventeen-year-old sister Cathy, a sister Emily, ten, and a brother Frankie, nine. These last two were always the babies. As I worked or started college, my own world overtook me. Ronnie was a natural mechanic. I relied on him to fix my bike and later my car, as did the rest of the family. My grandmother called him "Ronnie Fix." He always said we were wired differently. I stuck to books, and he worked with his hands, seeing how machines ran and how he could make them run faster. He left home after high school to attend a technical aviation school. He worked in Massachusetts and, when the draft threatened, signed on as an aircraft mechanic in a two-and-a-half-year Army tour in Germany. In our few talks after that he told me mostly about the fine women he had met. The Army looked like something good then.

Sacred Heart, a Catholic grammar school in Portland, was a tightly monitored environment where the Sisters of Mercy had near-total control of our minds and souls. Discipline, learning, and regimentation were absolute, and the parish priest was an unquestioned authority figure. The entire student body attended the Sunday children's mass together. Only a death in the family could excuse anyone from this. I joined the choir and became an altar boy, which was at least some diversion. I played every sport known to us. Our sixth-grade basketball team won the city championship. Two of my teammates led the local Catholic high school to the 1961 state championship.

Even with my 5-foot, 7-inch rugged frame, basketball was my passion. I developed a flat-footed but consistent two-handed shot and later evolved a jump shot. Maine's long winters had encouraged the sport's statewide popularity. In Little League and Pony League baseball from the age of six, I always played as a catcher. The big glove was an influence. I remember running down seemingly impossible foul balls for outs, but my batting was a mediocre .250.

Jesuits took care of my four years at Portland's Cheverus High School. These taskmasters doled out a solid classical education in an atmosphere demanding dedication and excellence and instilled a spirit of competition. In this all-boys' regimen, the honor student and the all-state athlete were equals, and we shared in the occasional humiliation of what then passed for discipline. At least four times a year some 400 of us assembled in the gym where the principal read everyone's grades aloud. He would berate a student for a poor showing. Entrance exams screened out those who could not do the work, and the weeding out went on continuously. I came to love all this: classics, history, English, and even Latin, and later majored in history at the University of Maine in Portland.

As a high school freshman in 1959, I tried out for the varsity baseball team. During early spring practice inside the old Milk Street armory in Portland's old waterfront, I discovered a new affront to my adolescent dignity. I was warming up sophomore pitcher Dick Joyce, a tall, rangy hurler of local renown for his overpowering fastball and good curve. He later pitched in college, in the minors, and in a single appearance for the Red Sox at Fenway Park. In the armory's dim murk, I could hardly see the ball when it left Joyce's arm. My dad hauled me to an eye doctor, who pronounced me nearsighted and put me in glasses. I didn't make the team and played a few more seasons in local leagues before work took me away from all that. By the time I entered the service, my vision returned to normal with the corrective lenses.

My personal war with the Army had begun the year before, as I wrestled with the draft system. I had been accepted to graduate school for a Ph.D. in history for the fall of 1968, and in June I went to the draft board in Portland with my acceptance letter to have my student deferment extended. The board office was located in the Customs House near the Armory. The Customs House was a four-story, solid stone and granite structure with all-hardwood interiors built into the side of a hill. Upstairs in the draft office, a steely-eyed woman clerk abruptly told me my deferment could not be further extended. I presented her with an interpretation of the draft law holding that if anyone had completed the first year of graduate study by October 1967, then he was eligible for four additional years to complete his program, all at the discretion of the local board. I met the requirements since I had completed one year of graduate school in June 1967 and would now continue for the Ph.D. at The Catholic University of America in Washington, D.C. I naively believed that if any draft board could legally issue a deferment they would not hesitate to do so. This fifty-something woman took delight in telling me that it was not the policy of my draft board to grant such deferments. She would sneer over any countervailing view or question about an appeal. Her scorn now gave me to realize she had me by the balls and was about to squeeze. Clearly she relished the power she had here. As my helplessness with her attitude rose to fury, a blind kid appeared in the doorway. He had just turned 18. On the arm of some relative, he was registering for the draft! Talk about bad timing. The draft board lady gratefully turned away from me to deal with this exaggerated patriot. Christ! The only thing missing was the Marine band playing the national anthem.

I sought out Judge Louis Bernstein, a former neighbor. For years I shoveled his walk, emptied his trash, and helped him load and unload his car when he came and went on trips to his summer cottage in Falmouth and longer sojourns in Florida. While he soaked up Florida sun each winter, I kept his sidewalk clear of snow, as required by local law. We settled accounts based on my say-so of how many times I had plied the shovel on his walk. It was a system built on trust. The judge had also gotten me an interview with Adam

Walsh, the U.S. Marshal in Portland and a Notre Dame player, when I wanted to apply there as an undergraduate. The judge and I talked in his office on Congress Street. He seemed pleased that I had gotten a master's degree, but he was noncommittal on my attempts to avoid the draft since he had done service in the Army during World War II. He referred me to a young member of his firm who was an expert on draft law. The young lawyer, who had recently completed three years as an officer in the Navy, advised me about an appeal to the draft board.

Optimism rising in my young breast, I walked past my favorite draft-board clerk again one evening in August 1968. In a private hearing room I sat to make my case before a five-man board. Never was such an assembly of flag-waving assholes collected in a single place. I asked for a deferment so that I could complete my studies. My 3.8 grade-point average at Niagara University should count for something, and I believed that a two-year absence from the books would limit or kill entirely my chances in a Ph.D. program. Without heeding what I said, one member took refuge in a stock argument, appealing to the example of a regional hero.

"Well, Ted Williams did it during World War II and Korea."

Everyone in New England knew what this fabulous Red Sox outfielder had done for local charities. His face appeared everywhere as a sponsor of the Jimmy Fund. I had passed the hat myself for that as a kid at Scarborough Downs race track. Every Red Sox fan in New England speculated about the records he could have achieved if he had the years back that he had lost in two wars. I could not believe what I had just heard, but for my inquisitors, the argument was a clincher. The irony also was that few remembered that Ted Williams had asked Senator Taft to keep him out of the Marines during the Korean War.

I told them I would sign any paper that would delay my service for three years, fully realizing during that period I would pass the magic age of twenty-six, the last year one could be drafted unless the country had declared war or was in grave danger. I again produced the paper favoring my eligibility for deferment. These guys had never seen or heard of such an exemption.

We were in a generational warp here. These were all veterans of the Big One or of Korea. They oozed patriotism and saw themselves as a damper on the generation that would not serve their country, even though by 1968 opposition to the war was rational and deep. One member pointed to the street to affirm that I was not like those kids out there. I had an education, he insisted, and could become an officer. He was talking about all of us "kids" who were subject to conscription. But, as a lieutenant in the infantry, I would not be better off than those kids, since reports from Vietnam indicated that lieutenants were not exactly immune to cannon fire. Trying to get across what I had at stake, I finally sighed that a few years ago, I was one of those kids. I worked myself through high school, graduating with honors, and then couldn't afford high-priced Bowdoin College. I worked some more to pay tuition at the University of Maine and then won a graduate assistantship to Niagara University.

No help! I had no connections or funds to get me out of the draft. This fellow was suggesting that I had done all this so I could lead other kids in Vietnam. Big fuckin' deal!

Though they hung over us like mist, the pros and cons of the Vietnam war never came up in that room. This was not the place to argue whether the leaders of the United States were making wise decisions. These otherwise kindhearted locals came off as tight-assed, right-wing clones with a single-minded mission of supplying manpower for the armed forces. For them it was country, right or wrong. They were not going to let me off, nor did they care that I actually had views about the war. I was not a conscientious objector and did not show even a faked injury. The board was unanimous in refusing the appeal. The hearing left me even more helpless and enraged. Five communist-hating flag wavers and an assassin bitch had refused to be swayed by what was in fact the law and had rejected the notion of setting a precedent.

I gave $10.00 to the lawyer as a token. He had treated me honestly and recommended the next highest appeal level. This was before a state representative, who turned out to be a retired Army colonel filling this state-level job. Christ! This deck was stacked! He repeated the decision of the local board and would not reverse it. Any further appeals would cost money, and I had none. Time figured in too, another two years of appeals with a solid possibility of losing.

I headed to Air Force, Navy, and Army recruiters to quiz them on officer candidate programs. The Navy and Air Force slots were completely filled, but an Army recruiter suggested I sign up for four-year enlisted status and after a year apply to Officer Candidate School (OCS). For me, four years' enlisted service would be living on a desert island for two years with the hope of being transferred to another island with five trees for another two years. I wanted the shortest time possible. Like many a desperate maiden aunt, this recruiter would say anything for a commitment. Once I was in the pipeline, the services could easily misplace paperwork, leaving me with four years as an enlisted, or finally gaining an OCS appointment with six months remaining in service. As it turned out, something just as bad happened later.

I asked the Army about a direct commission, figuring that my master's degree and a specialty in Soviet and East European affairs might qualify me for a commission in a language school or for an intelligence slot. The local recruiter, uninformed or lying, had never heard of a direct commission. There were such programs in intelligence and in other areas where the Army needed people. What he did have was a two-year, ten-month OCS delay program. This interested me for two reasons. I could escape being drafted by the Marine Corps, the only other service element taking a few here and there at the time. More important, I could delay my entrance into the Army for up to five months and complete a semester at Catholic University, which would ensure me a place at the school if and when I completed my tour of duty alive. I had to move fast. It was already late August 1968. Signing up for the delay program would negate the draft notice already in my hand. The recruiter promised an entrance date in February 1969. I could complete a full semester and take my final exams in the last two weeks in January, then to meet my fate.

As all this washed over me, the 1968 Democratic National Convention in Chicago exploded on the issue of the war. The forces of "law and order" battled with those of change and resistance to the commitment in Southeast Asia and the draft. This had been brewing for four years. During my sophomore year in college, especially after debates over the Gulf of Tonkin resolution of August 1964, I had formed some opinions about American policy. Intervention, even at the levels then being considered, seemed foolish. U.S. aid should have been in the form of several thousand Green Berets to train and occasionally fight with the South Vietnamese against the Viet Cong and their North Vietnamese allies. If adequate leadership or the will to fight for their own cause could not be established among the South Vietnamese, then all aid should have been withdrawn. In the spring of 1968 an older history professor at Niagara ran a seminar on the Vietnam war. Even he was particularly astounded at how little weight students and teaching assistants put on the fact that Ho Chi Minh was first and foremost a communist. We concluded that Ho was a forceful, charismatic leader, an ardent nationalist, everything the South lacked. The United States could not support the South Vietnamese government against determined aggressors forever. It was unprecedented for a country at the peak of its power to withdraw from a confrontation with a lesser country without some solid resolution to the crisis. This was the problem in 1968 and 1969. The United States had 600,000 troops in a country it could not leave without something it could call victory.

In September, with my delayed OCS program papers in my pocket, I had about ten days left before registering for classes in Washington, D.C. My brother and I took a lifelong neighborhood friend to the Allagash wilderness in Maine. Beautiful nature took us in with no one in sight for miles. We ate, drank, and fished a few miles from the Canadian border. I could easily have slipped across, even as an everyday tourist going through a checkpoint. I had relatives there who could have staked me for a time, but it was no long-term solution. Abandoning my country would also mean walking out on a graduate program and the possibility of a college teaching career.

One morning in the Allagash we guided the boat through a thick predawn ground fog about a half-mile out into the lake and cut the engine. We dropped our lines and drifted for a couple of hours in damp, quiet gloom. The rising sun soon burned off the fog, and day overtook us without a nibble. When we tried to start the ten-horse motor, the rope came off. A quick glance around confirmed our failure to bring the oars. It looked like we would have to swim and push the boat to shore. The adept Ron took a dime to the motor casing as a screwdriver, and within ten minutes it was working again.

I left for Washington for the fall semester and was soon lost in the workload. In mid-October, the Army sent me a letter. Screwed again! On that fateful page I read that the entrance date for the OCS delayed program was now late December 1968 or early January 1969. It would not be the last time the Army lied to me. After Christmas holidays there were still two weeks left in the semester, followed by a week and a half of finals. I had no choice but to withdraw from school, forfeiting about $300 in tuition. Back home, I repaid a good portion of the semester's loan. Then I sought out my friendly recruiter. I read him the Riot Act while he pleaded events beyond his control. He did not give a shit. This goddamned fucking Army, its war, and its draft just would not get off my back. Unless I was willing to do something illegal, like jump country, feign an injury, or commit a crime, I was in its mindless grip. There was no sense getting upset about the inevitable.

Things were still bleak when my sister Estelle's connections unexpectedly landed me a welcome three-month teaching stint at St. Francis College, Biddeford Pool, Maine. Hardly a hotbed of antiwar sentiment, the college saw no organized protests. Student energies that autumn went into a relay run to the Harvard University library, where the kids collected cast-off duplicate books for St. Francis. They even wangled rides for the 120-mile return trip.

VOICES FROM THE REAR

My first direct, and disconcerting, experience of a Vietnam veteran was at the school. A 22-year-old married undergraduate assistant (a junior) had been a Marine Corps infantryman in Vietnam. A genuine guy, he seemed troubled and unready for college. It seemed to bore him. One evening a group of us went to his home for drinks. As the evening wore on, he took out an old M-1 rifle and loosed off several rounds over the Pool. He was a mile away from houses, and the bullets could have landed anywhere. I never did like guns, and this behavior left us all cold. We finally convinced him to quit. I never asked if he was shooting at Vietnam ghosts.

Another confidante at the college added to my distrust of the Army. A German-born instructor who taught her native language once advised me never to believe what anyone says in the Army unless you have it in writing, and then make several copies, sending one to your grandmother and another to your parents or anyone else you might trust for safekeeping. She had worked as an interpreter for the Army in occupied Germany after World War II, and several officers had promised her civil service status. In one of the cutbacks she lost her job with no real explanation or notice. What the Army respects is paper, she quietly told me. Always have it in writing.

Then there was Nancy. If anything made up for my sudden departure from Washington in October 1968, it came in a November evening three weeks after I swung into Biddeford for the short-term teaching job. With a free weekend ahead, I had accepted the invitation of a friend in Boston for a couple of days of constructive bumming around. We were going to barhop and just spend time together. At the third or fourth neighborhood hangout in the dim hours of a new Saturday morning, we ran into a lively crowd of young singles. Four young ladies we started talking to were there together. One dark-eyed lass struck me immediately as more interesting than everyone and everything else in the noise, and my instinct drove me to the usual male ploy of buying her a drink. I had no idea if she was with someone and didn't know if this short-changed, short-time college instructor should make this investment

25

only to find her engaged with some burly sort when I returned. I mumbled what seemed like a command. "Wait here." Did I actually say that? Thinking about it later, it seemed more like a prayer.

Nancy . . ., Nancy Foote, she said. Her friends were all schoolteachers in Quincy, and they shared an apartment. She did social work. Less than an hour later, we were following her and her roommates in their Volkswagen through the streets of Boston. They promised us breakfast at their place. I had no idea where I was. Several times we lost each other at traffic lights and turns, but she was always waiting midway down the next block to lead this weaving caravan again. When we stopped, there seemed to be so much more to say. The sun was full up before we knew it, and then we were gone—never did get breakfast.

I spent the three-hour break before my swearing in at the "Forest Gardens," the bar of my youth on Forest Avenue, where I sat over a beer studying familiar faces and considering the prospects of seeing them again. A half-mile away was my home on Bedford Street, directly across from the university. On many a morning I spilled out of bed fifteen minutes before an eight o'clock class. When I became "legal" in Maine during my senior year, we hung out at the Gardens on weekends and after tests, basketball games, and the Thursday night fights. Ralph Salamoni, the owner, even posted the newspaper clipping about my graduate assistantship to Niagara University in New York in 1966. In the 1950s, the bar sponsored a semi-pro basketball team to run against another semi-pro bunch from Bubba's Cafe a mile away. The Gardens kept pace with its clientele. In the sixties, as the University of Maine in Portland grew and eventually became the University of Southern Maine, the place remained a watering hole for students and local blue collar workers who mingled freely and won or lost at dollar poker. Someone was always ready to talk.

Christ! I did not want to leave that stool. My stomach turned at the thought of going back. At the induction center, a sergeant noticed I was among the oldest and gave me about forty recruits to herd onto a bus for Portland Municipal Airport. The U.S. Govern-

VOICES FROM THE REAR

ment filled in the two-hour delay at the airport with lunch—at $2.00 a man. We had time to call home. I talked to my sister Cathy and told her about the day's events, and the gnawing feeling came over me again. Mom and Dad were out, which was just as well because it would have made it that much tougher to leave. If some of these guys were apprehensive, they did not show it. Some of them appeared to approach it as some type of an adventure, but one could not really tell. All I knew was that I felt pretty shitty and miserable.

At Boston's Logan Airport another twelve recruits joined us and the plane headed for Newark, New Jersey. An Army bus collected us there and ran down the Jersey Turnpike to the inprocessing center at Ft. Dix, New Jersey. The first command on this Army post required everyone to surrender any weapons. How many of these guys were armed! Knives of all descriptions appeared from coats and pant pockets. And those were only the ones turned in. As we filed into the place we confronted a sign three feet high and eight feet long with the exhortation: "Kill Charlie Cong." So it began.

The promise of eight hours' sleep was just one more Army prevarication. Around six in the morning, what we later came to call "O-dark-hundred," a scream in the night ordered us up and in line outside. Groggy, submissive sheep in double column, we trudged to a mess hall two blocks away. The low cafeteria-hall might have been a college dining facility except for the crazy people chanting.

"Hurry up you fuckin' scumbags."

"C'mon, you dip-shits!"

"Move it, slime balls!" This was breakfast. Amid the howling of cooks and sergeants along the walls, we gulped food while these tormentors ranged among us randomly selecting hapless fellows for some duty such as working in the kitchen. Some guys with two stripes harassed others, forcing them to do pushups and sending them immediately to some training company.

Haircuts were next. My head looked like a chapped football. Some longhaired dogs I knew as a kid were shaved completely to thwart a summer mange. They usually looked forlorn and embarrassed and hid under the porch. The dog adjusts; I didn't know if I

27

could. But I was trapped and despised being out of control of my own looks. Since we all looked equally idiotic, we resorted to catcalls as each newly skinned guy emerged from the inexpert hands of the Army barbers. Despite the hijinks, the process left me vaguely scared of what was coming. Too much easy graduate school life and beer had left me completely out of shape.

There was no time for self-pity or soul-searching. We were then assigned to a barracks, and no sooner had we familiarized ourselves with our surroundings and placed our belongings in our lockers when we were again ordered outside, this time for a half-mile hike to a test center.

The Army endlessly and gravely complained about the low test scores among its draftees and recruits. It never figured out that taking a test with 1½ hours' sleep in 35 is guaranteed to produce low scores. We perpetually exhausted and hardly cared how well we did. The tests supposedly revealed individual attributes, mechanical, general knowledge, language, and reading abilities. The tests were presumably administered to determine where the Army could best use an individual's skills. Testing continued until about 1:00 a.m. when a colonel walked in and ordered the enlisted cadre to cease testing and allow us to get some sleep. Rumor established the fact that one of our company, of influential heritage (his father perhaps being a politician), had called home during one of the breaks and related the story of our lack of sleep. To positively determine the accuracy of that rumor would be like reporting to the scientific community about spending a day frolicking with the Loch Ness monster without having taken any pictures to prove it. There would be too many doubters to support credibility. We could not care how it happened and we did not know who our savior was; all we knew was that through some unknown medium we were relieved from further testing and received some welcome sleep.

Rumor kept us alive, alert, and anxious throughout our stay in the inprocessing center. There was constant speculation on where we would be sent after completion of inprocessing. Some rumors claimed that we would be sent to Ft. Jackson, South Carolina, or

Ft. Polk, Louisiana, for basic training, because Ft. Dix was overcrowded.

On the third day we were marched another half-mile for clothing issue—boots, gloves, long underwear, fatigues—all the clothing we would need during training. The building was a long, single-story structure divided inside into separate rooms, one for each item of clothing. The half-door of each room had a small built-in counter. Each man stepped up and received his clothing allotment. The civilian employees in these cubicles constantly alluded to "Smokey the Bear," who would get us next. It all heightened the suspense at meeting the crew of drill instructors, the dreaded DIs.

At the door to the last section chaos began. Here people with duffel bags full of Army-issue clothes were expected to dress in the uniforms they had just received. The small enclosure teemed with struggling troops, all under the lash of several corporals and sergeants screaming at the top of their lungs.

"Get the fuck dressed."

"You motherfuckin' scumbags, you had better get you motherfuckin' lard-asses into gear and get the fuck out of here." I had already concluded that if the magical *f-word* somehow disappeared from the English language, the Army just could not operate. All this clothing was new to us, and of course the underwear was on the bottom of the bag, so we had to dump everything on the floor and fumble our way through the clothes.

Apparently my pace was not quite up to par, or the head corporal wanted either to have some fun or to kill his own boredom. He took some of my clothing and tossed it to the other side of the room, then ordered me to run and pick it up. When I got back to my duffel bag, he had taken another piece and threw it in another direction. The jeers of the other cadre signaled their enjoyment of the play. I was aware of dull, shocked, and staring faces of the troops around me as I calculated distances. I had slid into enough bases in my time, but this guy was just over six feet tall and more than 200 pounds. My flabby 193-pound frame could do the job. I spun and went for his knees, sending him sprawling. He was back on me in

29

seconds, but the other cadre was there to break up a brawl. The game was over, and nothing ever came of it. Their undue harassment was out of bounds. I did not give a shit. If they had beat me badly enough to cause injuries, there would be an inquiry. If they threw me out, so much the better. I relied for some moral superiority on the fact that I was also older than these guys, but I knew I was lucky. The other guys were too scared to jump in. If this clothing issue exercise got too screwed up, someone would land on the sergeants, too. I was beginning to understand how things worked.

That very evening at the barracks we met our first "short timer"—a person who was soon to get out of the Army. He was a stocky Sergeant E-5 about 21 years of age who had been in the infantry in Vietnam, and the Army had screwed him from an early Christmas out. He was drunk and speaking the language.

"Don't fuck around. If you fuck around and fuck me up, so that I fuck up my job, I won't get out of this fucking place. There's ways to fuck you up with extra fucking duties. So don't fuck up. I'm so fucking short you won't believe it, eight more fuckin' days in this goddamn fuckin' Army." The cadence of his phrases was now sounding right to me.

Most of the barracks stood back, mouths hanging open. In us he struck awe and envy. This man had made it through Vietnam—and he was getting out. At that point I had 1,030 days left.

Each day we assembled twice at the "red speaker stand" situated in the middle of a commons between rows of barracks. Actually a reviewing platform about 6 feet high, 15 feet long, and 10 feet deep, this structure had a chest-high railing in front and rear stairs as the only access. A thousand troops at a time would await duty assignments from a sergeant affecting an approved Army command voice. He called off names and numbers, sending troops to their basic training unit, and always named the unfortunates for Kitchen Police, still known as KP in the Army of the late 1960s.

I was always taken with thoughts of leaving the whole thing, and some did. Anyone could walk out of Ft. Dix just by putting on civilian clothes and waiting at the bus depot. Some left the base and caught a bus or a plane to anywhere. I had enough money for this, but knew I couldn't get a job in the United States. A professional job was nearly impossible to find. Every job interview I had at small colleges after June 1968 raised the inevitable question about my draft status. My parents still had three younger children at home and I would feel guilty living off them. Living underground was out, though the possibilities existed of an infantry assignment in Vietnam that might permanently put me there. My experiences with the legal system showed the difficulties of fighting it if I went AWOL (Absent Without Official Leave). I had to endure.

At the first formation on the sixth day, the red speaker stand called our barracks number. We were to gather up our gear for basic training. We hung around for six hours. At dusk we were hustled onto buses, struggling with our duffel bags. Unnatural quiet reigned on the quarter-hour ride, for the first glimpse of the DIs was at hand. For the next eight weeks we would be B-6-3-4th Platoon, Ft. Dix, New Jersey. Darkness shrouded the DIs' faces under their round-brimmed campaign hats. They barked orders.

"Hurry it up."

"Move it, shit bums," intoned one of these Canadian mounted police. Stragglers were subsequently kicked in the ass by these "round hats." I moved too quickly for that. In the barracks we each grabbed a bunk and started sorting clothing. Some of my colleagues were scattered in the scuffle to other barracks but in the same company, now consisting of five platoons, one to a barracks. Every platoon had four squads of 12 or 13 people. The whole company numbered about 250 people plus the cadre.

The barracks were creaking, post-World War I wooden structures. As near as I could determine, the heating system was a fuel burner, converted sometime before from coal. Only the headquarters building still had coal heat, and our duties eventually included firing it up. The inside floors were large hardwood planking, polished with a dark stain finish that required constant work. Each barracks had two floors with about 12 double bunks to each floor. Unlike what I had seen in the movies and various television series, the bunks on my floor ran parallel instead of perpendicular to the wall. I could only conjecture that it made inspections easier. The inspecting officer could go down both sides of a row of bunks and cross to either side with ease. It also made for easier exit, since the buildings were truly firetraps. Other refinements included a wall locker and a footlocker for each man. The footlockers were placed by twos under a window, and between two wall lockers. At the head of almost every bed a floor-to-ceiling pole sported a red cigarette butt bucket. At one end of our floor was a private room, originally used by resident DIs, but two company cooks occupied ours. I took the lower bunk on the right-hand side from the main entrance and the next to last bunk from the end of the line.

The company filled four other similar barracks, two of them across a road. The headquarters building as well as the supply and mess halls were one-story frame buildings of the same vintage across the road from us. An assembly area with its own red speaker stand was located about fifty yards from the headquarters shack.

On the next day, a Sunday, harassment started the day. The company filed into the mess hall for breakfast with an E-5 sergeant DI mouthing at us: "Don't open your fuckin' mouths." I went through the chow line and sat at a table for four while the sergeant continued his work with the next in line. Beneath his black hair, an intelligent face worked constantly. His six-foot frame ranged among us confidently in obvious enjoyment of his calling. He surveyed the room like a hawk preparing to pounce on some unsuspecting field mouse.

Then I became the mouse. He caught my signal for the salt to a tablemate across from me.

"You!" he bellowed. "Take your motherfuckin' tray and turn it in."

Instead, I walked directly out without a word. The unreal atmosphere reminded me of a book I once had to read, Bruno Bettelheim's *The Informed Heart*, which examines how some people retained a sense of inner self in the most dehumanizing Nazi prison camps. I identified more with descriptions of the initial shock of a middle-class German in such a place. Still, I had hopes this might all end if we came through Vietnam. German prisoners had little hope or relief. I did not need this kind of discipline. I also knew that if I could intellectualize some of my heaving emotions, I could relieve the pain, but in the meantime, I would have to play their game.

The days were mine to count. I knew then that any lingering commitment to the OCS program was gone. At the first chance, I would drop out of that and thereby limit my stay to two years. I was already under that. At least that arrangement had delayed my entrance, even though it cost me a semester of graduate school. It also kept me out of the hands of the Marines who, I later learned, drafted three guys on the spot the day I left the Portland induction center.

I finally got to see the company clerk about dropping my OCS commitment. After he filled out the paperwork, I went to see the captain for his signature. My captain made me step in and out of his office about three times before he was satisfied with the way I presented myself. I didn't care. I would have rolled over and played dead if I could have his signature on the paper. He signed the sheet and knocked 304 days off my Army service.

You never got used to the Army's treatment of basic human needs. There was no privacy for the daily routine of taking a crap. Each barracks had a bathroom with no door at the entranceway. Some six toilets were lined up in an L-shape with no partitions whatsoever. Everyone just sat on the hopper right next to a comrade while others were using the sinks and showers on the other side of the room; still others shifted impatiently, waiting their turn on the seat. I always held off as long as I could. In my entire life I had never had to shit in public. More likely it was too much trouble to maintain the extra partitions against graffiti and shot spots from trainees. It was also a way of breaking down anyone's individuality, but we observed wryly that the army that shits together fights together, or that regularity breeds tough regulars. The Army had also had a horror of homosexuals and perhaps sought to bring any tendencies out in the open by exposing all.

The first week of actual basic training was more orientation and familiarization with the Army through lectures by the DIs and other cadre, and sometimes through films. We did some Physical Training (PT) but for the most part the DIs started us off slow—calisthenics and brief runs around the company area. I was surprised and somewhat elated that I performed so well. I expected to lose weight, but not all in one week.

We forced-marched to each film session. The film topics varied from how to treat a sucking chest wound to general personal hygiene. Reaction to these presentations was always instructive. In a large theater with about seven other companies, we watched the 1965 edition of President Johnson's film *Why Vietnam?* It came off as absolute propaganda, a disgusting rationalization for a bumbling error. This was 1969, and the tide had already turned. Even Johnson had announced his refusal to run for another term in early 1968 after the Tet debacle. The film was full of obvious half-truths, the more evident in 1969. The South Vietnamese cause was portrayed as noble, yet no viable core of Vietnamese military leadership surfaced that had the force of Ho. Even our own revolution was a case in point: we had produced good military leaders with less than 50 percent of the population fully backing independence. About half the audience stood and cheered. I suddenly felt alone. None of the guys around me could see deeper than the banalities of the show. This left me more horrified than the first day in basic training.

Next an airborne recruiter took the stage to proselytize for jump school after basic training. He was a trim six-footer with an immaculately pressed dress uniform. His trouser cuffs bloused out of the top of his airborne uniform boots. The school required extended PT, he told us. For many in his audience though, the big draw, besides the small pay increase, was the look of bloused boots on dress uniforms. Regular dress greens came with pretty ordinary low-cut dress shoes. Infatuation with this sort of mindless detail was not unusual. A week into basic training, some guys were already sneaking out to the post exchange to buy the National Defense Ribbon. Some even bought expert rifle badges before they had even looked at a rifle in the Army. We were not scheduled to fire weapons for another three weeks, and if they were not going to wear them yet anyway, they were confident they were already marksmen.

An outbreak of spinal meningitis confined us to the barracks area during the first four weeks of basic. As part of this restriction, each member of the company wore a green tag on the outside of his field jacket while the infection ran its course. Other companies had different colors depending on the cycle of training they were in; the tabs distinguished one company from another. The quarantine also kept us out of the PX, really not much of a physical deprivation, but we couldn't gawk at shelves filled with goods from the outside world. Squad leaders were designated to take orders twice a week. Worse, we could not use the phones situated three blocks away. This was too much for us to endure. We risked the penalty of KP, extra duty, and other punishments, but we ventured out to the phone center at least once a week to call girlfriends and family. Platoon leaders would patrol the centers looking for members of their company whom they could identify by the colored tab. Troops quickly discovered how to trade their colored quarantine tab with those worn by trainees from other companies. I called Nancy in Boston. Just a few words from her carried me through the next days.

Oddly enough, sex was the farthest thing from my mind for the first four weeks of basic. The constant physical demands and the stress and apprehension of the whole process dampened any real urges. The training regimen wore me out every day so that I just hit the sack during the evening without even a thought of masturbation. The Army allowed no outlets for sex during the early part of basic training, and there was no leave until about the fourth week. One Sunday afternoon we were allowed to go to a beer hall set up specifically for basic trainees. A woman of perhaps fifty, judging from the wrinkles, circulated from table to table with a man her age and talking with some of the trainees. They were neatly dressed in civilian clothes. Rumor had it that she was selling blow jobs. If some of the guys were buying, it served to show that they were not experiencing the lack of sexual drive that I was. Younger men, and we had several under eighteen, reveled in the beer hall. They drank freely, without some cop barging in to check for an ID. For me, a veteran beer man, this was old hat, but a blow job while drinking beer wasn't my idea of a good time; I preferred conversation. At any rate, this was the level of entertainment supplied in the Army of the late 1960s. It could not offset the dull menial business of barracks life.

One duty I did not mind was fire guard. Since the barracks were firetraps, the Army ordered, and rightly so, a nightly watch outside the buildings. Each squad was assigned several evenings per week, one hour per man. For that hour, the individual walked back and forth outside the length of the barracks and then went back in to wake up the next man. In the proper heavy Army clothing, it was not an uncomfortable hour in spite of the New Jersey winter. Alone with myself, I paced off the time, thinking, dreaming, or reviewing a letter I had received that day, or even planning a theoretical escape, all a welcome reprieve even at the cost of an hour's sleep.

One recurring fantasy took me back to the happier times of a college beach party in Maine in my sophomore year. We were denied the pleasures of imbibing beer with faculty present, but we got around that rule. The beach was situated at the base of a steep, 200-foot rocky incline dotted with shrubs and trees that served to conceal furtive guzzlers. Six-packs multiplied in the nooks and crannies. As darkness approached and the beer took its effect, like raccoons, about 25 guys shook off the security of the hillside and captured a section of the beach about 150 yards from where the main party was engaged in a barbecue. We were bound to draw attention since a couple of guys were waist-deep in the ocean and calling for Christopher Columbus, to the jeers and applause of the others. Suddenly the college dean himself was making his way down the beach. Like a wave before him, panicked people retreated to the hill. About 25 yards towards the cooking fire I saw a girl from my French class on a large rock. I raced to her and put an arm around her while hiding my beer behind our perch. The dean was now in clear view and remarking on the number of beer cans littering the beach. I dutifully picked up a few empties, but impulse seized me as this authority went on his way. I raised my brew and sang at his retreating back: "Hey deanee! I've got mine, now you get yours." It seemed funny at the time, and I became a minor legend, but the next day the Student Activities Director placed my name at the head of a long list of students that the dean was considering for social probation. We did clean up the beach.

Mail call was the one daily event during basic that connected us directly to the outside world. I remembered television clips of soldiers in formation during mail call, and the one poor soul who got nothing. This was real. Watching some of the doleful younger soldiers go without news from home always impelled me to attempt to cheer them up. I was constantly looking forward to even the shortest of notes from outside. Our barracks had members from the New England states, Pennsylvania, Indiana, and Kentucky. An enterprising nineteen-year-old from Kentucky announced one evening that he had just received a letter from his girlfriend who had also sent along some addresses of several young ladies who would like to write to some of the guys. This gleeful announcement came with a price quote of $2 for each address.

For all their interest in receiving mail, some of the troops hated writing themselves. For the service of having my boots polished, I would correspond with families and girlfriends. After a few questions about their parents, girlfriends, and what they wanted to say, I would dash off some special love note. I wrote some pretty gushy stuff with amazingly lurid descriptions of what a fellow planned to do the next time he got home.

In the course of the inquiries, I also learned that some of the men had some type of criminal past. One had beaten his wife; another had stolen a car; yet another had gotten into one too many bar fights. At least one claimed a judge had given him the choice of joining the Army or going to prison. The fact that some jurist thought of the two as just about equal says something about the Army. But for the draft, the Army might have had greater numbers of derelict elements during the Vietnam war, but its composition in this century has always represented people escaping from something. The only thing wrong with the draft at this stage was that it was not fairly administered because wealthy or connected elements could buy or cheat their way out. Thus criminals were being drafted, and criminals were also getting out of the draft. The diversity of draftees, people with college degrees and those who were street wise, would prevent a uniformity of opinion and unionization of the military. It also represented the best deterrent against a military takeover in the United States. But this cross section of society would fight and die in this war.

One wiry high school dropout from Indiana had a typical hardluck story. Tough enough for the other guys not to press him or give him any shit, he was recently divorced and had two kids. His ex-wife called his local draft board with the ink still wet on their divorce papers to report on his new single status. He claimed he was drafted two weeks thereafter. Actually, he wasn't terribly bitter and seemed a bit relieved to be out on his own.

Steve Layer and Ken Myers were two more Indiana farm boys who knew each other and shared many mutual hometown acquaintances. They were both on my floor. Steve was a skinny six-footer with thick glasses. He took his lead from Ken, who was much shorter and built like a fireplug. They had each worked a year after high school before being drafted. They knew the same girls at home, and in the way of boys their age, each told elaborate stories about how he "fucked the shit" out of this married woman. Ken proclaimed her as "so horny that we did it twice on the dining room table before we got to her bedroom." Inevitably, Steve backed up Ken's yarns. Ken even had a letter from this insatiable woman that he read aloud, saying that she couldn't wait for him to get some leave. I just couldn't tell if they were bullshitting or not, but it sounded like another version of every adolescent's dream of meeting a nymphomaniac who owned a liquor store.

Steve was constantly in trouble with the DIs for "fucking around" in formation. He was always doing extra pushups or under orders to run around the platoon while the unit marched. These did not seem to bother him, but he was soon saddled with one of the more loathsome tasks in the place—the grease pit. This was a four-foot-square cement pond with a drain situated outside the mess hall. Here the cooks, or most likely the KPs, dumped the excess grease and most other liquid waste from the mess. The drain in the center of the enclosure was four inches lower than pit floor and occasionally got plugged up. Someone would have to wade in to snake it out with either his hands or some other means. As we marched into the chow hall one evening, Steve was in the muck laboring over the stopped drain. He was wailing uncontrollably. Ken edged out of the line and tried to console him, to no avail. Steve was still bemoaning the injustice that had befallen him. The DI had got the wrong guy fucking around, he told his buddy. It was more likely that he was mortified at this duty while the whole company paraded past him into the mess hall. One of the sergeants took pity on the wretch and quietly talked to him as the pit finally belched and emptied down the sucking hole. It was like a stern father finally relenting with a bad-tempered crying child. The episode seemed to quiet him down. He didn't fool around much after that.

During the second week of basic I developed a head cold and a sore throat from our activity and formations in the rain and chill. Coming off sick call, I pulled light duty in the supply room. There I met a private who had been in the Army about eight months and had gone AWOL four times. He was attempting to get out by any means. He was a short, dark-haired Jewish kid from New York City who never talked much. In our easy existence, I pried information out of him. He had found it real easy to go home when the spirit moved him. He was trying to get out by any means possible and, like most of us, had a terrible fear of going to Vietnam. His job sure interested me, and I envied him. Imagine spending his two-year Army duty there, close to home, and not getting shot at. I probed for any information I could about his present assignment, how long he could possibly stay there and not get sent to "Nam."

An hour of this and the supply room door opened to admit the supply sergeant, a huge black man, an E-6 about six-and-a-half-feet tall and 250 pounds. I immediately sprang to attention, wondering what harassment or new duties he would have for me. DIs half his size hassled us so much that I expected he would run my white ass around his supply room doubly hard. Instead he told me to sit down, take it easy, since all the weapons in the supply room were clean and ready for use by our company in a few weeks. He told me to write a letter home, and he commenced talking about his future plans. With 18 years in the Army, he planned to retire in two more and open a bar in northern New Jersey. He was already worrying about finding the right type of help, people who could be trusted. After my nearly two weeks in the Army, this was the first man in a leadership position who was downright human. He never harassed us. He treated us as individuals and showed a side of the military that I believed nonexistent. I remember this man to this day still. His sheer kindness and humanity made a lasting impression. He simply chose not to be a bastard and still got things done.

Harassment came in many forms, all demeaning and stupid. One morning standing in company formation in 8-degree weather, several of our number had reacted to the cold by putting down their earflaps.

"Who the hell gave you permission to put down your earflaps?!" yelled one of the DIs. He next ordered the entire company to put them up and stand at attention for fifteen minutes. Then he finally ordered them down and he admonished us never to put them down again without permission. Our company commander got into the act. The captain had received a head wound in Vietnam, which was partially corrected, everyone said, with the addition of a steel plate in his skull. One evening he ventured into our barracks where he discovered a man reading *The Naked Ape*, a then-popular anthropological study about the origins of man. The captain focused on the cover picture of a nude man and flew into a tantrum over the presence of what he assumed was pornographic literature. It dismayed me that an officer had no idea of what he was looking at and would not make an effort to learn. We respected the captain for his battlefield commission but couldn't help speculating on the depth of his wound and its effect on his brain, or if he had any left.

The captain had periodic visits in the mess hall from a friend, a major who seemed to have known him in Vietnam. The major sported a bizarre, nonregulation uniform. He had a white fur hat, a large gold buckle around his waist, and a white- or pearl-handled revolver. He preened around, showing off in that uniform. Some of the same trainees who had taken to the airborne recruiter earlier now had something else to gawk at. I had the feeling that this major and my captain, who also insisted on sharp clothing, thought they had reached a sartorial representation of some obvious mix of silver-screen cowboys and threw in their own imitation of General George S. Patton, whose pearl revolvers were the stuff of legend. The Army tolerated this among its officers, but it all added to an atmosphere of unreality in which time seemed endless. It took months to get through a week, and weeks to get through a day. We would pass other companies in training and realize that that class was in its sixth or seventh week while we were still in our second.

On January 24, we had our first trial PT test. It was a cold, misty day with the temperature hovering just above freezing. We were instructed how to perform the low crawl. We had to crawl in a sandpit, but we were told that the final test would allow us to crawl on mats, a much easier surface. Other events included the run-dodge-run, the hand-hang on the overhead bars, the 150-yard man-carry, and the mile run. In my best showing I carried a 170-pound man 150 yards in 40 seconds. Most grueling was the mile run. I had been a sprinter in high school; my best times were 4.9 seconds in the 40-yard dash and about 38 seconds in the 300, the most difficult long-distance effort I ever attempted. At that time, I made the finals in the 300, but the second race came too soon after the first. My time was dismal, hardly ever placing, and my guts came up after it was over. The Army's standard for the mile was 7½ minutes—anything more counted for nothing. I wheezed across the finish line in 10½ minutes. Everyone had to pass the PT test to get out of basic training. Failure meant being recycled. At the end of the trials I had a miserable 200 points out of a possible 500. I would need at least 300 points to pass the final test. The final was less than six weeks away. I stood there soaked clear through my long johns and despaired of ever leaving this vale of tears.

The next day produced another of those surreal events in the Army. At the late afternoon formation the captain with the steel plate in his head issued an appeal to support the Girl Scouts. Two tiny kids in scout uniforms stood up, the daughters of the First Sergeant, there to sell cookies. Nothing seemed more incongruous than the sight of these two innocents in front of our ragtag collection of military trainees. It was like the old Soviet Komsomols, the Young Pioneers, and the Hitler Youth all rolled into one, brought in to cheer the soldiers of the fatherland. In my fatigue and disappointment of the day before, I completely disassociated the Army from anything in the outside world. Bringing in Girl Scouts suddenly seemed ridiculously wrong. My only protest as we were marched by the girls was to refuse the proffered cookies. I could probably have scarfed down five boxes on the spot. Practically every man bought at least three. Those girls must have sold nearly 700 boxes. The traffic in these things went on for days, with those who hoarded their prizes selling them for double the price and more three days later. Truly this was capitalism at work.

In the late 1960s, the Army still drilled recruits in bayonet combat. We had to master three or four ritual steps with the weapon. All of it was unnatural for me. All the motions were supposed to be fluid, one melding into the next. I never mastered the trade and always had to think my way through the paces, looking robotic. It seemed rather silly, since the war we were preparing for did not allow for such diversions as hand-to-hand combat. If you were close enough to stick 'em, you were close enough to shoot 'em, some wise guy observed. I figured in close quarters that I would most likely swing the rifle butt from the barrel like a baseball bat. I memorized the movements but left this phase of training with the sergeant's dismissive assessment of my bayonet style.

On January 30, a freezing morning on the second day of weapons training, we fired a rifle for the first time. The day before, we had received instruction on positioning in foxholes and sighting and aiming the weapon. I recall the first echoes of the M-14 and the effect on 250 troops silently occupying bleachers near the firing pits. Christ! I wondered how I would ever qualify with a weapon that scared my socks off. With our issue earplugs, one by one we dropped into the foxholes to hit a target some 60 to 80 meters downrange. In the allotted six shots, I left the sergeant speechless: all six missed everything and flew off to endanger who-knows-what in the New Jersey landscape beyond. He stared down at the pristine marker. Even the white paper around the target had not a scratch. On jumping into the hole, I had slipped off my foggy glasses. The bulky Army winter clothing made it impossible to control the piece anyway, and at every shot the heavy collar shoved the steel helmet down over my eyes. With my new humiliation registered, the sergeants took turns showing us how, an exercise they clearly enjoyed. They were all combat veterans with at least one tour in Vietnam and could pepper the targets with amazing consistency. There was a fascination to this, but no way to really own the experience. I realized then that I might have to fire this thing in self-defense in the near future, and the thought was a frightening reason to master the art.

Marching and countermarching was part of the day during the aimed-fire programs. With each new rifle phase, the distance from the barracks to the ranges seemed to increase. The more experienced we became, the farther we had to force-march to the ranges. Eventually my Achilles tendons gave up. The pain was unbearable and put me on overnight sick call. A medic prescribed easy duty for another day, but the day after that another march laid me low again. One of my squadron mates, a dark-haired, quiet type from Hartford, Connecticut, came to the rescue. This guy claimed he had led a motorcycle gang in civilian life. He had gone AWOL once, but after a week had quietly rejoined the company in the same cycle. He handed me a little round pill he had somehow extracted from a government-issue painkiller. I was desperate enough to try anything. After breakfast I downed "Hartford's" dose and floated through the morning's eight-mile march to the range. I never let that man out of my sight. I thought the pain would return after the pill wore off, but I never hurt again. On some lucky days, we were trucked from the range in huge moving vans—no pain there.

Four weeks into this ordeal we got passes, with the promise of another at the sixth week. We went from a Friday in a cold hut before weapons firing to the euphoria of a 30-hour pass starting at noon on Saturday. We were expected back by 6:00 p.m. on Sunday. Several of us crowded aboard a bus to Newark airport and a shuttle flight to Boston. My God! There was Nancy, the girl of a million letters already. I carried each one around to read over when I got the chance, and I clung to each new one in turn.

Even with my spirits up on this cloud, the military regimen intervened. We went directly to a German place, had a few drinks, went back to her apartment, chattering at each other all the while. The Army tackled me there; at ten o'clock sheer exhaustion sent me sound asleep in my seat. Next day, Boston was deep in snow, a real Nor'easter. Nancy gamely trucked me to the airport where I would meet two others for the return trip. My world stopped short as I hugged Nancy. I was leaving everything I thought I wanted and needed in life for Ft. Dix. This was even worse than the first trip down to that abomination four weeks ago. I kicked myself for being a goddamned asshole incapable of escaping this thing.

Three of us in front of the check-in counter found that Boston was socked in, all flights canceled. We got a cab to the train station, hoping to get to New York and then catch a bus to Ft. Dix. We boarded in midafternoon for what was a fifteen-hour trip to New York. Nothing there was moving either. The whole Northeast lay blissfully under white, and we holed up at the YMCA. On the phone the company clerk at Dix placidly told us to get back as soon as we could. Nothing moved for two days, and we settled back to enjoy our extended reprieve. The USO bought our movie tickets, and we endured the leisure. Tuesday, February 11, 1969, at about 11:00 a.m. we straggled in to our company. There were no reprimands since many were still drifting in and others had not yet been heard from. We hung around on light duty because the scheduled final qualifying fire for the day was postponed.

Even the silver lining had a dark cloud. No one wanted to miss any key part of basic training if it meant being recycled. Nothing could be worse than this existence, so nearly everyone did their best to get out. A few of these "retreads" were in our company because they had been sick for more than two weeks or had gone AWOL too long. It took strength and sanity to survive all this. DIs hummed variations of this song incessantly. "Fucking up" would be rewarded with recycling. But our two- or three-day dent in the schedule hardly slowed things much.

With the fifth week, the pace picked up—more forced marches, PT, rifle ranges, night firing, and the hand-grenade toss. Finally I found something the Army needed that I was good at. In the grenade class, trainees were to chuck a blast-cap training grenade some sixty feet through an open aperture in a wood-frame dummy building. The regulation position for this was a squat exactly like the stance of a baseball catcher, and the object was launched from behind the right ear, just like the return throw to the pitcher's mound. With the platoon standing by, I arced the first practice bomb squarely through the window. The sergeant took sudden interest when my second grenade sailed right after it. It was almost too easy. When the third flew in directly after the others, I made his day, and mine, too.

The second pass at the sixth week of training took me back to Boston and Nancy again. Things had progressed far enough that we drove to Maine to stay with my folks. My folks loved her. We ate home cooking and caroused with my enormous and no doubt daunting family, but she took all this in stride. I kept checking weather reports in hopes of another snowstorm. Thirty-two hours wasn't enough.

Everyone I knew at Dix would rather have done a full march on a freezing day than do KP. The tour in the kitchen mess—4:30 a.m. to 10:30 p.m., eighteen hours straight—washing pots and pans, and cleaning grills and floors was hellish enough. Listening to the bullshit commands of the head cook and his subordinates made it insufferable. All the stoves had to be spotless after every meal, which was a bit of overkill because the next meal started a few hours later. One grand clean-up after the evening meal would have done it. One cook ordered me to clean out the rotten gunk in the inside drain in the back of the kitchen. I had no idea what was in there, and I made the mistake of asking the cook what we used to clear it with.

"Use your fuckin' hands, you fuckin' dumb shit." God! I was just too old for this bullshit. KP was horribly boring, and we got very few breaks. I believed that a week of this duty would be reason enough for a session with the psychiatrist, for the purpose of seeking a discharge for mental retardation.

I once peeled potatoes with a kid from Indiana and found another guy missing his girlfriend. He showed me a picture of the girl and his classic custom '55 Chevy. This girl was stunning, with long hair and great legs, and she was wearing a sweater that revealed all the endowments a man could want. The car was a dark metallic red hardtop convertible in gleaming mint condition. Holding the photos in his hand, he began to cry. He just wanted to go home and get out of this bullshit place. I tried consoling him by telling him that less than two weeks of basic remained. He whimpered on, head bowed over the pictures, fumbling first for the one of the girl, then for the image of the car. It seemed all the same to him, the bygone realities of home.

With me on KP the same day was a 6-foot, 3-inch athlete from western Pennsylvania. In the Army's methodical way, he became Moose. Anything but a dullard, this fellow with a 225-pound frame commanded attention, the last thing he wanted. His size belied a gentle and honest nature. Three years of college had exposed him to enough life that he cultivated a deliberately low profile behind which he hoped just to endure the Army. One day he showed us a deep one-inch tear in the skin near his crotch. He came off one of the forced marches with this thing, now deep, raw, and persistent. I told him to "go to Hartford" for the pain, but he did not care to. Like the most of us, he wanted to avoid the infantry. One day he

VOICES FROM THE REAR

subtly expressed to one of the mess corporals an interest in their culinary work after basic training. The head cook, a black E-6, thereupon humiliated and harassed the shit out of Moose for the rest of the entire day. This, I still believe, was to see if he had what it took to become a cook. Moose wound up cleaning places in the chow hall that I did not know existed. If he was out to prove he could take harassment, he succeeded. He also took a lot of the pressure off the rest of us.

Army life promotes bizarre behavior, and the company had its share of inspired scams based on how much punishment a young body can take. One Spec-4 (Specialist 4th Class) cook and his PFC (Private First Class) helper, both from Louisiana bayou country, were hardly geniuses but still could make a few quick bucks from KP trainees. The Spec-4 proposed that his PFC partner could gulp a 12-ounce bottle of Tabasco sauce. The six of us on KP raised a grand total of $5 to see it done. The rangy blond private downed the whole thing without stopping for breath. He calmly followed that with a glass of water while we waited for him to lose his innards. These guys enhanced their beer budgets like this with each new group of KP trainees. The Tabasco sauce was Army-issue, so the tent show was all profit.

During the last week of basic I had my first experience at guard duty and bivouac. Both would not have been bad if one had not followed the other. Along with six others, I was assigned guard duty the night before bivouac. The former entailed guarding a specific area or object for two-hour stints. My responsibility that night was a Quonset hut filled with some valuable machinery. Circling it was boring, and the cold night made it uncomfortable. The shift was easy enough, but sleeping afterwards proved difficult. It took about forty-five minutes to fall off, usually an hour before we were stirred for the next watch. This was endurable, but heading back to the company and strapping on sixty pounds of equipment and hiking ten miles was not.

Bivouac was supposedly optional during the winter cycle of basic training. But our gung-ho captain was like a kid who looked forward to these events without a clue to what sort of labor it took. Taking the company out on a 70-degree day would be fine, but at 12 degrees, with a wind-chill factor making it 5 below zero, it seemed unwise. We marched in, set up camp, and ate supper, fully anticipating settling down for sleep and guard duty. Wrong! Suddenly we broke camp, packed our gear, and prepared for another forced march to nowhere. After two more hours we set up our tents, this time in pitch darkness. The worst it could do now was snow.

Snow it did. Christ, it was cold. Once we were inside our good-quality sleeping bags, body heat helped keep us warm. I passed out for seven hours. In the morning, four inches blanketed our encampment. I often wondered why there were not more cases of pneumonia and exposure caused by that sojourn. I do not know what the captain was trying to prove except that he could say he bivouacked his troops in sub-zero weather. He could have canceled it by regulation and because of inclement weather, but no, he probably wanted to make major. Maybe he just wanted a change of routine. He slept in a large tent with a heating unit.

Some of the troops saw this as a great accomplishment. It only seemed stupid to me. The constant lack of reason or purpose gnawed at me. There was no sense of mission to mentally carry me through this thing. How was this cold weather encounter going to prepare us for the Vietnam experiment?

Around this time the prospects of our next assignments began to crowd us. Those who had signed up for three years were fairly well assured of their next assignment after basic, or at least of what school they would be attending. The rest of us would be assigned according to the needs of the Army. I still felt I was wasting time, and doubts about all of this kept running through me during the long runs, sometimes slowing me down.

After bivouac we qualified with both rifles in the Army inventory at the time. The older M-14 was a long, heavy piece with a large slug. I really preferred the new lightweight M-16—it felt like a toy but had a high rate of automatic fire and a nasty, small round. I got better with each range session, fired well with both weapons, and attained sharpshooter status with the M-14 and expert with the M-16. The showdown for the last week was the final PT examination. After passing all the written exams, this was the final hurdle. I had improved steadily since my initial test, nearly reaching the required 300 points. But on the test day I made a mistake. Seeking out "Hartford," I wanted to be doubly sure and took two of his little round pills at about 6:30 on the morning of the test. The kick was not long coming. I began to sweat buckets as dizziness and nausea rolled over me. I put a damp cloth on my forehead and paced the barracks trying to shake it off. I wanted to lie down, but I had to go out and pass that damn test to clear basic training. I never got through it. At the end of the mile run, my breakfast and I parted company in an open field. That cleared my head, but I was involved in a return bout with the PT test the next day with fifteen others. This time I coasted in over the margin by twenty points.

That afternoon we were supposed to process out and get orders for our next assignment. There was to be no leave between basic and the next step—advanced individual training, or AIT. This was a disappointment for all of us, especially those who lived on the East Coast, because if sent farther south or west, we knew we would never make it home on a weekend pass. We stood in the usual cold waiting for the usual paperwork when my head started swimming again. I was running a fever. By the time I got back to the company I was high as a kite.

At the base hospital an excited doctor found me registering nearly 103 degrees. I felt drunk and an I-don't-give-a-shit aura overcame me. They pumped me with antibiotics and drew blood. In a quiet room I slept for twenty hours. In two days I felt better, fit enough to travel to a hospital annex. With twenty other enlisted men I arrived at a World War I-vintage medical complex with a long head building and some 25 wings running perpendicular to it. In this drafty old barn, we walked hallways to eat, call the outside world, and use the facilities. Prowling around in bedclothes and bathrobe ran my fever up again to 102 degrees. The care was decent, with temperature checks every two hours. The men in the ward all seemed threatened with dehydration, and we drank prodigious quantities of liquid, grape Kool-Aid being the mainstay. To this day the sight of Kool-Aid makes me sick.

Five days of this and I was well enough to help clean the ward. My stay could have been depressing, but I rationalized it as all good time to be added on to my now less than one year and ten months remaining in the Army. One guy had his girlfriend visit him, a rather large young lady whose size made her look much older. An orderly announcing her presence in the ward loudly declared to the man that his "mother was here to see him." No one let up on this poor guy after that, but he was the only one who had a visitor.

On the seventh day I was released to my company to find all my friends scattered to various assignments throughout the country. I had been scheduled to go to Ft. Leonard Wood, Missouri, for combat engineer training along with other members of my company and barracks. Everyone left the evening I went to the hospital.

I spent another five days in my old company doing such things as sawing up old tree limbs that had fallen on company grounds. I processed out a second time and drew the same assignment to Ft. Leonard Wood. Everyone I knew there would be in a different company and well into his second week. Even on the way out, a civilian clerk issuing airline tickets at the post could not resist harassing me about missing the earlier military flight. It cost the government extra to send me commercial. Here was a middle-aged flack, probably another retired "lifer" who had wrangled a government job to suck two pay checks a month in addition to his pension. It took some restraint not to punch out his lights. "Fine," I told him, "I'll see if I can avoid 103-degree temperatures and taking vacations in military hospitals after this." I really wanted to cash in the tickets and head for Maine.

I hung around the company with other holdovers and some of my basic training cadre. Even the hated DIs suddenly seemed human. They had done their best in little time to prepare us for the worst, despite the harassment. A couple of them sought me out as I was leaving. "You're a good troop," they told me in what seemed an Army accolade. For all their bullshit, this produced for me a rush of some odd kinship with them. Actually, I had not been a bad troop and gave them little trouble and attempted everything ordered. If you really tried, I found, they generally laid off. It never ended, though. Right through the end of the cycle, a DI would signal me out of formation.

"Watson, get your shit together," he would growl before sending me as quickly back to the ranks. We were welded enough by then to snicker at the Army's methods of making soldiers of us, and the tension relaxed.

I was not disappointed with leaving this place, only sorry that I had missed saying goodbye to some fellow troops I had been rather close with. My bout with the fever abruptly ended some friendships because I got no forwarding addresses. I was no wiser, but I was in better shape than I had been in four years. I was of course relieved at the end of an ordeal, but I never acquired a sense of commitment. I didn't know it then, but this was the first step toward the war zone in Vietnam.

Chapter 2

Advanced Individual Training

Two weeks after basic I was headed for the nation's heartland and the enormous engineer school at Ft. Leonard Wood, Missouri. The flight from Philadelphia to St. Louis, with stops at Pittsburgh and Indianapolis, was uneventful. But at Lambert Field in St. Louis I had to run to the Frontier Airlines connecting flight to the post, 120 miles southwest of St. Louis, not even a hour by air. An ancient DC-3 fitted out to accommodate 40 passengers had about a third that number already on board. I had the luck to sit next to another of the many characters that the Army threw me together with, a PFC from Hudson's Bay. A Canadian citizen with no obligation to be where he was, he had volunteered for the United States Army as well as duty in Vietnam. In my sheer astonishment at this guy's whole being, I never got his name. He needed some excitement, he told me. I would have thought that surviving a winter in Hudson's Bay should provide enough of that. He had a wife and an infant child. The U.S. Army had all kinds.

The aircraft descended into a landscape dotted with patches of green, a true harbinger of spring. It was March 14, 1969, and the 60-degree weather in Missouri contrasted with what I had just left at Ft. Dix.

I checked into my new company E-3-1 (AIT), Third Platoon, that Thursday evening and immediately drew KP for the next day. It seemed like shit followed me wherever I was in the service. The company had not fully assembled, and the training cycle would only begin the following Monday. In a new organizational wrinkle, the unit here was managed by special squad leaders fresh from two weeks in leadership school after basic training. These fellows became squad, platoon, and company leaders. In basic training, the DIs appointed squad leaders on the spot. In the AIT phase, companies had an established submanagement group in place, people with some sort of training in what they were doing. These squad leaders answered directly to the DIs. This organization seemed better, but everything depended heavily on how well this cadre got along with the rest of the troops. Examples of how good or bad this could be fell into place from the first.

A black private, Jim Haines, checked in when I did. Haines kept a fine, even distinguished appearance in a tailored uniform. Squad leaders ignored everything about his squared-away frame and focused immediately on his delicately trimmed mustache. It looked good to me, but they got on him to remove it during the training cycle. Jim had obviously heard all this before and was citing Army regulations permitting it when a sergeant emerged from an adjoining room and ordered him to shave. We paced side-by-side back to the barracks with him repeating "Goddamn fuckin' Army" at each step. At each utterance in this litany, I offered "Amen."

Warmer spring weather had already set in at Leonard Wood. At the first predawn formation, I heard birds singing and stole glances at two robins cavorting nearby. In the midst of this wonder, we figured we would soon be building bridges and roads and becoming demolition experts.

KP here was easier than KP at Ft. Dix. We endured much less harassment and were given several breaks throughout the day as

53

well as a shorter workday—five in the morning to seven in the evening. The head cook was a fat but refreshingly pleasant white E-6. He never raised his voice or dished out harassment, but he gave matter-of-fact orders. I formed the notion this place would be more civilized than Dix. On day one I was knee-deep in pots and pans with a Mexican named Sam, another "offshore" fellow who was in the Army for reasons of his own. He was no fool. He had signed on for three years instead of the usual two because of the promise of going to a missile school and the possibility that his service would give him American citizenship. He was obviously duped by another snaky Army recruiter filling a quota. Sam, though intelligent, had no command of written English and couldn't get past basic training exams. The Army then transferred him to combat engineer school! We got on well in the kitchen, usually finished early, and our friendly cook let us take extra breaks. We even went on supply runs with one of the Spec-4 cooks who treated us like equals as we all loaded and unloaded boxes.

The physical surroundings were by now familiar. The barracks and company area were similar to the ones at Ft. Dix except for their color. At Dix, buildings were all white; at Leonard Wood, everything was a deep yellow. The two-story wooden barracks were newer than those at Dix, but this meant they barely predated World War II. The bunks were now kept perpendicular to the walls instead of parallel as they had been at Ft. Dix. I again grabbed a bottom bunk. The company compound was rectangular and situated on the crest of a hill with a road leading up one side of the area. This hill made the PT runs memorable and difficult. A large open assembly separated two sides of the company. My barracks and one other were on one side; three more were on the other. The mess hall, headquarters, and day room were single-story buildings on one end of the rectangle; the supply building was on the opposite end.

More than anything, I missed Nancy now. I was nearly a thousand miles from her. I wrote feverish lines to her, usually at night, in the realization that I could never get to Boston on a thirty-two hour pass which was being promised us within two weeks. I did not have the money anyhow, and the $92 the Army paid us each month was a joke. I wouldn't ask her to pay my way, and I couldn't ask my folks for this favor either. I had financed my way through private high school and then college. With three younger kids at home, my parents just did not have the money. Down East practicality also ruled: *never spend what you don't have.*

The basic routine stayed the same. We were up at 4:45 a.m. and outside in company formation to start the day with a forced-march mile run followed by PT. Lights went out at 9:00 p.m. That first week we were issued equipment that was much the same as I had just turned in at Ft. Dix a few days previously: helmets and helmet liners, canteen, belt, mess kit, shovel. All this stuff we would keep in our lockers, which would be subject to inspection. It was so disheartening to think about the possibility that this was going to be basic training all over again. By now, though, we had gotten used to the Army's whimsical ways, and no one suffered such a fear of the unknown as we had at Dix. There was even less sense of urgency.

The training and propaganda films continued. At one of the meetings, the company commander, a young lieutenant, attempted to squelch any rumors that we would all be sent to Vietnam following our training there. He held out the hope that some of us would be sent to Korea or Germany. All of us eligible were fairly certain that it was "the Nam" for us.

Our DI actually interviewed all his platoon members individually. He was a short man who mumbled, but he had been an Army professional for a long time. He inquired if we had any problems. I made a point of mentioning my Achilles tendon problems. He promised to remember this. True to his word, after one two-mile hike, he sought me out with a question about my heels. This amazed me at the time, and I never seemed to have any more pain. The head sergeant, a Master Sergeant E-8, was an older, wiry, black six-footer in great physical shape. A holdover from World War II and the Korean War, he commanded everyone's respect until he required us to sign up for United States Savings Bonds. This meant another allotment taken from our already short pay, and his audience risked

55

some pretty vocal arguments about living off the pittance remaining. The married guys needed every cent; their families were on welfare to survive. The sergeant was adamant, beating down any protest about the $19.75 a month to be withheld from our monthly pay. He was more concerned with total company participation, and he threatened rough going for those who did not get onboard. None of the married troops signed on. I didn't either, but I never heard any more about it.

The second-ranking enlisted cadre was a lanky, 35-year-old white E-7. He forced-marched and ran effortlessly all day long. He fumbled through incoherent lectures as diverse as the communist threat and first aid. It wasn't his job to make great speeches, but rather to push troops, and that he did. A standoffish sort, he nevertheless took questions put to him in earnest. I once asked him why I hadn't been selected to attend a special missile school which didn't require extending from two-year status. He allowed he didn't know for sure, but he speculated that my mechanical and motor maintenance scores were not that good. At least, he didn't put me off and seemed sincerely interested in helping troops within the confines of the world he knew.

The company commander was a genuine ass, a young engineer graduate who had a college ROTC commission. He deferred to the First Sergeant and the E-7 on most issues, but every once in a while he would try to get gung-ho to remind himself of his exalted status. One trainee in another platoon, a college graduate himself, once foolishly called the lieutenant by his first name. Everything stopped cold, and the lieutenant ordered the man to report to him on the following Saturday morning. The lieutenant ordered the excavation of a grave-sized hole. Once this was done the officer walked up to the pit, threw in the butt end of a cigarette, and ordered it filled in again. I don't think he smoked, but he lit one up for the occasion. Instead of instilling a due respect for rank, it opened a chasm between the leaders and the led that became a really raw issue for the field Army in Vietnam. These guys were not the best and the brightest. The older, wiser, enlisted leaders who had endured a couple of wars and could outrun the rest of us were respected. But these young lieutenants who did not know their asses from their elbows wore their authority ignobly and to no good effect.

My own run-in with "Jerry," the lieutenant, came with a double-time two-mile morning run. At the mile-and-a-half point he upped the pace just at the bottom of a hill. A couple of us fell out of step and proceeded to walk and trot back to the formation. Before we got back, a young holdover PFC assigned to this duty by the DIs started shouting in my face to get down and do pushups. I did some pushups, then stood up.

Next he wanted us to double-time it back to the formation. I refused to do that or any more pushups. I yelled back at him that I was doing my best, and that if I could double-time it, I would still be with the formation. There was no reasoning with an idiot. As we arrived back at the formation, the PFC was tattling excitedly to the lieutenant about my transgressions. The lieutenant did nothing then, nor did the DI. I knew better than to press my luck with this PFC by sticking anything in his face. For the rest of AIT he never bothered me again. The message was clear: stay off my back and I won't bother you. Later that day the lieutenant asked me what the problem was. I explained that I could not maintain his pace, fell out, and was heading back to the formation, walking and trotting, when the run-in with the PFC occurred. He seemed ill-at-ease and dismissed me. What could he do to me anyhow, send me to Vietnam?

The first week of AIT passed rather swiftly when compared to basic training. We learned about electric and pneumatic tools. Rigging was a whole science of knotting and sling work for emplacing rope bridges. Tying diagramed knots was not difficult, but doing it from memory the next time eluded me. The written tests after each series of classroom instructions were relatively simple if you paid attention. The tests were supposedly geared to a sixth-grade level. Many of us more theoretically educated types still had trouble with terms and tools we had never seen before. I had too little grounding in the practical elements of life and thought my bother Ron would have made it here. Some of us envied the people in the missile training classes. We figured those guys would never go to Vietnam and carry a rifle.

In one class I asked the instructor what the casualty rate was for combat engineers in Vietnam. During a one-year survey of 1,000 combat engineers, he revealed, nine were killed, and five of those were in a jeep accident. He also indicated that the Viet Cong did not usually attack engineering units because they built roads and bridges, an asset for their country. The same roads built by day could very easily be used by them at night. He maintained that if one's orders read for a specific engineer company in Vietnam, then that person would be a combat engineer, but orders making you a general replacement could land you in the infantry. Everything he said seemed to make the point that most of us would be going to Vietnam and most likely to infantry units.

Other harder statistics were against me too. About half of my company, Echo, or E-3-1 (AIT), consisted of officer candidates, people who would not go to Nam immediately. Another 20 percent were U.S. Army Reserves (ARs) and National Guards (NGs), and another 5 percent were 17-year-olds, which kept them out of the war zone for another year. This left the last 25 percent which seemed certainly destined for Vietnam. The chances of my going to Germany were slim. With my knowledge of modern European history, I might enjoy myself there, and for that reason alone the Army would never assign me there. I would be assigned according to the needs of the Army.

In the second week at Leonard Wood, the temperature dropped to the 30s and high 40s. During that week we participated in the night map-reading orienteering course. We went out about nine miles that night. Several guys got lost. The object was to find our way back through completely unfamiliar area to a specified point using a compass and a map. If you did not panic and went carefully, then you could pass with ease. Some guys ran helter-skelter through the woods, missing reference points and losing themselves for hours. The exercise reminded me of summer camping trips my family took all over New England. The outdoor toilets were usually some distance from the campsite, and that distance seemed farther at night. My brother and I would take a flashlight, tramp through the woods, find the outhouse, do our duty, and find our way back, losing each other and leaping from behind a tree to scare one another. Dark woods were not intimidating, and I never gave in to panic. I felt I could blend in and lose the rest of the people and still get back.

The usual human burlesque followed us too. Our platoon had a 17-year-old white kid from rural New Jersey who through God-knows-what accident had lost all his teeth, and now sported a set of false ones. He was a short and wiry tenth-grade high-school dropout with a marvelously comedic sense of mime. On impulse he would spit out his teeth, seize a broom, and do a shuffling routine of a dim-witted sort who was trying to whistle a tune as he tripped over the broom. During one platoon formation, our DI was pacing back and forth in front of us repeating his conviction that we were smarter than the infantry and perhaps would not be sent to Vietnam. In the middle of the platoon this kid pocketed his teeth, and every time the DI faced away from him, treated the ranks to his patented toothless grin, the mark of the obviously smarter combat engineers. Physical comedy may be among the lower forms of humor, but it goes a long way in the Army.

Near the end of the second week Nancy surprised me with a package of chocolate-chip cookies. I shared some of them with the guys, but I really wanted to hoard them, keep them secret, and savor them only once in a while. Nancy was an obsession now. Every time I got a letter I smelled it, read it quickly, then read it slowly, devouring every word and nuance. I carried each one folded in my shirt pocket to read several more times until I got the next one to start the cycle again. I saved everything she sent—except the cookies. Mail call was the same ordeal as at Dix. At day's end we lined up in company formation and anxiously waited for our names to be called out. It was the only time in the Army you wanted to hear your name called. About the second week I was lining Nancy up to spend much of my anticipated leave following AIT with her.

We only had about three weeks, so I wanted to make most of it. She was the real reason why I wanted to make it through this thing. I proposed that she stay at my folks home in Portland.

On Saturday morning, March 29, the entire post staged a huge parade in honor of President Eisenhower who had died earlier in the week. Some twenty thousand troops of many companies and battalions assembled. It was pleasantly warm that day, and I found some purpose in the event. I knew of Eisenhower's military stature and grew up during his presidential years, and so found this a worthy tribute.

We also were issued our first pass that day. Even here the Army practiced its curious way with incentives. Since our platoon had finished last in total performance for the week, our passes were not issued until five o'clock. The first-place platoon got passes at noon, and the second-place platoon at three. I did get ten hours of sleep that weekend, something that I had not done in ages. I went to a movie with some of the guys—*100 Rifles* with Jim Brown. It seemed as if in every scene someone would be shot, not the most pleasant thought.

I got my hands on Harold Laski's *The Age of European Liberalism* at that time, and its thesis found resonance with my own worries about going to Vietnam. Laski elaborates on the decline of single-church control in temporal matters and the rise of religious toleration, a general mood of live and let live. The gradual waning of divine-right monarchy in turn enabled individual commoners to amass greater wealth and hence political influence. I asked if the next phase could be toleration among all creeds including from capitalism to communism. One or both sides would have to take a first step. Could not the United States do this by gradually pulling itself out of Vietnam? I hoped President Nixon would keep some promises and start pulling people out of Vietnam.

During my second week at Leonard Wood, the Army was running us through a series of booster shots when I learned that my medical records had been lost between Ft. Dix and Ft. Leonard Wood. At the first station, the status of our medical records was loudly announced by a couple of medics behind a table. As I stepped in line inside the large gymnasium, the medic informed me I had no shot records. A bit too joyfully, he shouted down the line that I needed the works. Getting the works involved passing between two rows of guys armed with pressurized immunizer guns. The victim advanced down the line as the orderlies with the instruments literally fired medication directly through the skin of both upper arms, a process vastly speeded up, and much to be desired, over the days of the single needle. A man with shot records got only the gun he still needed. I got it from both sides, full loads on both shoulders. My arms were limp, and I could barely get my shirt back on. The pain would subside, but not my anger with the Army. If I had carried the records myself, this would not have happened, but the Army could not trust a stupid private to carry his own shot records. Someone at my old company should have forwarded my records after I got out of the hospital. Once a person gets off the track as I did by being hospitalized at Dix, though, the system goes haywire. The shot records were never found in my entire two-year Army career. At least I had a new set and resolved to keep an eye on them.

The threat of infantry service was a constant theme in the training. During the third week, the DIs lectured us about flunking the training tests. Half the company was flunking, they maintained gravely, and we had better get on the stick if we did not want to become "grunts" in Vietnam. Combat engineers "had it made" compared to infantrymen, they repeated, and we would not see much action. This encouraged me, especially since *Time*'s issue of March 28, 1969, gave a body count in the war zone of over 1,000 for the most recent three weeks. The same article quoted some U.S. generals as saying that the United States was not succeeding in containing the Viet Cong because the Viet Cong's last offensive proved they could strike anywhere at any time. The ARVN (Army of the Republic of Vietnam) had not improved as a fighting force in a year, and it was losing about 13,000 AWOLs a month. None of this boded well for us. Our professed objective was for the ARVN to take over the war and eventually enable our U.S. troops to withdraw. We were hearing that this million-man Vietnamese Army could not stand alone against the communist threat. We had achieved our goal of a stable government in South Vietnam, since the Thieu government had retained power for seventeen months. Thieu seemed the best politician of a shaky lot, representing a consolidation of vested interests, but his staying power rested on retaining that balance. However, the possibility also existed that the slightest incident, fraud, scandal, or battlefield defeat could upset that balance.

Thoughts of that country haunted us all, even those whose sense of geography was way off. One 18-year-old from Cicero, near Chicago, had a booming voice in which he was always either boosting Chicago's virtues or calling the wrath of God down on something. When we discussed assignment possibilities in Vietnam, he would inevitably shout that he didn't care where he went with one exception, he did not want to be sent to Hanoi. When we asked him why, he couldn't answer. He also knew of no units or personal friends that had been specifically assigned to Hanoi. Chicago, as we called him, was either dumber than he sounded or he knew something we didn't. On a world map he couldn't tell Turkey from Tokyo, but he expounded with such authority and conviction that he convinced some of his younger comrades he knew what he was talking about. Chicago could outperform most of the platoon in physical activities, but he fell asleep without fail five minutes into any lecture. The sergeants devised special tortures for him, running him around the area with rocks in his backpack while everyone else took a break. This was to energize him into staying awake or to provide an incentive to keep awake. Nothing worked. He had all the stamina in the world for physical activities but nothing left for mental exercise. We wisecracked that if he ever took a wrong turn he'd end up in Hanoi with a knapsack full of bricks and drive the North Vietnamese crazy.

In the third week, we built Bailey bridges in night and day exercises. A British invention of World War II-vintage, the bridges were an engineering marvel made of interlocking cantilever panels bolted together in various configurations capable of carrying over 30-ton loads. The panel sections each weighed about 650 pounds and were moved around by eight sweating troops. At night we worked by moonlight, and the danger of catching hands or feet in the shifting parts increased. One evening a man caught a thumb between two steel sections being bolted together, but he returned to duty the next day. I hoped that we would never have to build one of these bridges at night in Vietnam. It would be difficult enough to see at night, but I had the impression that the enemy was more difficult to deal with after sundown.

One instructor had his own routine for teaching bridge assembly, and it came off in the Army's usual high-minded way. He picked a trainee and inquired if he knew the difference between a female and a male. The wary candidate said he thought so.

"Good, asshole!" said the sergeant, "Now come up here and explain the male and female parts of the bridge." The instructor sent the bewildered soldier to his seat. Now the sergeant took one of the long "male" bolts and held it up.

"For all you assholes who still think your dick is to pee through, you are dumber than a dumb cunt. This bolt is the male end, and to build this bridge you are going to have to do a lot of fucking. These many male ends go into these female holes." He was so outrageous we laughed the whole time, but we got the picture. This guy had a potential career when he retired from the Army as sex education instructor.

During these exercises, the instructors pitted squad against squad in bridge-building contests. Our squad leader, Nelson, was a blond Minnesotan with a college degree headed for OCS after AIT. A decent sort, he had a cheerleader's approach to leading men. He reasoned with his people to do what he ordered because it was the right thing to do. I could never get up for his rah-rah attitude. He was fair and tried to get us information when we asked about the future. He wouldn't bullshit anyone, and I really thought his sincerity and enthusiasm would make him a good officer. I couldn't be that sincere about something I didn't believe in. The closest I had come to exercising this kind of suasion was as caddie master at the Portland Country Club. I managed to train a bunch of young caddies in proper green positioning, how to hold the pin, how not to allow your shadow to cross the hole or the line of the put, how to clean and smooth the sand traps, replace fairway divots, where to stand on shortcuts and many other aspects of caddying. Eventually even the 12-year-old caddies could estimate distances and suggest clubs. Even now this seemed like more of an accomplishment to me than motivating troops to make bridges.

My psychological opposite was bunked next to me. Bill was a tall, thin Marylander who was anxious to get to OCS. He was not just enthusiastic, he could almost taste it. He wanted to make his father proud of him by becoming an Army officer. His father was delighted with him for graduating from college, he said, but becoming an officer would earn him additional respect. Bill liked to lord it over guys he thought were not as bright as he was. On several occasions I pointed out that demeaning people was a poor attribute for a quality officer. If he continued to browbeat his troops, he would never command their respect. Like many others, he confused rank with power and success. If you were on line in Vietnam it would seem that this attitude could be unhealthy. From what I had seen in the Army thus far, the enlisted man was doing the work anyhow, and the more pragmatic officers looked to the enlisted men for direction on how to get a job done. This was my impression after about twelve weeks at the lowest levels of the Army.

Army chaplains tended to support the whole program, too. One afternoon the Catholic chaplain came to one of our classes and talked to us about the gratitude we should all have for being physically fit to join the Army and serve our country. If he had stayed much longer he would have had us all wearing large printed crosses on the front and back of our uniforms to better fight the holy war against the infidels in Vietnam. He rambled earnestly about the U.S. Army keeping peace in the world and doing a great service for freedom. After his remarks about the fit being in the Army, I resented again those who had escaped the draft with faked injuries. After this war a whole generation would be composed of cripples, and the only physically fit people would be Vietnam veterans, miraculously uninjured. Then, if that were the case, many jobs should be waiting for the returning healthy veterans because so many people back in the states had physical profiles. But we all knew that such catastrophic injuries tended to heal miraculously after people reached the magical age of twenty-six. The majority of our company remained polite in the chaplain's company. In the barracks the older cynics among us made me know I was not alone in my thinking. As a Roman Catholic, I was rather embarrassed by the speech. The next Sunday some of us went to a Protestant service to hear their party line. The Protestant minister gave us the same similar rhetoric: the evils of communism can and must be stopped, and we were the forefront of that effort. I felt much better knowing that the Papists and the Protestants had reached common ecumenical ground in the Army.

We learned about fortifications, starting with foxholes and protective concertina wire. We made bunkers, some stronger than others, but we also found out how vulnerable we would be to direct hits from enemy rockets. Cement bunkers overlaid with dirt would serve as little forts, proof against small arms and mortar fire, but they could not protect us much from direct artillery fire. In this context, during the fourth week, a sergeant with Vietnam experience as a combat engineer gave us a new set of survival statistics. Of 160 men, 6 were killed and nearly 100 received some type of wound, a figure he said was not that bad compared to the statistics in some infantry companies. That did not sound as good to me as the previously quoted statistics, especially since I now had 29 days left in AIT.

Also during that fourth week, we spent a five-day training period on mines and demolition. In a week's time we were to become demolition experts. Rumor had it that if any combat engineer was assigned to an infantry company, he would automatically become the unit's demolition expert. We also had to probe for mines on our hands and knees, a frightful process even with the benign training mines we worked on. These things, equipped with blasting caps, gave off a sharp snap when activated. Anyone could easily imagine what a real mine would do if it wasn't detected. We probed the earth for the buried charges with an instrument that looked like an elongated ice-pick. When my turn came I moved very slowly, imagining the effects of a real mine and dreading the mini-explosion of the cap. Painstakingly I slid on my knees in the dirt, expecting contact with something solid in the ground before me. Suddenly I gave an involuntary shudder and my heart and stomach seemed to reach my mouth. I thought that a cap had gone off, but as I regained my senses I realized that Louis had tiptoed behind me and jammed his thumbs into either side of my ribs. We rolled on the ground laughing. Totally focused on millimeters of dirt in front of me, I never expected something might come from behind.

Louis was a very lanky black fellow from Mississippi. You got an education about the American racial divide being around him. He was very defensive when people told him to do something, especially the whites. Around other black soldiers, he would talk about getting his "black ass" going, but never resorted to self-deprecation around whites. He would take no bullshit. None of us liked to take orders, but he particularly disliked it. A man with a wildly funny side, he could also go into a rage over small incidents. Once we were assigned to construct picnic tables. He could not get it right and stood around laughing about his lopsided table, generally fucking around so that the job slowed down. If we finished our allotment, we could all take a break. Sam, an OCS candidate with a degree in engineering, went over to Louis and took the hammer out of his hand.

"Come on, man, we can get this done," he said. Louis flew into a rage at this.

"You motherfucker. Don't you ever take this hammer away from me." He threatened to hit Sam with the hammer and might have succeeded had Sherman White, another black man, not stopped him. Sam should never have snatched the hammer away, but Louis was not playing with the team.

Sherman White was big, 6 feet, 4 inches tall and about 220 pounds, and was among the decent men I knew then, given to reflective, quiet speech. I often talked with him about our upcoming adventure in Vietnam, and he said that he wasn't sure that he would go. He would make up his mind later, unfazed that he would be charged as a deserter or AWOL if he did not show up. I saw Sherman pissed only once. After lunch at an outside training session we had a few moments before the next activity when a real white-trash idiot turned to Sherman.

"Hey, why you standing around here acting like a lazy nigger?"

Sherman moved with easy purpose. He seized this wiry white smartmouth off his feet by the collar and slammed him just as quickly nearly headfirst to the ground. Sherman was his own man and liked order and fairness. Even when some of the brothers would attempt to jump to the front of the chow line, he would join the rest of us in pointing out where the line started. There was always some idiot who had to be shown how team ethos works. It was always nice to have Sherman on your side. Race relations in the Army were as tense as anywhere else in America in 1969, but some of the damnedest fights started in the enlisted clubs over music. Hard rock and soul music contrasted harshly with the country and western songs favored by many of the southern whites.

One glaring Army prejudice that became evident in basic but showed up more in AIT was the dislike among the regular cadre for members of the NG and the Enlisted Reserve (ER). Even the easygoing cook would yell when the chow line was about to form, "NGs and ERs at the end of the line." These people were considered "candy asses" for staying home from the real war after basic and AIT. They just weren't considered real soldiers. If someone would ask a sergeant a dumb question, the incredulous sergeant often demanded: "What are you, scumbum, some type of NG or ER?" These people were really second-class citizens, really Jodys in drag. (A Jody is the guy who stays home from the war and steals your girlfriend.)

Near the end of the demolition training week, we learned how to assemble charges and then blow them up. The scenery at the demolition range was spectacular. It was a very fine day, warm with a slight breeze and a deep blue, almost cloudless, sky. The range

67

itself was bordered on one side by high cliffs dotted with pine trees. I was again reminded of some my family camping trips. A couple of large turkey buzzards plied the updrafts near the cliffs, the only visible sign of wildlife. They seemed ominous, eyeing us or searching for smaller moving prey. It dawned on me they were waiting for some trainee to make a mistake with the demolition exercise and give them a meal. We watched some engineer experts set off some powerful plastic explosives. The whole thing was fascinating but daunting. I figured it would take quite a lot more training for any of us to be able to do that without maiming ourselves. If we had to blow up things in combat with what we knew at that moment, we would be more lethal to our own troops than to the enemy. The whole week with the mines, a sergeant reassured us, was supposed to be a familiarization program preparing us for our next station and more explosives training.

The next weekend, April 12, we all had extra duties, and mine was to help plant new grass. It was easy work in beautiful weather. The Army was getting some real cheap labor on some cleanup and base beautification projects. That afternoon, with the detail complete, about twenty of us went to a nearby field and played softball. The soul brothers busted each other every time one came to bat. No one knew what the score was, it was just a good time. Afterwards we went out to get a steak and some drinks and partied until midnight. The only thing missing was girls. Some of the guys took care of that at whorehouses off-base and came back with tall tales, but it just was not my style. One short black kid was legendary for having a huge dick. After all these big guys had gone in to see this one particular girl, he marched inside and took off his pants. At the sight of his equipment, the lady burst into tears. All the others backed him in every detail of the story. I sure did miss Nancy and spent a lot of time pouring out my heart in letters.

Squad tactics dominated the fifth week. In a series of maneuvers, we attacked a variety of fixed positions. One side played enemy while the other attacked. In one scenario, we advanced up a hill toward an open spot, each man spread ten meters from the next.

VOICES FROM THE REAR

In the clearing, we suddenly took fire from the top of the hill. We all hit the ground and then provided cover for each other as we moved slowly up the hill in classic Army fire-and-maneuver. Rushing forward in leaps and bounds, we searched constantly for any indentation in the earth or rock to use for cover. At the top the sergeant gave us high marks. He figured we would not have lost too many in the assault and would have taken the position. Of course this was all done with blank cartridges.

One evening my bunkmate Bill and I went out to play Charlie Cong. We were to sneak through the woods and get a good position in front of the company and ambush the advancing column. The flaw in the plan was my malfunctioning M-14. My sergeant finally peered into it before we went out, and he pronounced it fine. We killed time in one ambush for thirty minutes with me assuring Bill that my rifle would surely fire this time, but no one came our way. We ran around some more in the woods to a better place. Here some "enemy" troops stumbled into us, and the rifle jammed again. Bill got hysterical over my "Oh-fuck-shafted-again" expression, and he soon had me giggling. We ran from that position to another, and the damn thing finally fired. I was so pissed that I just kept blazing away into the dusk until my last ammunition clip was empty.

It began to look more like real combat now. On these squad tactics we were intermittently schooled in the M-60 machine gun, the 3.5-mm. rocket launcher, the .50 caliber machine gun, and the M-79 grenade launcher. The M-60 machine gun impressed me because one man could carry and set it up to command a field of fire out to 1,100 meters. It was easy to fire but hard to master. At 126 pounds, the .50 caliber was unmanageable for one person, and its rounds were about half as thick as my arm. It penetrated three-quarter-inch armor and would certainly kill a man, even obliterate him, but it really had to be mounted to be effective. We all got to fire one round, and I recall the kick. The entire company watched the 3.5-mm. rocket launcher fired at a distant object. We were drilled in how to position ourselves to use it, but we were never allowed to fire it. The light, compact M-79 grenade launcher was

69

most impressive. Even on the run, a soldier could elevate the weapon to drop a round behind an obstacle. It had a decent range of 300 meters and a killing arc of about 5 meters. After several practice shots, one could easily figure out the trajectory.

The weapons instructors were a different lot, all of them having seen Vietnam combat. They were fairly gruesome in the detail they gave us about the effects of the ordnance. One guy still had a glazed look. His eyes were watery and distant as though he was still seeing something terrible and was stunned at the sight. I did not rule out the possibility that he might have been on something or had a rough previous night. They seemed callous about human life, but I supposed that is the only way one can look at it when one is under fire. Another instructor related how his company was ambushed and he fired his weapon until the barrel became too hot to use. He had lost some of his buddies and had seen others wounded, but he lay there and kept on firing. He said it was over rather quickly, with the Viet Cong pulling out after initial contact, and they really could not tell how many of the enemy had been killed.

After the field exercises we could frequent a beer hall with an outside seating area and just relax, sip brew, and shoot the breeze in the late afternoon sun. The enlisted men's club on the weekends took on a more raucous atmosphere. It was always too crowded, with a go-go girl on a small stage gyrating to a band whose only virtue was volume. All these horny guys would ogle the one female in the big space where no one could hear himself think, let alone talk. If we were lucky, on weekends we were off duty at noon on Saturday until 6:00 p.m. Sunday. I seemed to pick up more than my share of KP duties, manning the company phone in three-hour stints, with general clerical work for the sergeants thrown in too. You couldn't get anywhere from Leonard Wood overnight. On the fifth weekend, Bill, Nelson, and I headed to St. Louis for a Cardinals game. It wasn't close, but we enjoyed being with other people and drinking a few beers. Nelson took us to the chapter of his old college fraternity at St. Louis University, hoping the brothers would show us a good time or tell us where some action was. Nobody there was too receptive, leaving me uncomfortable and actually feeling bad for Nelson. These kids obviously had no use for soldiers and didn't want us around. We walked to the waterfront, ate something, and finally got a cheap hotel room and just fell asleep. After breakfast the next morning, Sunday, we took an elevator ride to the top of the St. Louis Arch. Being out in society still left me with doubts about going back to the post, but thoughts of going AWOL were more distant now. I rather wanted to finish AIT and get the hell out of there and start getting my life into shape. A cabdriver driving us from the base bus station to our company area insisted on preaching against draft dodgers and war protesters. He wanted all these people in prison. Nelson stopped me from getting into it with this guy, a forty-something draftee during the Korean War. Nelson quietly observed that we were not going to change his mind. We had more important things to do.

Five weeks were already behind us. I was certain they had passed much more quickly than the time in basic training, which had seemed like two years. One thing was worrying all of us who were not NG, ER, or going to OCS after AIT: where was our next assignment? Some hoped for Noncommissioned Officers' School, which would ensure them of another six-month stint in the states at Ft. Leonard Wood; some held out hope for assignment to Europe or even Korea. Most of us resigned ourselves that we were going to Vietnam. Even the DIs started telling us that the first duty of a combat engineer is that he is an infantryman first and a combat engineer second. I had no delusions that I would be going anywhere but Vietnam.

I passed the PT test with flying colors, even running the mile in under 7½ minutes. I scored 380 out of the 500 points. I had no problems as I had in basic training. I was in the best shape that I had been in years.

By week seven, it was bivouac again. We marched to the camp area and set up. The first night we had no winter sleeping bags in a sudden cold snap, so we froze in the tents without much sleep. In the morning a couple of brothers entertained us. One was hobbling along with a stick because he was so stiff from the previous evening. A couple of the other guys got on him for looking like Uncle Remus. The camp outhouse was a long, narrow, wooden building with about ten latrine seats in a line. At each end was a door. Clients in true Army fashion lined up at one end, entered and sat for business, and, when finished, left by the opposite door. Seated on the thrones, each group of ten could look out through a screened-in front wall, and everyone else could look in—no privacy, inside or out. DIs who happened by felt obliged to supervise even this activity and move the crowd along. It could be worse: we might have had just an open pit to bend over and shit in. We spent the nights on exercises firing weapons and chasing each other around in the woods, the good guys against Charlie Cong. After the first cool night, we were rewarded with mild weather, and whatever sleep we did get was really welcome. When we just sat and waited for something to happen, it was easy to drift off in reverie.

    One night I sat dreaming about a beach party at Ferry Beach in Maine in late May 1966, my senior year at the university. A hundred of us had been out there from five in the afternoon well into the evening, drinking beer and talking. I remembered the girl of the moment; we had just patched things up after some months of taking it easy. My best buddies were there, and all was just fine with the world. I was a couple of weeks from graduating, accepted already for a resident assistantship at Niagara University. I wanted to make time stop and keep all these people within reach. We were all getting pretty mellow on beer and good company. Why grow up? Couldn't we just talk about the war and not have to witness it? One of these guys was soon drafted and sent to Vietnam, but he made it back. Another joined the Peace Corps for two years, but he was still badgered by the draft board when he got out. He eventually got deferred by claiming he picked up some exotic disease in India. That malady lasted only until the magic age of twenty-six. A third guy was two years behind us and had completed his undergraduate degree. Lucky enough to draw a high draft lottery number, he never had to serve and sailed unhindered right through law school. The crackle of those infernal blank rounds in the night brought me abruptly back to where I was. The platoon was moving out again. On the last day of bivouac, we took some relatively simple written tests and boarded trucks for company headquarters. Tension prevailed that day, for the whole platoon was on the verge of getting orders to our next assignments.

Mine seemed to fulfill some dread destiny. I opened the paper, already knowing what the future held. The glimmer of hope for assignment to Europe died right there. The word leaped off the sheet: *Vietnam.* I was to report to Oakland Army Terminal, California, on June 5, 1969, but I could look forward to a twenty-one-day leave starting May15. I felt down about the assignment, but in no way surprised.

Well, at least I got a break and a chance to get rid of my bad feelings about the assignment. Six of us, Nelson, Bill, Sam Goldhammer, Dick Henderson, and Pete Wilson, little known to me but a bosom buddy of Henderson's, got a car and left Saturday at noon for the Lake of the Ozarks resort area. Henderson usually ran the mile with combat boots in about five minutes flat. We rented a cabin on the lake at $66 a night. We spurned the pool to swim in the lake and even skated at an indoor rink. The resort's French restaurant outdid itself that evening, and with fine wine we laughed a lot and tried to forget the sentences the Army had just passed on us. I stole out several times and tried calling Nancy, but I couldn't raise her. I just wanted to commiserate with her about the Vietnam assignment.

Propaganda films and some lectures filled the last few days of AIT, with more of the bullshit on why we were fighting this war. The Army was barely coping with the war by this time. At one of these last briefings, though, the Vietnam-bound troops were wonderfully entertained by remarks on sexual hygiene. A young black captain had a straightforward opener.

"I'll bet you guys think if you don't use your dicks your sperm will build up inside your body until it passes your eyeballs and eventually blows your brains out." He wanted us to be very careful with "our guns," he said. "There are isolated places in Vietnam where there are guys with diseases that they will never get rid of." He made it sound like a leper colony on top of everything else. Selective fucking seemed the watchword, or else it was total abstinence for us.

One positive result of the loss of my records was that I had to refire the M-16 so I could leave a set of official training scores. I made sharpshooter in basic with that rifle and appreciated the additional time to practice with it since that would be the main weapon we would use in Vietnam. Eight of us trucked to the range and zeroed in the rifles. The thing felt comfortable now. We had taken it apart and reassembled it endlessly during classes. It was my friend and protector. The day was warm with little or no breeze, and the drill included a series of pop-up targets appearing at increasing distances from the shooters. The close targets were easy and went down with a single round. Then in quick succession I drilled the 100- and the 150-meter targets. Man! I was hot! Then the farthest target sprang up. Christ! It must have been 300 meters out there and barely visible. I squinted down the sights and fired directly into the center of its mass. A second round followed the first, by now some kind of a record. The sergeant announced I had just fired expert. I was relieved to be so confident of my marksmanship on the eve of my departure for a war zone, and a little proud of myself, too. The Army had made me a master of the weapon in only 16 weeks. As the NG and ER members of the company drifted off for their homes, we stood in ever smaller formations. During one of these after the firing exercise, a newly minted E-7 sergeant first class (SFC) asked me why I was not going to OCS. He thought I took direction well, was confident with weapons, and would make a good leader. I told this earnest fellow the time was not right, I had things that I wanted to do and that the shortest distance between two points was a straight line. OCS would delay me for another year. I wanted to get out as soon as possible. He thought I was making a mistake, but I knew too much about the survivability of an infantry lieutenant in Vietnam.

VOICES FROM THE REAR

By the strange workings of the human mind, one other thing that kept me going at the time was the Boston Celtics. My dad and I were addicted to broadcasts of the games. Johnnie Most, the partisan radio voice of the team, always gave gripping, purple descriptions of the action. Listening to him, we just knew Bill Russell was the first bionic man. "Russell is being punched," Most would holler into the mike. "He is bleeding, he was tripped, slapped, belted, it is a WONDER the man can WALK!" Televised games had none of this color. If you tuned in to Most and watched on television at the same time, it was always two entirely different games, and this phenomenon became ritual to many New Englanders. Most made the Celtics the good guys, and all else was evil. The Celtics took nine regular season Eastern Conference Championships in succession from 1957 to 1965 and eight straight National Basketball Championships from 1959 to 1966. After Philadelphia won the NBA in 1967, the aging Celtic team came from behind the following year to take the title. With the team down three games to one before the fifth game in Philadelphia, the pundits pronounced Celtic glory at an end. Banners in the Philly Palestra proclaimed "The Old Men Are Dead." The inimitable Russell dominated the day and pulled out a magnificent upset. Boston knocked off three straight to win the series. I was in tears in the final minutes of the last game. Even now, in the Army, I took sustenance from that tableau of morality, resurrection, and redemption. If the Celtics could do it, so could I.

A few days later, my stint at Ft. Leonard Wood, Missouri, was over. We had turned in our equipment and started saying good-bye. Nelson and I exchanged addresses. I was glad to be going home to see Nancy and my family. Again, the people just sort of vanished. The NGs and ERs had trickled out a few days earlier. There was no mass exodus. We gathered our duffel bags, signed out of the company, and then got transportation to the bus depot. While I would not miss this place, I would always remember the pleasant weather conditions that made it just so much easier to train. I was in real good shape. The time had passed much more quickly than at basic training. Yet, I did not feel bad leaving. Ft. Leonard Wood was but an interlude before the real trial, Vietnam.

A bunch of us boarded the bus for the St. Louis airport. After arriving we split up to go to various airlines. I was the only one on that bus going to Boston, so after eight weeks I was riding alone again, this time heading east. I was anxious to see Nancy and my family.

Nancy met me at the gate. We hugged and talked a bit and headed back to her place in Quincy where she picked up a few things. We then drove to my folks' place in Portland. The weather was warming, and we had a couple of great outings at the beach with my sister Estelle and her boyfriend Skip and a few others. At one memorable cookout on the rocks near Biddeford Pool we had a huge supply of lobsters and clams. On another occasion a group of us went fishing with my sister and Skip and Mark Alden, the guy who went with me and my brother to the Allagash the previous September. The fish still weren't biting, and the diversion could not alleviate the anxiety of my next move. Shit, I just did not want these good times to end.

Nancy took much of her leave during this time, working only a few days. We spent some time with her parents in Agawam, Massachusetts. They kept the one and a half acre grounds surrounding their small but neatly maintained house superbly landscaped. They were concerned about my upcoming Vietnam tour. It was pleasant chatting with her father and mother. Apparently they had accepted me and liked me. I just did not have time to care or think about how they would receive me. I did not have the time, and what little I had I wanted to spend with Nancy.

Nancy and George on the rocks at Biddeford Pool, Maine, in May 1969.

From Agawam we drove to see my friend Brud Higgins and his wife Joyce in South Hadley. We were graduate students together at Niagara University. I was his best man at their wedding. We hung out a lot at his tiny apartment in Niagara Falls, New York, during the two years that we attended the university. He had a history department assistantship and did not have to live on campus, whereas my resident assistantship required that I live in one of the dorms. So his apartment was a refuge from dorm life. The four of us went out to eat and dance. After an evening of fun we decided to get a cup of coffee at a restaurant along River Road in West Springfield. On the road, I took a left turn in the face of a road sign clearly prohibiting that maneuver and was almost immediately pulled over by a policeman. I pleaded with the man: I had never seen the sign. As we went on, I had to tell the officer I would soon be leaving for Vietnam and could not make any court appearance. He let me go. I wondered, if I had been arrested, would I then be AWOL? It was not a bad thought as I believed it would be easier for me in prison than in Vietnam. So, for the first time in my life I did not fear a confrontation with the police. What were they going to do to me anyhow, send me to Vietnam?

Nancy and I got engaged during that summer interlude with the cloud of Vietnam hanging over me. We got a ring at E. G. Foden's in Portland. She chose an opal and I paid for it with my last $400. We could pick it up in two weeks. I told the clerk that I was bound for Vietnam and really needed to have the ring on schedule. Two weeks later, there was no sign of it. I had to leave without being able to present this token. Instead she received it in a cardboard box. The way things were going, I figured the box would also have my shot records.

We also saw another old friend, Buddy Boomhour, and his wife Margaret. I had also been Buddy's best man. He had just returned from a tour in Vietnam. We did not talk too much about his year in Nam, and he either could not or did not give me much encouragement about my prospects. It was different now that he was married and I was with Nancy. It just was not the same relationship. We would always have a lot of good times in college to remember.

As I had anticipated, the twenty days of leave swiftly passed, very much unlike the time spent in basic training. The last day was particularly brutal. Nancy was at my parents' home. We had breakfast. My dad and mom drove us to Logan Airport in Boston. The TWA clerk at the ticket counter noticed my uniform and asked if I wanted to fly military standby because I could save about $50. He assured me that I would have no trouble getting on the flight—nice of the guy to be looking out for a soldier, especially one that was going to Vietnam.

Then the time came to say good-bye. I hugged my mom and shook hands with dad. They quietly backed off to leave me alone with Nancy. I hugged her to me. She was crying, and I was doing my best not to. I promised to write as soon as I could. I turned glumly away and walked to the plane. I felt like a dish rag. I got to my window seat, and the tears came. I did not care if the plane crashed on the way to California. I was so tired of saying good-bye, I just wanted to get this fucking war off my back and get my life back to normal.

The airplane to San Francisco was half full. About halfway through the flight another private walked down the aisle and sat in the empty seat next to me. He introduced himself as Tom and said he was going to Vietnam. We quickly established common ground. He had just left Leonard Wood and was reporting to the same place I was, the Army Overseas Replacement Station at Oakland Army Base no later than 1200 hours on June 5, 1969. Among the thousands of people going through that place, he had trained to be a heavy equipment operator and figured he would never draw infantry duty. Talk seemed to divert him, and he poured out his identity to me. He was from New Bedford, Massachusetts, and had dropped out of high school in the tenth grade. He was nineteen years old, about five feet, ten inches tall and solidly built, was dark haired and had a face scarred by adolescent acne. He was a truck driver. His boss had fired him for a traffic accident. While he was nursing his feelings over this insult, his draft board added the injury of a call-up. Since we would be landing at about 5:30 p.m. local time and then had a whole evening to kill, we figured on getting a cab to San Francisco and stay the night at the local YMCA.

We had no sooner hailed a cab when we ran into a guy I knew at Ft. Leonard Wood. John Fish, who always went only by his last name, had a college degree and two years of law school. It was always unclear why he left, but the draft soon took him, too. Fish was a short guy with glazed green eyes and a haunted look. He was in another platoon of my company at AIT, but his reputation as a wit preceded him as far as our unit. He quickly joined the two of us in the cab. We settled in, ate aimlessly, and got some beer to go for an evening of TV and contemplation about our upcoming ordeal.

Would we be combat engineers and would we be assigned as a combat engineer in an infantry unit? Tom kept repeating his assurance that he would not be an infantryman because he had signed up for three years with heavy equipment. Fish and I could only guess about where we were going.

The next morning we checked out, headed for a deli, and walked around for three hours. As we waited at one corner for a light to change, a dirty, long-haired guy in a faded blue-denim jacket and pants wandered over to us, surveyed our uniforms, and began shouting obscenities. "Warmongers!" he kept on. In the middle of this tirade he launched a wad of spit, most of which hit me. Without a thought I leaped on him. With odds of three against one and us going to Vietnam, he was the one taking chances. The guy was about twenty years old and just my size, but slighter. He was under me on the curb and I wanted to prolong his agony before beating the shit out of him. Could I work up the biggest "lunger" possible, and spit it in his face and make him say that it was the best meal ever? It never occurred to me that this asshole might have a concealed weapon. This shit-for-brains was abusing me for heading off under orders to an unpopular war while, as I figured it, he had some contrived deferment. I suddenly wanted to make him pay for all the inequities of the world. He was a mouse and I was the cat, and I was going to play with him. Tom hastily yanked me off him. Here was the irony: a young, unlucky, high school dropout pulling me off this piece of scum to keep the peace. It struck me later that any incident might have delayed or even prevented my going to Nam had I been obliged to answer to assault charges in San Francisco. The frightened rat scampered off. Tom and Fish wanted no trouble. "Shit, what trouble?" I went on for a while.

An hour later we were at the Oakland Army Base, the predominant color of which in 1969 was a light pistachio green. Everything visible on base was neatly manicured. In a large classroom with desk chairs, a major told us we would be staying here for no more than a few days, but we had to show up at mass formations three times a day to see if our name would be called. After more form-filling we found bunks in Building 590, a huge warehouse and temporary home while we were in transit. Unlike the barracks in basic training and AIT, the warehouse had vending machines. We were free to walk around the base but not away from it. Chow was decent, but I was too anxious to eat much. I was also hoping to avoid a KP assignment or some additional duty. At the processing station, we were told we would not be staying more than forty-eight hours.

We were issued some clothing and told we would be given additional boots when we got to Vietnam. We put on our new, loose fitting fatigues that we would wear overseas. The boots were much more flexible than the all-leather ones we had been accustomed to in basic training and AIT. They had cleated rubber soles and black leather uppers, but a strong porous light-green mesh cloth extending above the ankle to the leather top of the boot.

In the first mass formation the next day at 7:30 a.m., the impression was much that of a prison yard. It was an eerie feeling to see some of the grim-faced men called out for Vietnam duty, like doomed people being shipped off to their deaths. These replacements left Oakland for Travis Air Force Base and aircraft bound for Vietnam. I would never see them again. My name would be on one of the next lists. While waiting, I pushed a garbage can on wheels around the area, picking up cigarette butts and grass in the yard. In the idle discourse that was part of this, a sergeant in charge of the detail revealed he was being shipped to Thailand. I envied him.

At Oakland Army Base we could see returning veterans, usually conspicuous by their faded and worn uniforms. Fish found a clothes bin where these guys turned in their old uniforms. He pulled out a shirt with a unit shoulder patch. Even the returning cadre, thinking he was one of them, would approach to trade experiences. They would name off places in Vietnam and ask if he had been there. Fish tried bullshitting some of them and told the truth to others; he did not care. What were they going to do, send him to Vietnam? More in disappointment than anger, some of the cadre finally saw through all this and made him turn the shirt in.

Tom's name came up at the next formation. I never saw him

again. Like basic training and AIT, people came and went and were assigned according to the needs of the Army. We never built any attachment to each other or a sense of unit identity. My name was called at the next formation after that. I said good-bye to Fish and wished him well, gathered my things, and boarded a bus for Travis. I was on my way.

CHAPTER 3

CHERRY

Where I was now headed seemed a cauldron of indecisive activity producing mounting casualties without real results to show for the sacrifice. By early June 1969 a press uproar continued over the assault a month before on a mountain in Vietnam called Dong Ap Ba, overlooking the A Shau Valley. The 101st Airborne Division's deaths during the ten-day battle exceeded fifty men, with hundreds more wounded. Democratic Senator Ted Kennedy now railed against spending American lives for military pride. It was senseless and "irresponsible to continue to send our young men to their deaths to capture hills and positions that have no relation to ending this conflict." Critics further argued that the battle ran counter to Nixon's "Vietnamization" program, another buzzword of the moment, for turning over the fighting to the South Vietnamese. The contest over Dong Ap Ba, or "Hamburger Hill," as it later became known, directly contravened professed administration and military policy. In reality, the military did not believe the ARVN (Army of the Republic of Vietnam) Army was ready to go solo against Viet Cong and North Vietnamese regulars. Rampant ARVN desertions and inadequate leadership were definite deterrents against any hope that the

ARVN would stand and fight on its own. Nixon doctrine held that the South Vietnamese would have to do just that, ready or not. The new president had promised that he would begin the gradual withdrawal of U.S. forces in August 1969 by sending home 50,000 troops.

Hamburger Hill struck only fear into the minds of general replacements. The 101st had sustained substantial losses and would have to replenish its numbers, and the possibility of an assignment to the division and a commitment to future dogfights like this weighed on our minds. Army doctrine maintained that every soldier was trained as an infantryman first. My combat engineer training certainly qualified me for the infantry, as well. If the Army needed me there, that's where I'd go.

To add to this, *U.S. News and World Report* was speculating on a North Vietnamese offensive in July. Nixon was scheduled for a talk with South Vietnamese President Thieu at Midway Island on June 8th. I hoped that Nixon would preach the necessity of Vietnamization to Thieu and then begin the promised troop pullout. In my optimistic moments, this might reduce American casualties and increase my chances of survival if not shorten my tour.

The bus from Oakland dropped us at Travis Air Force Base. Inside a terminal soldiers were milling around. Young captains and lieutenants wore faded jungle fatigues marking them as Southeast Asia veterans. They were headed back for a second tour or coming off some type of emergency leave. The mood was solemn, with no one saying much of anything and no bullshit coming from the officers. Most of us new general replacements wore no rank chevrons on our new fatigues. We were told we would automatically become a PFC when we got to Vietnam. There we could have our camouflaged, or subdued, unit insignia and rank sewn on. Those in faded fatigues seemed confident, at least less apprehensive, as if they knew where they would be going. How many of this crowd would return wounded or in body bags?

Several hours dragged by before we boarded the privately contracted World Airways jet. The twenty-five-hour trip would take us to Anchorage, Alaska, to Yakota Air Base in Tokyo, Japan, and then

VOICES FROM THE REAR

to Saigon. Two hundred and twenty uniformed souls packed themselves on that plane. The stewardesses were women in their late thirties and early forties, not as good looking as the women on regular commercial flights. This airline seemed to use these seasoned volunteers to fly the Vietnam runs, and they were a sober lot engaged in delivering young manhood to a war zone. I figured that return flights of homeward-bound veterans were much more exhilarating.

Five hours later we arrived in pitch-dark Anchorage. We were on the ground for about two hours. On the nine-hour leg to Tokyo, I couldn't sleep. My mind kept churning about Vietnam, and all the possibilities of assignment. I dozed off a bit but could never quite shut down. I did not want to die for the Vietnamese people. Why could I not just have a nice visit and leave in about two weeks?

With several hours to kill in the Tokyo terminal, I had another of those improbable eerie coincidences that assails a man in a military career. A voice from my past jerked me around with: "Hey, little fella!" I was looking at a redheaded kid with a broad smile—Eddie Lynch standing there in uniform. This bit of banter got started years before when I called at his house in Portland looking for his older brother, Joe, another caddy at the Portland Country Club. With no Joe around, I needed to leave a message with Eddie, but I couldn't remember Eddie's name. "Can I speak to the 'little fella'?" I inquired. He wasn't around, either, but next day at the club Eddie reported in. "Here I am, the little fella." It never let up all summer. "Do you have the little fella's lunch?" he would ask plaintively. "When do you think the little fella can get a double loop?" We went on yelling at each other at every chance meeting after that with "Hey, little fella!" Now I heard this half a world away.

It turned out that Eddie was waiting for transportation to his new assignment in Korea. He had signed up for three years and would complete his enlistment in a year. I asked, "How the hell did you get assigned to Korea?" He said he did not know but he was not going to turn it down. We caught up on news of the people we knew who had been drafted, who had been to Vietnam, and who had returned.

The plane left Japan with me as sleepless as ever on the last four and a half hours to Vietnam. We expected to put down at Bien Hoa Air Base at about seven o'clock in the morning. About four hours airborne, I heard one soldier asked the stewardess for a blanket because he was cold. She told him that he would be landing in fifteen minutes, and he would be warm soon.

Right! Several hundred feet short of the Bien Hoa runway the plane pitched upward. A disconnected voice on the intercom announced that the field was under rocket attack. We were going around until that cleared up. I had heard about such incidents, but I was hoping at least this air base where commercial aircraft regularly landed would be safe. Our plane was practically a sitting duck, unarmed and vulnerable to a rifle shot, much less a rocket attack. Not much effort would be required to down it. This was not a welcome sign or harbinger of things to come. The passengers were silent. I held my breath and thought, what a way to go, to be shot down before even setting a foot in Vietnam. About twenty minutes later, our aircraft safely landed to the relief of all I am sure.

An all-pervading damp heat took us by the collective throat. Before I was off the plane's ramp I was soaked. A military bus shuttled us from Bien Hoa to Long Binh, a massive base just north of Saigon where the Military Assistance Command (MACV) was headquartered. Shanty houses and fields bounded by metal fences dotted the road. Once inside the replacement station area, we were hustled to a tin-roofed hut and ordered to seats. Screens opened the hut's interior to the oppressive atmosphere. A young Spec-4 announced that we would have unit assignments within two days. We were to expect extra duties, the usual area policing. After some more paperwork, we got to the chow hall.

This far into Army life, eating facilities usually came with some goons screaming at any new entrants, but things changed with the terrain. Vietnamese women were doing the KP—serving food and cleaning up. Hot beet dishes, meat, some type of potato, and even a dessert arrayed themselves down the line. Overwhelmed with the first assault of Vietnam's cloying temperature and the effects of a two-day trip, no one wanted much. We dutifully carried still loaded trays outside, where Vietnamese women waited around a couple of 55-gallon-drum garbage cans. It seemed an efficient process until I realized that the people outside were there to skim off what we produced as garbage. They took food from the GI's trays and scraped it into small containers to be brought home for their use. What was in the big drums was also fair game. The raw filth of the business soon overcame me. These Vietnamese were the privileged ones, allowed to work on a base where they lived off the droppings of the American forces. There was more to come, but it reminded me of dinner-table exhortations of long ago about the starving Chinese children. I never understood how cast-off vegetables would get to the mouths of these unfortunates, but somehow it suddenly seemed to fit.

Among the staples of our training in the states were stories of these Vietnamese women whose husbands and sons were in the ARVN army or gone forever. They got these sinecures providing services of all kinds for American troops on the basis of a weird sort of veterans' preference. If these were the fortunates, what did the really unlucky ones have? How could these people support a government that was itself sustained by monetary and military aid from a foreign power when that side could not provide enough food for its people. It seemed logical that it would not be long before the Vietnamese people would side with their own people, the Viet Cong and the North Vietnamese, to rid themselves of their own corrupt government and the foreign intruder. I walked to one of these hovering figures and handed her my practically untouched tray. She smiled and immediately scraped every morsel into her waiting pots. I assumed she was taking the food home to feed her family, but many sold it to other Vietnamese for a few extra bucks. She must have done all right that day on the bunch of new arrivals I was with.

After an afternoon of more inprocessing I claimed my usual lower bunk at the barracks by throwing a duffel onto it. Still brooding over what the next days held for me I found the enlisted men's club for beer and whatever scuttlebutt was around. After sundown the temperature was not as oppressive. From the barracks just before dark, distant shelling beat a background tattoo. I could not tell if the shells were ours or theirs, but everyone around me offered an opinion. At this point, we had no M-16s and could offer no defense to a sudden onslaught. Finally sleep overcame me.

After breakfast next morning, I ran into Joe, my former AIT company trainee leader from Ft. Leonard Wood. With the exception of Fish, neither of us had seen anyone from the old company. He had been assigned to the 1st Calvary Division and was leaving that morning. He came to the formation to see if he knew anyone. I told him he was lucky not to be associated with the 101st Airborne Division. You learn not to say things like that.

No sooner were we lined up for unit assignments when my name came up paired with that dreaded unit. Watson was going to the 101st as a replacement! "My shit is weak," I thought, and cold shivers shot up my spine. Here I am in Nam, and now assigned to the very division that is seeing the most action. Joe uttered a solemn "too bad," and headed off. I gathered my gear from the barracks and boarded a bus with about fifteen other guys who were also assigned to the 101st. The half-hour trip again took us through fenced-in fields and shanties bordering a red dirt road.

My thoughts wandered off, back to more pleasant days. I was gripping the reins tightly in my hands and leaning into the sway of a horse-drawn hay cart. Ginger, the mare up front, maneuvered her careful way down the red dirt road winding tightly through the hayfield. The passage was just wide enough for the lumbering wagon. One mistake and the whole load would topple. Ambrose, a distant family relative, was next to me. His father owned the farm where we were staying in the Canadian province of Prince Edward Island. After twenty minutes, Ambrose had gained some confidence in my performance with Ginger. I guided the horse into the barnyard and then into the barn and felt quite pleased with myself—not bad for a nine-year-old kid. At lunch my brother Ron asked Ambrose if he and I could release Ginger from the cart and take a ride. Ambrose never realized Ron's aptitude. He had the thing figured out in ten minutes, and the two of us were riding bareback in the barnyard and out the red dirt road. Ambrose was amazed, and my dad, dumbstruck. Damn! Those were simpler summers. I wished I could be back there again. That red dirt road was much more amenable than the road I was on now. It was too late for an escape to Canada now.

    We entered Bien Hoa through a different gate from the one we had left a day earlier. The bus circled the perimeter of the base and halted before a large billboard with a rendition of a huge eagle, the logo of the 101st Airborne Division. THE HOME OF THE SCREAMING EAGLE, the board advised us. We were at Camp Ray. I didn't know who Ray was, most likely a hero who had died defending the area. We learned in our first briefing we would stay in this camp about a week for five days of P-training, the term used to describe a reorientation of the principles of basic training. We would do PT, receive M-16s, zero them in, take marches to various ranges, and undergo simulated battle conditions that included ambushes and attacking an artificial Vietnamese village. The cadre at this P-training unit all wore black baseball hats. All were veterans of real Vietnam combat. This was fine with me, another week to gather my senses about where I would be stationed, and if I had to go to the line, any additional refresher course would be useful. Besides it would be one more week off my total year in Vietnam.

Camp Ray, Bien Hoa, Vietnam, July 1969

Our barracks was the dirtiest place I had yet seen in the Army. There were no sheets or blankets, just a moldy, smelly mattress. There were no lights, and the odor of an open urinal out back permeated the area. Well, one more week, I thought as I tossed my duffel bag on a bunk.

Inprocessing didn't start until the following day, and the Army kept us busy. I drew extra duty with a couple of other guys. We drove to a perimeter bunker to help fill sandbags, pretty easy work, but it gave me another look at life in the country. With the bags in place, we carried ammunition. Among us now were about thirty Vietnamese children, mostly girls from eight to fifteen years old, helping with the project. A grizzled sergeant wanted us to fill more bags and shift ammunition. He told us privately that these kids received about $1.25 per day, which I did not think was too bad considering what I was making. The sergeant had this little Vietnamese girl and her even younger brother hanging around his bunker. I think the guy lived out there. After a while the sergeant asked us bluntly if we "would like this little girl to suck us off." I thought he was kidding but he wasn't. She would give us a blow job for a dollar, he repeated matter-of-factly. My stomach turned; the girl was about eleven years old, her brother, about seven. No thanks, I told the sergeant. None of the other guys wanted any either. Later when the sergeant was not looking I called the girl and her brother over and gave them the equivalent of a dollar and told them to keep it. I nearly gave them a 50-percent raise for the day. I wondered what stake the sergeant had in this process. Was he getting half the money? Was he just helping us adjust, or was he helping them? Was this what Vietnam did to a man? What were his values in the real world? Did he have younger sisters at home? I wanted to puke. We were here saving a population that had to let its children do these things to survive. I did not even know if these kids' parents were alive.

I was happy to start refresher training. Next day we formed into a class of eighty-five soldiers for five days of training. Our first task was paperwork through the division's two branches, personnel and finance. We lined up with our records outside the personnel shack, another long, tin-roofed, half-screened affair sandbagged halfway up its sides. As we stood in formation before the shack, a Spec-4 gave an orientation and handed us forms to complete. One of these was the "dream sheet," a list of assignments choices for after our Vietnam tour. The form exuded optimism in the assumption we would all be going home, whole and entire. The speaker was a slight guy, who because of the heat wore only his olive drab T-shirt. He told us that we would be assigned in our MOS. My spirits rose. I still clung to the belief that combat engineering was less dangerous position than the infantry. The next words out of the man brought me back to reality. He added the qualifier that we would most likely be assigned in accordance with the needs of the Army. In other words, an infantry assignment was still a real possibility. The last thing our guide asked for was college graduates to help inprocess this group I was in.

Never volunteer, ran the enlisted man's code, but what the hell, I thought I'd see what the duty was. By this time, the Spec-4 was inside the hooch. I followed him in and confronted a line of GIs seated behind a row of long tables down one wall. A lieutenant sat behind a desk in the far corner opposite the tables.

"Where do you want the college volunteers?" I asked the first GI in the row. He surveyed the room and ventured that they had all the people they needed, but since I was here he would take me first. I produced my records and 201 file, the all-important personnel record. He ran an eye down my job history with the master's degree listed. He sent me to the lieutenant, a kid at least four years younger than I. More scanning of the record, and the lieutenant demanded to know if I had really taught in college.

"Okay, complete your inprocessing." That over, I was sent next door to finance. I completed finance rather quickly and then had the rest of the morning off.

That afternoon in P-training we heard several "captured Viet Cong" explain how they had survived in the jungle without much food, lived off the land, and used much of what the GIs discarded, such as C-ration cans, for booby traps. We were wide-eyed before these guys, the real "McCoy." These were the people we would soon be out searching for. They even picked up pidgin English so quickly. We were still in our seats when the two Viet Cong "Black Hats" came back out for their bows and turned out to be a couple of airborne troopers. We reacted like kids at a circus and cheered their whole act.

Training moved apace. I wanted everything to slow down. Every day spent here was one less I had to spend in the field doing the real thing. Most of the new arrivals found themselves concentrating on the work at hand. Regardless of anyone's politics or fears, we were in the presence of people who would gladly shoot at us. Still, there was one kid who thought all this was a playground. One Black Hat singled this guy out on the marches to the various ranges to zero in and fire our recently issued M-16 rifles. The noncom stood this redheaded fool, caught playing grab-ass one last time on the march, out of the formation, loaded five bricks into his backpack, and ordered him to run alongside of the formation where he could be watched. For all my attitude on the Army, my sympathies were suddenly with that sergeant. I figured in a week my life could be in the hands of this kid who treated this as if he were on a scout trip.

The cadre lectured us on ambushes. In one of these encounters, a sergeant told us we had to unload everything we had. "You must cut the enemy to pieces. Make him into hamburger. Keep firing at him until he is hamburger." When closing in on the enemy we were told to check for body count and make sure the dead enemy was hamburger. He screamed this again and again. "Kill these motherfuckin' gooks and make them hamburger." We all got the point: this was the real thing.

During P-training I met Dave, an Asian college graduate from Los Angeles. He was as concerned as I was about making it through this year. We hung around together on maneuvers. On one exercise we were searching some "dead" enemy for booby traps. Some Vietnamese teenagers simulated the casualties, more privileged locals who worked part-time for the cadre. If we saw anything suspicious such as a hand grenade we were supposed to yell "fire in the hole" and hit the dirt. As I turned one of these kids over, he released the pin on a hand grenade. Dave and I jumped for the ditches, yelling the warning and uncorking some blank rounds at the kid for good measure. Everyone else in the patrol stood dumbfounded. Our instructor was livid. "You guys are dead," he raged at them and went on chewing out the lot until he ran out of insults for them. If that grenade had been real, they certainly would have been goners.

One night we were on perimeter guard, manning a bunker line. We had our M-16s, an M-60 machine gun, hand grenades, the M-79, ammo, and some flare rounds. The controls to some Claymore mines ran back into our wire. These things acted like huge shotgun charges and were an effective thing in defense or an ambush. The enemy respected them enough that he often crept in to turn them around so that they would discharge their loads in the defenders' direction. Four men were assigned to a bunker. Guard duty began at nine o'clock and included two men up and two men down (sleeping). The bunker was built right into the berm line, a mound about seven feet high and about twenty feet thick at the base. The foot-high, four-foot-long embrasure at the front of the bunker offered a 180-degree view over rows of concertina wire interspersed with Claymores. Every hour we checked in with the command post on a direct phone wire.

As the sun slowly disappeared we realized that there were no lights on the berm line, as the defensive perimeter was often referred to. It was soon black and silent, and all we could do was listen to the quiet. We started to hear and see things. One guy in the next bunker saw an elephant in the wire, another a monkey.

Midnight. Sirens began a plaintive howl that ate into the night. Their pervasive song signaled a mortar or rocket attack! I jumped to the bunker's opening and poked my M-16 into the night. Behind me someone was calling in to ask about the situation. A voice on the phone told us to fire flares to see if there were any enemy in the wires. In the distance came three distinct thumps, then maybe a half-dozen more. After that, nothing! The descending flares on our perimeter revealed nothing on the wire, and the pretty lights made us all feel better. Serious enough, this was only a stand-off attack, aimed at hitting something big, like a fighter aircraft, at the Bien Hoa base. In a half-hour my heart slowed down. We were supposed to spend two hours down and two hours awake, but every sound drilled into my soul. At first light the eerie shapes of the night became familiar bushes and trees. Our own fears played on all of us. Heading back to the company one guy from a neighboring bunker, still shaken, was convinced he had seen a Viet Cong in his bunker at two in the morning.

"Did you shoot him?" I asked.

"Nah! He looked right into my eyes and was gone in a flash," he carried on. If he had seen a "gook" at that range, then he was lucky to be alive. That night another fellow from the bunker line woke up screaming that the Viet Cong had shot him and he didn't want to die.

In another attack during these P-training sessions, the rockets came closer. I was in a barracks hooch when the siren started. We raced to a long, enclosed two-foot-deep trench covered with sandbags. Benches on both sides of the bunker seated fifty or more people. Actually I felt quite safe. At Leonard Wood we learned that a direct hit could do substantial damage to the people and equipment inside. While I pondered this, a sudden crash outside preceded what seemed to be a power saw ripping wood. When the shelling stopped, we ventured out. A shell had blown off part of the upper roof of a nearby hooch. The sandbags showed shrapnel damage, but nothing had reached the interior. You could easily survive anything but a direct hit if you stayed flat on the floor inside. A rocket had hit an oil storage area about a quarter of a mile away, sending 50-foot flames and black smoke spiraling upwards. Luckily, no one was hurt.

Time passed easily, with the heat the only discomfort. The beating sun reduced us to sweaty lumps before breakfast, and threatened the unwary with dehydration. Even the C-rations seemed better than edible. We simulated an attack on a Viet Cong village, looking for booby traps. And again some of our number missed the traps and were counted as casualties by our cadre.

The 101st's chaplain was a captain whose military reputation exceeded anything involving a relationship with God. Shit, in this division even the chaplain was gung-ho. In the unit's lore, he had also become a combat leader for regrouping some men under fire and standing-off an enemy assault. Unlike the stateside chaplains, he never once mentioned God and our holy mission against the communist world menace in his speech, but he told us to keep alert and remember that if we did, it would help keep us alive. It was pretty good advice. His spiel actually sent me to the division chapel for some serious contemplation about my fate. I threw it all into the hands of the distant God. There was no use trying to hope for something I couldn't control. If I had to be assigned to the infantry, then let it be. On the last day of P-training, I was in the best shape of my life and I could handle the M-16 with confidence. Now let's get this motherfuckin' war over with.

Next day, our orders took this group all over the division's area. We scattered to artillery, signal, medical, and various infantry units. With another engineer, Ronald Charlton, I was to report to the 101st PRB Company, a mystery unit. Charlton's orders made him a 71H20, a personnel specialist, replacing a specific person heading for home. His engineer MOS was changed on the spot. He was another case of the draft system's erratic workings. Coming from Minnesota, he had a master's degree in education, was married, and was teaching school when drafted. That combination would have gotten him deferred in another area of the country. My orders were to the same unit but with no change in MOS. Charlton couldn't shed any light on what was next, but a Black Hat thought PRB meant Permanent Reconnaissance Battalion, not bad, he reasoned, if I was stationed in this area. The reconnaissance battalion worked around Bien Hoa and Long Binh, places fairly much under our control except for the enemy night forays and random rocket barrages. Base transportation took Charlton and me a mile and a half to the administration company. I thought that the reconnaissance battalion would not be bad duty; others were being shipped to the airport for transfer north to where the majority of the division's units were.

We reported to the company command post and the crusty old master sergeant, a guy who had seen the downside of forty some time ago and sported a big gut and gray hair. He stood us in front of his desk and told us that we were to be assigned to his company as personnel specialists and would be maintaining the records of soldiers in the 101st Airborne Division.

Records? No permanent reconnaissance battalion? Did I hear him right?

"If you work for me and keep out of trouble I might even get you into Saigon for a day or so," he intoned. "If you fuck up, you can pack your bags, and I will personally send you to an infantry unit." I barely heard this because I was still looking for a dignified way to kiss this man's living ass.

"Yessir, yessir," I babbled on in my bliss. He wanted hard work, he said. "Where and when do I start?" All the nervous sweat over the PRB was for nothing—it stood for the Personnel Records Branch of the 101st Administration Company. All those guys in my class including Dave were going north to the various divisional units, and I was staying at Bien Hoa. That lieutenant must have passed my case to a captain at the processing center who looked at my 201 file. I just happened to be at the right place at the right time. It was June 19, 1969, my tenth day in Vietnam. I knew I could make it through.

A clerk took me across a road to a row of hooches until I got to one marked PRB. Here a Staff Sergeant E-6, second in command of the branch, told me I would monitor a set of enlisted records. My schedule ran from 7:30 to 11:30 mornings, then from 1:30 to 4:30 in the afternoon and from 6:00 to 7:30 in the evening. We drew no guard duty except for general alerts and, best of all, no KP. He marched me down the row of desks and file cabinets to confront a Spec-4.

"Hey!" this fellow shouted in jubilation, "my cherry is here. I am truly short." In the language of the country, a "cherry" was the newest guy on the block. Getting right down to it, that also made me the FNG—"Fuckin' New Guy." *Cherry* could refer to anyone with less than three months in country. The overjoyed guy I was replacing had thirty-three days left in Vietnam.

He took me to the barracks to drop my bag. The two-story quarters looked like every other one since basic training except for the screened-in sides. With some calculation, I got a bunk on the first floor. Outside, the sandbags ran around the place about shoulder-high. One of those rockets might pepper the wooden siding of the second floor without penetrating the sandbags surrounding the first. About twenty-five single beds in the barracks ran heads to the wall, with a standup locker between them and a wooden footlocker at the foot. The upper bunks were empty because of the danger of the blast to anyone in them. Several bunkers lay about sixty feet from our hooch, not as big as those at the inprocessing section, but as effective. A guy later pointed out the siren might not go off before the first rounds hit. You would then be taking a chance running in the open from hooch to bunker. Setting myself up in there put me in touch with another level of service by Vietnamese women. I drew sheets and another pair of boots. Hooch maids cleaned our uniforms and polished our boots and cleaned up our area for $10 per month. You wore one pair of boots while she cleaned the other. Even a PFC could afford this. A base Vietnamese shop later sewed on my PFC stripes and the 101st Airborne shoulder patches.

As the FNG, I had the rest of the day off and immediately wrote a letter to Nancy, giving her the news of the day and starting to plan for an R&R (Rest and Recuperation) trip sometime in January, ages away. I begged her for letters and some pictures as soon as possible.

That first evening I met some of the guys in the barracks. One guy, Paul Vey, was from Nancy's home town, Agawam, Massachusetts. He had been a guidance counselor at the girls' junior college there, and his wife taught high school in Springfield, Massachusetts. He had arrived on May 20th, another trained combat engineer who was awarded a change of MOS after completing P-training. At company formation next morning it occurred to me that the enemy could do some real damage to this massed soldiery with a morning rocket attack. Many of the guys speculated that Vietnamese women had already paced off the distance from a hooch to the company formation area.

Next morning I set about my job. I updated records by adding award citations, change orders, promotions, and status changes when people shipped out either after their tours or were wounded or killed. A high school typing course gave me the fundamentals without ever making me a speed demon. I had barely practiced as an undergraduate and paid to have my papers typed in graduate school. I figured I'd get by and my speed would improve. The rest was mainly paying attention to detail and keeping ahead of the correspondence.

VOICES FROM THE REAR

The guy I replaced made most of my presence by disappearing, or "greasing," and running some elaborate errand affecting his outprocessing. He reappeared in time to check my work at the end of each shift. At 11:30, we could eat or head for the hooch and snooze or read. He followed the same routine during the afternoon, and after dinner he didn't show for the last hour and a half shift.

Over beer on the second evening, I debated four other guys on the war. They had spent nearly a year in the country and were really short. They wanted us in Vietnam and were entirely for bashing war protesters. They believed that every college was infested with hippies carrying war protest signs. In the year they were away, times had changed, I argued. Tet turned the public against the war, and the debacle at the 1968 Democratic National Convention had soured people even more. One guy worried that as a Vietnam veteran he couldn't study on a college campus because of all the antiwar protest, and he had to fear for his own safety. I didn't think he would be bothered and suggested that the protesters might even ask him to join them. As the beer and the talk flowed, they wanted to fight. I declined any fisticuffs, hoping that I could get along with them better if I did not stir them up. I was the "cherry," and they would beat me up for that alone. I gave up trying to mollify them.

On day three I met SFC E-7 Don Carpentier, a 28-year-old with a flattop, at one of the back desks in our work hooch. He was a ten-year Army veteran from Hallowell, Maine. I wasn't going to get too familiar with him at his rank, but he was from my home state and I was happy to talk with him. Next day he took me with him to "in-and-out-processing" which he was going to command. I had just come from this same function less than a week ago. He wanted me there next day, too, explaining that it was an easier job with no formations. I got up early and thumbed a ride down to the new office. Carpentier lived where he was and commuted back and forth, but he suggested that I move where the work was. The only drawback was with the guy I originally replaced. Now he had to stop "greasing" and get back to work, looking all the while for another "cherry."

As a humble PFC, I couldn't commandeer a truck to lug my footlocker and duffel bag to the new location. For a couple of days, I hitchhiked and walked back and forth to the new job. One morning I set off and got caught in the open when the sirens went off. I dove for the gutter at the side of the dirt road and climbed into a small gully. There was enough light to see everything in the depression, but if I was seriously wounded, no one would think to look for me there. A few shell bursts and everything went quiet. Shaken and relieved, I later heard that the shells had in fact hit a morning formation, scattering troops everywhere. Several were injured badly enough to be hospitalized; some had minor scratches. No one was killed. After that, formations were less frequent and never on the dot of 7:00 a.m.

Transferring over left another ordeal. I finally was able to get a truck so Charlton and I could load our gear and drop it in our new home. I gave Paul Vey $3 for the hooch maid, figuring since she only worked for me seven days and her fee was $10 per month, this would have computed to something like $13 on a monthly basis. Since my days as a paperboy I was always sensitive about paying my bills and paying people their due, especially since several of my customers forgot to ante up when they moved out of town. Paul informed me the next day that the hooch maid threw a tantrum and would not accept the money and demanded more. Paul did not know how much she expected, and he basically wanted to stay out of the argument, so the next day I hitched back at noon time and offered her $5 in "P," what everyone called piasters, Vietnamese currency, which she accepted without chatter. I guess I was responsible for her pay until a replacement came in. Like everything else, a welfare system existed in the name of people we seemed to be exploiting anyway. I do not know what she could have done if I gave her nothing. But I knew the helpless feeling of being on the other end.

Jerry Poire from Worcester, Massachusetts, the same short guy who asked for college volunteers on my arrival at the processing center, was the first person I sat next to in the new job. He had completed a business degree and was teaching high school when he was drafted. He signed up for three years and had served stateside for over a year and a half before being shipped to Nam. Jerry had a DEROS—a date of expected return from overseas—in late March 1970. This date was something everyone lived by in Vietnam. His DEROS was two months less than his ETS—his estimated time of separation from the armed forces. So at the end of March 1970 Jerry would leave Vietnam and the service.

Whenever two GIs met, exchanges of information on hometowns, politics, race or creed, and even women came after the establishment of their mutual DEROS and ETS. Many GIs had their own personal short-timer's sheet. Most common were those featuring a voluptuous nude with 365 numbered boxes on her ample form. At each passing, day the troop would color in the number of the day just elapsed in the countdown to release. The last number, one or zero, was right on the woman's vagina, signifying that the man had now arrived at the promised land. When a guy had less than a hundred days in country left, he became a "two-digit midget." A cherry like me with 345 days left to go would always be questioned as if he were serving a sentence for killing some big shot. The diminutive Jerry hung around with a six-footer, Larry Hollenbeck, who accepted his partner's nervous patter with interested diffidence. Company lore retold the story of Jerry's excitement when he began to break into meaningful statistics.

"Larry, did you know that I recently broke the three hundred mark?" Larry gently assumed an owlish look. "Yes, Jerry," he always repeated in soft deliberation to all of these exchanges. Larry was from Dowagiac, Michigan, a small town near Lake Michigan and about twenty miles southwest of Kalamazoo and eighteen miles northeast of South Bend, Indiana. The details impressed themselves on me because Larry would constantly but patiently repeat directions to Dowagiac whenever asked. With that same patience, Larry would listen attentively to people, ask questions, and practically give you the shirt off his back. At 21, he had two years of college, had married, dropped out of college, had a daughter, divorced, remarried, and finally got drafted. He really loved his daughter and told me that he had made a special trip to Saigon to call his wife and daughter. I wanted to call Nancy from Saigon, and he promised to lead me to the phone center at the USO in Saigon.

Larry worked next to Jerry at the center of the line at the inprocessing section, endlessly filling in DA-41 forms and the Servicemen's Group Life Insurance Election Form (VA 29-8286). The DA-41 was an IBM card recording emergency data and addresses for the dispatch of a serviceman's remaining money if he was killed in action. Parents or other next of kin were identified, and the existence of a will was noted. This simple card affected much because many enlisted men changed their status while on leave after basic and advanced training. They got married, got divorced, got into fights with beneficiaries, and changed the conditions of a will. Our operation was the last place a man could review and change all this in his Army records. His company clerk could initiate some changes, but his official records would remain at our admin branch. My job at the end of the line was to review the person's file and discover if he had any brothers in Vietnam, was a sole surviving son in a family, or had any other profile affecting his being sent into combat. A "yes" answer to any of these questions could affect the assignment of the individual. Sole sons and brothers of GIs already in country were usually sent home to stateside assignments. People with still-mending injuries, back conditions, or other long-term ailments could also be diverted to lighter duty. In the Army's arbitrary way, it chose some in this way for survival and sent others into harm's way. I found several with brothers in Vietnam, but they usually did not want to be sent out of country. If a man's brother was injured, he wanted to be able to get to him without the prospect of a trans-Pacific flight first.

VOICES FROM THE REAR

The inprocessing team at Camp Ray, Bien Hoa, Vietnam, August, 1969.

It was fairly easy to spot more cadre for the clerical work we were doing. GT (General Test) scores recorded in 201 files generally revealed the level of a man's math and verbal skills and, as expected, would almost always be higher when a guy had more education listed on his sheet. If I saw a viable candidate for a possible clerical job, I would note his abilities and make a suggestion that he might be used in a capacity other than infantry. A captain situated at one of company hooches "back up the road" would have the final decision, but it never hurt to bring such promising people to his attention. I just began doing it one day and nobody ever told me to stop. It was apparently what had happened to me when I inprocessed. My final task was to record each man's name and serial number in a large green line ledger.

When a man completed P-training and was assigned to a unit we would get a copy of his orders and record their assignment in the space next to his name in the green book. We had our own local record on the whereabouts of every single enlisted man, E-6 and below, in the 101st Airborne Division. Every man's complete record was maintained up the road at the main Personnel Records Branch, which handled officers' records as well. The green logbook was the only continuous record that we kept at the inprocessing station. Directly across the room from me was a fingerprinting station for the occasional straggler who never got his prints taken from the day he entered basic training or lost his records somewhere between then and now.

Staff Sergeant E-6 Ben Blakely and PFC Steve Radford rounded out the inprocessing team. Blakely was a short-timer and would leave for home in mid-August. He was tall, medium build, and had thining red hair. Ben was outgoing enough, but not well liked. It later came to me that he had angled too obviously for a promotion to E-6. Larry observed drily that he had sucked up for it. He had signed up for three years but now had a definite short-timer's attitude. He didn't work too hard, but Carpentier stayed on top of him constantly, which produced in him a tendency to sulk and whine. He just didn't seem to fit his rank, and the others picked that up. I had met Radford when I in-processed. He was temporary already then, but waiting to go up the road to work with officers records. Ordered to our operation for a month, he left within two weeks and showed up only in periodic company get-togethers.

Carpentier sat catty-corner from me at his desk, equipped with a phone connecting us to the main administration company. He periodically reviewed 201s and recorded assignments in the green book. At the end of the day, he went up the road and took the inprocessed records to the captain's office for the individuals' assignments. It usually took five days to process assignment orders while the new guys were enduring P-training.

Outprocessing was in another hooch fifty feet from our back door, where Carpentier also monitored the flow. In outprocessing were Bill Ferguson, Johnny Bradley, and Eddie Warbeck, joined by Charlton, the guy I arrived with. Charlton turned out to be a sort of cold guy with a smirking laugh for everything. He usually had a scheme for getting something on the cheap. He worked well, but he never hunkered down and socialized or communicated with the rest of us; he was above everything, just not there. He had his own contacts, usually involving some deal. In one arrangement, he got extra regular-issue camouflaged blankets and had the local tailor make them into jackets, then sent them home.

Ferguson was a tall and wiry Coloradan, with long, rangy arms that he plied expertly in legendary fights. He had a special animus for Ben Blakely, and their bickering never stopped. His father was a rancher with over six thousand acres. Coming from New England, I couldn't imagine such an expanse of open land, but he said it was mostly arid and it took a lot of ground to feed livestock. A three-year enlistee who signed on as a personnel specialist when the draft threatened, Fergy also had a prominent beak of a nose. Vietnamese women loved this thing, he claimed. This may have been so, for he was a daily customer at the base bathhouse, or "steam and cream," where local women provided all manner of perverse services. On a Spec-4's pay, this routine was prohibitive, and we figured he was getting much of it free.

Fergy's counterpart in these many escapades was Johnny Bradley from Hattiesburg, Mississippi. A judge there listened to Bradley's story about "accidentally getting drunk and accidentally burning down a forest with a bunch of other guys." John thereupon had a choice of a two-year prison term or the Army. Adopting the lesser of two evils, he dropped out of college after his sophomore year. He was a marvelous personality, a born leader, I thought. People flocked to him seeking fun or just commonsense talk. He and Fergy often teamed up outside with a liquor bottle and then defended their honor against all comers. He had worked summers building large oil piers to be sunk in the Gulf of Mexico. He explained to me just how these piers had to be hauled out to sea, submerged in place, and stabilized by divers.

Twenty-year-old Eddie Warbeck from Johnstown, Pennsylvania, had signed up for three years as a personnel clerk. A wiry, friendly guy, he disdained violence, drank little, and read some but did not discuss it. His consuming occupation in Vietnam was cookies. He wrote to every cookie manufacturer he could get an address for and asked for free samples. When his mother or some relative sent him a supply, he would sample, assess, think about the quality, then write favorable letters to the manufacturer telling how much he enjoyed their product. Would they please send him some free samples for the guys? His pitch had a patriotic side, pointing out that GIs could not afford these luscious things. Ed's file system cataloged which cookie company had responded with samples and those that had not. A low "Oh, shit!" from his corner usually greeted a cookie rejection letter. More often than not, though, he scored, and the samples passed around our hooch.

My new place was across the road from the processing area. Anyone crossing this two-lane dirt strip then had to surmount a four-foot-deep drainage ditch on a piece of pierced steel plank, the famous PSP alloy strips of which airfields were built. The single-story hooch perched on a cement slab placed parallel to the road. The tin roof structure sported the usual wooden siding halfway up and screens on the upper reaches of the walls. A door at either end gave access to the road and most other human services in the area. About six feet from the building, sandbags rose about shoulder high on all sides, with breaks allowed for the doorways. A four-foot-wide hallway went from door to door through the middle of the hooch. Individual cubicles led off each side of the passage. To my initial surprise, we each had separate areas containing a bed, a footlocker, and a wall locker. Thin as they were, the walls gave a great illusion of privacy. Each cubicle door consisted of a curtain of beads. These spaces also had one overhead pull-chain light. The interior walls were plywood that nowhere extended to the ceiling, but we were all happy with the small territory we had to call our own. At the far end of the hooch was an open space the size of four cubicles with a plywood bar, a couple of small tables, and some chairs. "*This* is fuckin' Vietnam?" was my first impression. One corner held a small, creaky refrigerator to chill the essence of life, beer. Eventually a small portable black and white TV graced the top of the bar. We each pitched in about $12 for it. One Army-run channel carried programs like "Gunsmoke" and day-old sports from home. The

VOICES FROM THE REAR

Army stationmasters had to throw in commercials extolling the benefits of military life. One had an American girl with a come-hither look confiding that she "always liked to tinker." After a pregnant pause, she adds "with gadgets that is." This was a pitch to join the Army to become an electrician. It soon paled. The shows were outdated, and most news was edited or censored. The box sure looked authentic on the bar, though, a reminder of the real world.

The inevitable girlie pinups covered the wall behind the bar. Some of the best of *Penthouse* and *Playboy* were there, but other raunch competed with the tastefully arrayed centerfolds of the big slicks. One of these had a woman in a garter belt and shiny black, elbow-length gloves and matching high-heeled boots running to mid-thigh. With hands on hips, she thrust her bare pelvis forward in one of the first "full frontals" I had ever seen. Shoulder length hair framed a reasonably attractive face. We could not take our eyes off her. She bulged the shorts many a GI who looked too long. While monthly selections from the racy press came and went, this one hung in its place for the duration of my stint in that hooch. Fergy once took it down, claiming it was his, but the outcry made him relent.

Sandbags decorate the "hooch" area at Bien Hoa during summer 1969.

A line of Vietnamese graves behind the "hooch" area.

An American GI doing some of his best work.

The "Hooch" Bar.

Our hooch had some interesting features. Some of the individual cubicles had crawl-out bomb shelters, created when previous occupants knocked out man-sized holes through the siding just above the cement slab. Just outside, a three-foot-deep trench offered protection in an attack. This shelter was usually about five feet long and held one person comfortably, two in a pinch. The original architects variously installed sandbag roofs across wooden beams, and the proliferation of these things also showed the inventiveness of troops in danger. In an attack, anyone could roll out of the bunk, out the hole, and into the bunker. Only a direct hit on the bags would threaten life and limb. Jerry was really proud of his and described his precautions in his taped messages home, letting his parents know he was safe. My cubicle had no such exit, but Jerry said I could share his. Fergy argued these holes attracted snakes, but this seemed largely for the hypersensitive Jerry and to justify not building one himself. I don't like snakes, and, anyway, I figured I had enough time to low-crawl over to Jerry's shelter.

A urinal outside the hooch consisted of a barrel sunk into the ground and surrounded by three four-foot-high aluminum sheets set about ten inches off the ground. The wind occasionally carried the smell into the hooch, but we got used to it. On the other side of this facility was another hooch exactly like ours, housing the finance people. Beyond their hooch was a three-hole outhouse used by us and finance. Beneath the holes were large metal wash tubs, the kind that are used at picnics to store lots of soda, beer, and ice. The tubs could be reached via small doors behind the outhouse, and periodically we would have to drag them out and burn the contents, a duty that we did not look forward to. A few short yards from the three-holer was a makeshift shower, with a water reservoir above it resupplied every few days by pumper truck.

Beyond this outhouse was a field of large graves resembling four-poster beds, each surrounded by a stone wall. Bien Hoa Air Base sat on land that was once a rubber plantation. The tombs were those of former wealthy landowners. Some evenings we would sit on the gravestones, sip beer, talk about life and our futures back in the world, or just simply contemplate the significance of our navels. Out of respect, Larry, Jerry, and I policed up the empty beer and soda cans. Larry even managed to involve two of the hooch maids in the cleanup after a lot of palaver about how the Vietnamese respected their dead. Whether they felt obliged or were just humoring the big and slightly inebriated GI, they fell to in any case.

In four more hooches across the road, the guys outprocessing spent perhaps two days while their paperwork proceeded. The nearby enlisted men's club helped them kill the hours and their anxieties about whether they would see that "freedom bird" or not. Bien Hoa wasn't called "rocket alley" for nothing. It was hit frequently, and the possibility of a fatal injury while outprocessing was the final irony visited on these guys. In this club Fergy would pick his fights. I think he did it just to get some exercise.

Beer was a bargain at 15¢ a can in Vietnam, and a pack of cigarettes cost the same. Beer came from the enlisted club or one located at the 101st Administration Headquarters. Fergy usually brought it home for the refrigerator, and a rough honor system prevailed. Occasionally Fergy came back to the hooch late at night ranting and raving that someone had not left the proper amount of money in the refrigerator. On those occasions, he most likely had not seen enough action that evening, and we had to settle him down.

Near the enlisted club on the same side of the road was an above-ground swimming pool 120 feet long, 60 feet wide, and an even 5 feet deep. Though it belonged to another unit, Larry got permission to use it, and we sometimes swam away our lunch break. The water was refreshingly warm. We could sit up on the sides, swim, do laps or whatever. There weren't any girls lolling around, but I had no complaints. I had pulled one lucky assignment.

I was 25 years old on July 3, 1969—a quarter of a century old—but I felt like a kid. With the sometimes odd calculus of military service, there was a possibility I could be here for my next birthday. I would have to spend an additional 56 days in Vietnam to have the minimum of 150 days left when my tour ended to allow me an ETS in August 1970. If I extended to August 1970, I could leave

Vietnam and immediately get out of the Army. This was depressing, but the only other option would be to go home in June 1970, get a month's leave, and then have to serve an another six months in the states. That could put me as far away from Nancy as I was now. From a base in California or Texas, the travel time and costs back to New England would break a PFC. My six months in the Army seemed like years. So much had happened so quickly that it was tough to keep a realistic view of time. Spending 56 more days in Vietnam seemed to outweigh the 180 days in the stateside Army, and based upon my previous experience in basic training and AIT, the additional time might seem endless. I just didn't know which way to go at this point. Rumors about extending the early-out to 180 days was as exciting as those about troops going home early in a general withdrawal of Americans. Realistically, I thought the war would drag on for another three years with the president ordering 25,000 troops home every three to six months, just to mollify the home front. My guess was that the real peace negotiations would not take place in Paris, but in secret between the Viet Cong and the South Vietnamese government. The South Vietnamese had to do something with the American presence scheduled to be entirely gone within three years. If Thieu's government could not lick them, he would damn well have to deal with them. The Viet Cong was still a viable field force despite the million South Vietnamese men in arms and the backing of the United States of America.

In late July, SFC Carpentier brought in Spec-5 Kirt Finney, Blakley's replacement. He was the skinniest 135 pounds of soldier among us. His devilish smile made you think he was always up to something. From Bell City, Missouri, he had been in the service for over three years of a four-year hitch and would finish his obligation in early May 1970, leaving him ten months to go in the service when I met him. Finney was married, but his relationship with his wife by his own admission was never good. When he found out from a friend that she had been sleeping around, Kirt immediately went to finance and shut off her allotment check and spent everything on expensive items like a camera. His wife complained to the

VOICES FROM THE REAR

Army, and a chaplain showed up to plead with Kirt to reconsider. "Too bad," he told the padre, "let her boyfriend pay her." When Finney got a real case of the ass, he was stubborn.

Finney fell in directly with Bradley and Fergy, who always referred to him as the "Ding Dong from Bell City, Missouri." Finney and Fergy became the Mutt and Jeff of the unit and found equal joy in drinking and fighting. Finney's size was deceptive, and he was agile enough to dodge most punches. He absorbed punishment with that huge grin, and then he dished it out. A couple of drinks would fire Finney for combat, and he often led the attack, sometimes so fiercely that Fergy actually restrained him. If he was working off his frustrations this way, Finney couldn't do anything else about his wife, at least not until he got out of the Army.

He could be dangerous to himself, and us too. With a fair share of beer, he would decide it was time to clean his M-16. We didn't know if he would kill himself or someone else in the hooch. We would try to convince him to wait until the next day to clean the weapon. He would sweep the room with the weapon, that shit-eating smile on his face, and holler: "No, goddamn it! We had best do this because you never know when the fuckin' gooks are going to attack, and I am going to be ready." We never knew if he had a round in the chamber or not. Everyone was afraid to get near him in that condition. Finney was crazy at these moments, or as I sometimes thought, he liked to make us think he was.

Finney developed a daily routine with the mamma sans. Two of the cleaning women came by every day to sweep up, wash clothes, and polish boots. One was in her forties, and the other seemed to be no more than a teenager. Both had relatives in the ARVN. The younger one was definitely cute, but modest in bearing. Practically every morning Finney would leap stark naked from his cubicle, snapping his towel at the young girl. She screamed and ran to the next cubicle with Finney chasing her and yelling, "Mamma san, you come in here and give me morning wake up." "No, No, No!" she protested loudly each time, clearly embarrassed. Finney figured this was all in good fun, but if anything came of it, he wouldn't refuse her. It was the gentleman in Finney.

Finney displayed a better nature around the hooch, but he could fight like a caged tiger at the slightest provocation. An E-6 staying with us for three weeks was much bigger than Finney, a six-footer weighing around 210 pounds, but a peaceable guy. One evening, he and Finney got into an argument and were soon wrestling on the floor. Three minutes into it, the E-6 was on the floor and gasping for breath. Finney, outweighed here by probably eighty pounds, had managed to wring himself free of the guy and shove him into the bar. The larger man took the edge of the bar full force in the ribs. Two guys finally helped him to the clinic, where he found that his ribs were badly bruised but not broken. He was still taped up when he left two weeks later. Finney once started with Fergy, claiming that the "great nose" had stolen about a hundred dollars from him. This went on for weeks, without interrupting their evening excursions to the club. They were best pals on the way to the club but fought relentlessly in the hooch. One night Fergy dramatically located some money in the wall behind his bed. No one believed his version of things, but he gave some of it to Finney. Fergy never admitted taking the money, nor did Finney ever press the issue further. It seemed to end the ongoing argument, and peace returned to the house at night.

Finney decided that we needed a hooch pet. Larry found a puppy and suggested that they take a look at it. The next day the pair had brought home a light-colored, cute and friendly female mongrel. Finney and Larry had decided after much hooch discussion to name her "Bitch." Finney's mean streak showed itself when he teased the dog by repeatedly cuffing both sides of her face. He didn't hurt the dog, but it caused her to growl and attack Finney. Finney warded her off, then repeated the process until the infuriated Bitch barked and snapped at everyone. If someone did not ask Finney to call the dog off, he would eventually do it himself. Actually Finney loved the dog. When our unit had to move to Phu Bai near Hue and we couldn't take the dog on our assigned flight, Finney stayed behind with Bitch until he talked a transport pilot into letting him sit next to one of the pallets while holding the dog. He couldn't bear to leave Bitch behind, but she was crushed by a truck in Phu Bai. Kirt took several weeks to get over that.

Larry H.

The "hooch" pet named "Bitch."

As if my military life was not full of enough characters, life in Bien Hoa threw me in with one of the all-time great showmen. The draft system, for all of its eccentricities, is a great leveler. No one in the Army of the time could predict what stupidity or cunning intelligence he would run into next. War reveals some of the most abject behavior in men, but it also enlarges on some of the most amazing personalities.

On a hot afternoon that July, Denny Macfee blew into our lives. Just back from lunch, I heard someone declaiming at Carpentier's desk. If the word *fuck* had lost its shock value for me in the Army, Macfee raised it to an even higher art form.

"I fuckin' tell you, Sarge, I just got the fuck off the plane and it was so fuckin' full. Landed in fuckin' Ton Son Nhut, and it was so fuckin' hot I couldn't even think about fucking, although I kind of fuckin' knew I wasn't fuckin' going to get fuckin' laid there. Had a fuckin' great time on fuckin' R&R, absolutely fuckin' great. Well I am fuckin' back and fuckin' ready to get to fuckin' work." I couldn't (fuckin') believe someone was talking that way to Carpentier.

The incomparable Denny Macfee from Chicago—Mr. Chicago—was hard-core Irish, about 5 feet, 11 inches tall, with dirty blond hair combed in a wave up front right out of the 1950s. He was a tight 175 pounds, good looking, and accomplished at life. After high school, he worked for a couple of years until joining the Army to get ahead of what awaited him if he were drafted. Personnel Specialist is what he opted for. Macfee was on his second tour in Vietnam and knew the ropes in ways I never would. He had just returned from leave following his initial tour. He had gone home to his family and now would ETS the following summer.

Macfee kept the same pace as did Larry and Jerry. When he humored Poire, Macfee revealed the timing and punch of a stand-up comic, Chicago speech patterns woven into a line of patter that stopped me in utter fascination.

"Er, yes, Jerry, I did go back to the fuckin' states and I did manage to survive there."

"How was it there?" Jerry asked, and Macfee moved for the kill.

VOICES FROM THE REAR

"Pretty fuckin' unbelievable, Jerry. Too bad about Woochester, Massachusetts," Macfee added, knowing that Jerry was from there.

"What happened there" Jerry demanded, hooked as always.

"Oh nothing fuckin' much, just a big fuckin' earthquake and fire that killed a fuckin' lot of people and wiped out the fuckin' entire Poire family. But they never knew what the fuck hit them because they were listening to a fuckin' goddamn tape from their fuckin' son in Vietnam, telling them how tough he had it."

"Oh shit! Macfee! Can't you give ever me a straight answer?" Jerry pleaded.

"Er, sure, Jerry, if you can stop fuckin' whining and fuckin' keeping me awake at night crying on those fuckin' goddamn tapes."

Macfee's girlfriend had sent him a Dear John during his first few months in Nam and then got married several months later. Macfee kept this to himself, but he told Larry he had gone to see his now married ex-girlfriend during the day while her husband was at work. He told Larry in a smiling way she couldn't resist him and he had fucked her several times. Overhearing this, I was shocked and set myself up for one of Macfee's routines. It was always my attitude that if you lost the race you would necessarily leave the other guy's wife alone even though she had been your girlfriend at one time.

"How did you do that?" I inquired, leading with my chin.

"Er, well you see, George, I just walked into her fuckin' apartment after she let me fuckin' inside and told her how fuckin' much I missed her and how much she must have fuckin' missed me. And then I put my fuckin' arm around her and grabbed her fuckin' tit and started to fuckin' kiss her and, as fuckin' expected, she could not fuckin' resist me. I carried her into the bedroom. Are you fuckin' following this, George? Then I fuckin' took her cloths off and then fuckin' took my fuckin' pants off and fuckin' placed her on the fuckin' bed. And with her fuckin' moaning 'No, No, No,' I proceeded to fuckin' give her what she really fuckin' wanted, fuckin' wonderful fuckin' me. Do you fuckin' follow this, George?"

Bingo! I tried to retort with something more affected. "Oh, I thought you were going to say something a bit more expansive like she could resist me no longer, and begged me to embrace her, and we clutched each other warmly as we wandered off to the bedroom where we soon became most intimate."

"Er, well, ah, no, George, I didn't fuckin' think of it that fuckin' way, but let me fuckin' close by saying that I fuckin' fucked the shit out of her, and she fuckin' enjoyed it and she fuckin' told me that she had made a big fuckin' mistake by not marrying me." In vintage Denny Macfee, a sentence always started with "Er, well, ah, yeah, you see it's like this." Depending on who he was talking to, he would add "asshole," "douchebag," or just plain "motherfucker." Macfee was every inch a veteran, and he looked and acted like one. He wore the most faded uniforms that I had ever seen. Mamma sans had washed them so many times that they were tinted white. In Nam, this was status. He could have replaced his uniforms and probably was issued some new ones on his second tour, but Denny Macfee had a reputation to uphold. I am sure he had mamma sans wash his new uniforms every day even though he didn't plan to wear them until they had been properly seasoned.

The unerringly consistent thing about Macfee was his love of Chicago. He would always brag about Chicago. At the inprocessing formations he would interrupt Jerry's presentation with "Who the fuck is from Chicago?" To any show of a hand he would say with the certainty of a preacher: "Good! And you best be proud of it, man!" If he felt especially good that day, Macfee would yell, "Get up front here, man. Since you're from the greatest place on earth, I'm going to inprocess you first, and you damn well better be fuckin' proud you're from Chicago!" The bemused guy would walk to the front of the line. Jerry inevitably added nothing. Nor did anyone else. Macfee's presence was enough to convince everyone that this is the way things were done.

Jerry with our captured AK-47, as Macfee would say, "working on another tape for home."

He took some occasional guff about Chicago. If some lifer gave anybody some shit, Bradley or Fergy would pipe up, "Oh, that asshole must be from Chicago." Macfee was rapid on the uptake: " Well, ah, er, you see, shitface, if he was from Hattiesburg, Mississippi, he would be swinging from a fuckin' tree or saying something really fuckin' smart when asked to sign a fuckin' form, like dah, what is a pen." To Fergy, Macfee would intone: "Well, er, ah, dick face, if he was from fuckin' scumbag Colorado, he'd be crawling on all fours looking for something to eat off the fuckin' floor, and if we gave him the fuckin' form to sign, he would probably start fuckin' chewing it and think he finished fuckin' inprocessing when he shit it back out."

These litanies were always inventive, always delivered with the same matter-of-fact inflection. Anyone sitting in inprocessing would soon be convulsed. Macfee paced to the front of our line entering the door, scratch his ass, and rattle the hooch walls where eighty or more guys wrapped themselves in a sitting line around the outside, "Who's from douchbag Hattiesburg, Mississippi?" This usually got no answer, and Macfee with Bradley standing right there would say

"Good, no fuckin' dumb shits in today's group." Just as deliberately, he would shout "Who's from the greatest fuckin' place on earth, Chicago?" More often than not, someone outside would answer "I am."

Macfee, like a man possessed, came back, "Good, and you best God damn well be fuckin' proud of it." One guy, already in the spirit of the plan, answered through the walls "I am, I am, it's God's city."

When the tableau played itself out, Macfee would turn to Bradley and Fergy, scratch himself again, "Well, ah, er, you see, sperm breath, God answered my fuckin' call, and you know fuckin' why, turd breath, because God is from fuckin' Chicago, case closed." Like a ringmaster he took his quiet applause.

Macfee knew many of the mamma sans and paid attention to them all. When he walked around the compound or down the road, mamma sans would muster the only English to shout his name, "Macfee! Macfee!" He had the same response for all of them in Vietnamese, something that sounded like "Laudi manoi, homocai." I asked him once what that meant. "Come here, darling, give me a kiss," he carefully translated.

On a couple of occasions I walked back to the hooch during lunch break. Rhythmic thumping betrayed what he was doing inside. I peeked through the bead netting and saw Macfee busily humping a Vietnamese woman. It was the only time I caught him speechless.

VOICES FROM THE REAR

Johnny Bradley, a gentleman and a genuine nice guy.

"Well, er, ah, yeah," I intoned, in my best Macfee voice. "I think I'll come back another time when you're not so busy." His "laudi manoi, homocai" had gone a long way for him this day. But he was good to these women as well. Several times I saw him with the medics, asking, not telling them, to see mamma san's baby who was very sick. Macfee walked with the woman and her baby and did the interpreting as best as he could for them. They felt reassured with Macfee because he had been there so long and had cultivated their friendship. I really never knew if he had to pay for their favors, but I did see him giving one women some money on several occasions.

Denny did not take shit from anyone. One story about Spec-4 Macfee early in his first tour followed him around and became lore. He was riding shotgun in a jeep with another Spec-4 driving. The driver stopped to pick up a friend of his who was a Spec-5, a grade higher than Macfee. The guy insisted on sitting in the front because he outranked Macfee. Macfee would have none of it, arguing that a Spec-5 was not an E-5, or a hard five, and therefore could not push troops around. It was charitable on the part of Macfee to give the guy the opportunity to back off, because he would not have gotten

121

out for an E-5 or an E-6, either. The guy insisted, and Macfee pointed his locked and loaded M-16 at the guy: "Well, er, you motherfucker, either you get your fuckin' ass in the back of this fuckin' jeep or start fuckin' walking because you ain't never going to get in this fuckin' front seat, and even if you're fuckin' dead, I am still going to throw your fuckin' ass either in the back or leave you right here in the fuckin' road."

The guy got in back. Nothing more was said, but the guy reported Macfee for the lock and load. Macfee was subsequently called in, given an Article 15, and busted in rank. He was later promoted back up to Spec-4, but this mark remained on his record and prevented him from making E-5.

These guys were my life for a good portion of my tour in Vietnam. Individually, they were more or less likable, but most of all they collectively made a family of sorts for the first time since I entered the Army. Through basic and advanced training I had met a lot of commendable characters, but they all soon departed to different assignments. I wondered if this was the Army's intention. I would think the Army would want to build a cohesive force, but as a general replacement you could not do that until you finally attained an assignment.

None of these guys resented my assignment as a personnel specialist without having signed up for an additional year or two. Larry was a two-year draftee and had attended some type of clerical school. I was assigned my MOS on the spot with the wave of a wand. None of them was really antiwar, but all were anti-Army. They were living through it as unavoidable until they would be allowed to return to their world. Finney, Jerry, Larry, Bradley, Warbeck, and Fergy would all ETS in less than a year. Macfee would ETS in a year, as I would if I chose to extend. We could put up with the Army bullshit until then, and I had to acknowledge that time went much faster now than it had during basic training.

The one thing that we all had in common was the draft. No one would have volunteered for this. We were all from working-class or lower middle-class backgrounds. I would never meet an American

VOICES FROM THE REAR

"aristocrat" during my entire tour in Vietnam. The "Perry Puffins" of the world or "Muffin Smith's" older brothers were not in this war. I had figured this out much earlier in my attempt to fight the draft system. The monied classes would not fight this war. And they never really fought in past wars unless they desired to or sought some leadership position that would enhance their career afterwards. We made the best of the situation and tried to make the system fit our needs. All the guys in the hooch were Spec-4s except Finney, a Spec-5, and the cherries, Charlton and I, were PFCs. Blakeley was the fluke as an E-6 who was scheduled to get out in August or in a few days.

By early August I had felt comfortable with all these guys. One evening as I walked back to the hooch with Jerry, I saw Larry, Macfee, Fergy, and Finney playing a game of hearts. Jerry went to his cubicle to cut another tape for his parents, Warbeck was reading a cookie rejection letter, and Charlton was by himself as usual. Blakely was not in the hooch. Johnny Bradley had walked in just before me, and both of us started watching the game. We stood behind the players. It had just turned dark, and since it had been sunny and hot that day, everything was dry. It was too early for Finney and Fergy and Johnny to go to the club.

An unearthly swooshing sound I had never heard before commenced outside. Before any danger registered on me, Larry was screaming, "INCOMING, HIT IT, HIT IT!" Within an instant, I was the only one standing—everyone else was on the floor. A hot flash seemed to overtake me and penetrate my entire body, as if I had blushed from head to toe. Adrenaline drove my next moves. From the floor I felt the first impact. Shit, that one was too close. Through intermittent screaming, another flash erupted, this one a little farther away. The fright awakened every cell in me, and I made for the underside of my bunk on my belly. Jerry's strained voice from his bunker hole pleaded, "George, come join me." I didn't know if he was looking out for me or if he was just so afraid that he needed someone to stay with him or jump on top of him for extra protection. I was staying put. Even Fergy was on the ground, not

123

doing his usual lying down on his bunk routine. This was a serious attack, we knew it was close. A few seconds after the second blast, the in-coming siren went off, which meant that more rockets were on the way. They were aimed at the Air Force fighter planes snuggled tightly in their thick cement revetments, but they could land anywhere, even 500 yards from the field, where we were.

The aftermath of an attack at Bien Hoa, Vietnam, 1969.

Jerry was whining louder now. "How many more do you think will be coming in?" Larry hissed back at him, "Shit, Jerry, if I knew that, I wouldn't be here." Macfee pitched in. "Well, er, ah, you see, Jerry, it's fuckin' like this, I don't fuckin' know either, but I hope the fuck one lands on your fuckin' whining tape recorder." Fergy piled on, too: "Jerry, why don't you just shut up. If this damn attack doesn't soon let up, I am going to have to walk to the club anyhow." He went on about the protective umbrella of his nose. We were soon giggling from each protected cover. Bradley had another problem. "I wish this would let up. I have to take a shit." Macfee "Well, er, ah, you mean you haven't fuckin' shit already? I thought you fuckin' did, because I can fuckin' smell shit from fuckin' somewhere, or was that fuckin' Jerry? Jerry why don't you put the fuckin' tape on and tell your fuckin' folks that you just fuckin' shit yourself during a fuckin' rocket attack." Finney chimed in, "Fuck this shit, I was just about to win that fuckin' game." Charlton even managed a laugh, "With no power, we'll have to drink warm beer." As usual the juice quit during a rocket attack, so all this chatter ran on in pitch black with everyone on the floor either in or near their own cubicles. A few more rounds hit on the other side of our hooch and closer to the runway. Good, I thought, the "gooks" are finally zeroing in on the airport. Now that they hit both sides of us, would the next one hit right on top of our heads? Ten minutes later, the all-clear siren sounded.

An F-100 at Bien Hoa after an attack, 1969.

With the dying wail, commotion carried across the street from the outprocessing barracks. Blakely was missing, and Fergy offered that the "asshole is probably whining to someone about how short he is and that he hoped that he wouldn't be hurt or maimed with so little time left." Fergy took a quick check and came back in ten minutes. One of the outprocessing hooches took a hit, and about eight guys had been hurt, several critically. Ambulances came and went. Although I never saw the bodies, it was stated, not rumored, that several guys had been killed that evening. We were lucky; those rockets had come across our roof, probably missing us by just a few feet.

The burning remains of an attack at Bien Hoa in 1969.

Blakely showed up to report that he had made it to one of the trainee bunkers. Fergy snorted, "Too bad! I was hoping you would have to stay in Vietnam until your wounds healed, especially the big hole in your head."

"Thanks, asshole," Blakely groused right back at him.

"You're welcome, douchebag," Fergy shot back. Fergy wouldn't have cared if Blakely went home in a "glad bag." Blakely left Vietnam in a few days after that, and no one missed him.

The chatter took our minds off the danger. I started to calm down, got a beer, and contemplated surviving another rocket attack. We had no warning. Larry at least recognized the distinctive sound. I was too scared to join the repartee, but I figured I had shed my cherry skin. I was now a veteran, or at least no longer a FNG. The sound of that rocket remains with me still.

CHAPTER 4

THE BEST OF BIEN HOA

The attack that took my cherry status and claimed several lives and some more wounded produced one stroke of good fortune. One rocket hit the shit house directly, and it burned to the ground. Johnny Bradley and I were scheduled to service the huge wash tubs that filled with human excrement under the toilet holes. The duty entailed pulling the tubs through the trap doors behind the outhouse and igniting the contents with something flammable. The rocket not only burned the existing shit, but also buried the whole structure without a trace. A new outhouse arose nearby within a couple of days, but the shit-burning detail now fell to the mamma sans.

The morning after the rocket attack, Johnny Bradley strolled over from outprocessing and stood in front of Macfee's desk. Macfee saw this as an invitation and inquired, "What the fuck are you doing here—you lost?"

"Yeah," Bradley came back. "I thought I would come slumming and find out if you are still as ugly as you were this morning."

"Well," Macfee retorted, moving with the beat, "bend over and put your fuckin' face between your fuckin' legs and pull on the cheeks of your ass as hard as you fuckin' can until you see that big fuckin' crease which starts after your balls, and that is a better fuckin' reflection of your fuckin' face, and in fuckin' case you're too fuckin' stupid to figure out what it is, it's your fuckin' asshole."

Bradley wouldn't back away. "Macfee, you have probably got the letter *C* tattooed on your ass and nothing else because you don't know how to spell Chicago."

A row of inprocessing soldiers was now in stitches, and, just to add to the rumble, Ferguson, who by this time missed Bradley in outprocessing, heaved a rock on our tin roof and yelled, "Incoming!" Jerry hit the cement floor.

"Larry, is it for real?" he wailed in a high voice.

"No, Jerry," came the dry windup from Larry, "it's only Ferguson with one of his famous rocks, you can come up now."

Without warning, a nearby crash of musketry cut the banter and laughter like lightning at a picnic. We were all on the floor in a trice, including the guys inprocessing. Two more blasts in succession made the silence afterward seem almost palpable. It was midday. Jerry peered out to find some Black Hats before a firing party that had paid a twenty-one gun tribute to those killed in the hooches the previous evening. With that gratifying news, we broke for lunch.

For the average young troop, women are always around in spirit. The Army could do nothing about the hormonal levels of these captive workers in a great military hierarchy. A war zone presents endless opportunities for sexual creativity and release, but sometimes it was easier to get laid than it was other times. One afternoon after lunch, someone, maybe Finney or Macfee, arranged for a mamma san to fuck three guys for $10.00, yet another benefit for the available Vietnamese women. Saigon prices were $50.00 and up. But you get what you pay for. This woman was around forty, an estimate hard to nail down with Vietnamese women. The betel nut all the locals chewed blackened her teeth. She stationed herself on her back on a mat in one of the cubicles, with her knees cocked and her black pants off and fully exposed. All of us were in the bar except for Jerry and Fergy. Jerry was outside making another com-

VOICES FROM THE REAR

bat tape for the home front and, Fergy was at the "steam and cream," checking to see if his nose still retained some purchase.

I wasn't interested, and Carpentier moved off. But Finney figured he'd give it a go. He dropped his trousers, entered the cubicle. About three minutes later he was out, yelling "Goddamn it! I just couldn't get it up. This ain't what you call appetizing. I tried, guys, but it just wouldn't go." No one else wanted any either—Bradley, Larry, Warbeck, or Macfee. She was just too old and ugly—just uninviting. Minutes after this, mamma san came out fully clothed, collected her ten bucks and said "I come back anytime and bang-bang three for ten dollar." She did all right. All she had to do was lie on her back for twenty minutes with her pants off. She most likely added 25 percent to her week's pay. It was difficult to know if she had come to prostitution recently, but this was one legacy the American army left in Vietnam during the fight for the South's independence. Perhaps these local Vietnamese felt that like the French and others before them: we would soon be gone and they had better make their profit quickly.

I personally needed a little bit more rapport with a woman. I might just as well jerk off. Perhaps an additional deterrent for me was the fact that I retained a tremendous fear of shots, the Army's all-purpose cure for sticking your tool into that chasm. She was not government-inspected and would willingly share diseases with any horse's ass who went to the well too often. Shots never bothered Finney. Back from Saigon, he would march to the medics for a routine penicillin shot, a contribution to preventive medicine. Needless to say, more desirable women were available and willing all over the place, but the attendant troubles made up for the apparent windfall.

Bradley had the best sense of what was up that day. "Shit, I would rather masturbate than stick my wick into that!"

"What!" yelled a disbelieving voice, "you'd rather beat off?"

"Shit," he came back, "I'll beat it in the morning, beat it at noon, and at night, anytime I feel the need. But it's better than flailing my cock inside that." His peroration came at the right moment in the proceedings. Case closed—the woman never came back.

Army chow in Vietnam was a surprise. Everyone at the admin section of the base, including the P-training classes, crowded into the same chow hall. Food was overly plentiful and, for me, always better than acceptable. Breakfast eggs came in standard American, scrambled, fried, and poached, with huge mounds of sausage or bacon. Hot cereals, grits, toast, juice, milk, and coffee accommodated every soldier's taste. We usually skipped this, though, and bounded out for work with a cold Coke from the refrigerator. In the evening, the Army cooks put out a proliferation of assorted meats, chicken, potatoes, vegetables, and dessert day after day. The wholesome, planned diet never offset demands among the troops for junk food, hamburgers and pizza, and the abundance always made the grim and silent local women the more poignant as they collected from a single troop's discarded tray enough to live on for a week in the Vietnamese scheme of things. We got spoiled. Even the two-hour dinner session each day, which usually handled the whole crowd with no waiting, could put us off if it occasioned the slightest delay. Sometimes if we found a line waiting, we skipped supper and headed for the hooch and a nap. Then the couple hundred yards to the mess hall seemed too much to bother. Lunch was a problem of a different sort. All the P-trainees, outprocessing troops, Black Hats, and other cadre including officers in the camp were in the mess hall at the same time. Officers went in by a different entrance and ate in an area separate from lowly enlisted. We had an hour to return to work, and at the outset got behind a lengthy line of 100 or more people. Carpentier arranged with the head cook to allow his admin staff to go to the front of the chow line at noon every day so we could get back for work. "Excuse me," we would plead in low voices to the waiting multitudes and their occasional moans and groans. One afternoon, after this system had worked well enough for a few weeks, a large E-6 black cook ordered Jerry and me to the end of the line of nearly 150 people after we showed up in our usual way. Mortified, we walked back down the entire length of the line.

Carpentier had to renegotiate the whole thing again to clarify the situation. That cook recognized us afterward, but it was another embarrassing example of one guy in an Army hierarchy not getting the word.

Haircuts were another human service that emphasized the subservient status of many Vietnamese in the presence of the American host. A Vietnamese barber cost 40¢. I once had one of these fellows insist I owed him $1.35. I had gotten a massage, too, he said. He had done some kind of unsolicited 20-second back and shoulder rub, which I thought was part of the haircut. I forked over the money, but told Carpentier. I suspected this guy was trying to charge what the traffic would bear. Many Vietnamese were milking this American cash cow while they had the opportunity. Talk of an American drawdown prompted sharp practices among them, though the amounts involved were petty. If that were the case here, I had only to walk a little farther to another barber who didn't run the massage scam. The first guy's haircuts were not great anyhow. Other things concerned us with the Vietnamese living and working among us.

Long before I got to Vietnam, the troops lived with the assumption that many of these locals were working for the enemy. The first barber shop was only twenty yards away across a drainage ditch. The guy operated out of an ancient two-story weathered building that once housed more shops. Part of the roof on the far end of the structure had collapsed, leaving a broken-down barn of a place. The shop was so hidden that you had to be led there the first time. I never saw the barber come to work or leave the place, but only about 200 yards of growth separated this ruin from the barbed-wire perimeter of Bien Hoa Air Base. He could easily transmit any intelligence about numbers and takeoff times of Air Force planes. I later shuddered to think this barber had stropped his blade before applying it to my face. All we had to go on was the word of other GIs that he had been a barber there for a long time and that he could be trusted. How often or how recently he had been checked out? He could have measured off the distance from his shop to the outprocessing hooches and provided that information to Viet Cong rocketeers in the field, the same bunch that just claimed several lives and could easily have taken mine. In AIT and in P-training we learned everybody could be your enemy, so you never really knew who could be trusted.

On our way up the road one day, Larry and I dropped into the company day room. This hooch had a pool table, card tables, and several other games. On one wall were bookshelves filled with paperbacks—westerns, mysteries, and literature and history. I hovered over the history section and found I could take anything I wanted. Book publishers sent remaindered books for the GIs in Vietnam. Even a guy on line might want to squeeze a book into his pack or pocket for some leisure reading.

I picked up George Kennan's memoirs, a book on the Spanish Civil War, and *The Ugly American*. Someone had thrown away a damaged copy of *Seven Russian Short Novel Masterpieces*. I taped it up and enjoyed Pasternak, Dostoevsky, Tolstoy, Chekhov, Turgenev, Gogol, and Andreyev. I looked for their views on a society headed for the Russian revolution of 1917. A year before, I was studying Russian history at The Catholic University.

Nancy also sent paperbacks, including John Steinbeck's *East of Eden*, which I couldn't put down. Nancy and I got to discussing the literary merits of the story and its exploration of a virtuous if naive man involved with an amoral woman. Inevitably at the time, I found a resonance even in fiction with our situation in Vietnam. It was a welcome reprieve to get lost in a book. The books were always an escape to a life away from the war zone. I sometimes hated shutting off the lights at night.

A mile from the 101st Administration Company Headquarters was the Bien Hoa Education Center. Larry had wanted to sign up for a course to continue toward a degree, then finish part-time when he got out. Required for instructors in the Center, the warrant-officer director told me, was a master's degree in a particular subject. I mentioned my background, and he asked if I wanted to teach an East Asian history survey course for the University of Maryland Far East Division. The university would provide contents of the exams, but the instructor was permitted to use his own ideas for lectures and the method for teaching the class. This could be interesting, given the proper sources.

I quickly perused the small library that was attached to the education center and discovered about five books related Far East Asian history. Larry said he would take the class if I taught it. Carpentier egged me on since the classes would be taught at night. The fourteen-week class met once a week for two and a half hours.

I started immediately. With only two graduate semesters of Far East history at Niagara, I was no expert in the area, but I figured that most of the class would have had little college experience. I had about three weeks to prepare, since the course started in mid-September. My classes were built around a lecture on the history of Japan and China and then an introduction of some history of Vietnam. Sessions left room for the class to discuss why we were here and then draw on local history to infer how the Vietnamese really viewed us. Were we just another conqueror or occupying army in a long historical succession? How did the class members see themselves in this ongoing narrative? Were they doing any good? Was the South Vietnamese regime worthy of preservation or propping up? Did they believe the South Vietnamese would survive? What role was the United States playing in Vietnam? How did they perceive future historians would view our involvement in Vietnam? What was the history of Chinese-Vietnamese relations? If the communists took over both Vietnams, would they seek closer ties with China or the Soviet Union, or would they try to play off the pair against each other and preserve their own autonomy?

We had no textbooks and could rely only on the library. I had checked out most of the books to prepare the course. Heading for the first class, I was a bit nervous. I figured Larry would be the oldest student and would lead the class. Seven more people showed up, including four officers, all with bachelor's degrees but none in history. One officer was a veterinarian. Two of the four remaining enlisted guys had undergraduate degrees. The first lecture seemed to please everyone, and I let the class go early after defining questions and issues for next time. The course work kept me occupied and intellectually stimulated for eight weeks.

The Viet Cong supplied their own emphasis to the session. One dark night I was walking and thumbing alone to the class when the siren blew. Into the deep roadside gully I went again, with thoughts of where I'd wind up if something hit me hard. We'd been here before, though, and I was soon rehearsing the night's lecture in the ooze of the depression. All-clear rang off, so I walked on to class less fazed by the attack than with the content of the evening's presentation. It went off without a hitch, and I had a story to tell about the hazards of teaching a college-level course in Vietnam. Like so many ephemeral happenings in the Army, events overtook the course. The 101st Admin Company was soon to move north. With six of the eight weeks done, we had to terminate the class. Most of the participants were from other units that would not follow us. It paid well enough, about $5 an hour for classroom time, or about a penny an hour counting preparation time. Money was not the object, though; it was hard to believe the Army would sponsor a program that supported critical thinking about why we were in this country.

For the first month or so at inprocessing we did not get our usual half-day off because of the large influx of troops into the 101st. It appeared, and rumor sustained the view, that the 101st had been building up because of the withdrawal of the 9th Infantry Division. The 101st might have been only repairing itself from losses sustained during the Hamburger Hill operation. I couldn't prove any of this, but I started maintaining my own figures on how many we were in-processing into the 101st. There was no great disappointment because of the loss of the half-day off. With that little time, all one could do was catch up on a letter home or read. You couldn't leave base without special permission, and a PFC couldn't go very far in a combat zone, anyhow. The half-day off was a small change of pace and a chance to be alone.

Finally in August and September the flow of new people broke for a few days. One day we had twenty men instead of our usual hundred or more. Carpentier sent us all outside for softball. We didn't have enough people to play a real game, so we just took turns at hitting and shagging balls outside the inprocessing hooch on the flat hard dirt area. Carpentier pounded out some long ones. Here I was, shagging fly balls in the Republic of Vietnam, grateful not to be out humping the boonies with the infantry. This was another of life's deals—I got sent to Vietnam in a combat MOS, but I was pulled back and made a personnel specialist. "Fair is foul and foul is fair." There were few enough days when we got a chance to hit softballs to our buddies. Most weeks we put in seven days.

Then came jungle rot. In this climate, as one Army medic explained it, any break in the skin that does not heal normally quickly becomes infected. A small abrasion on the top of my right hand and wrist started with a mosquito bite and spread alarmingly into a large welt. Medics bandaged me and had me back every day for a couple of weeks before things mended. Newcomers questioned me about my "wound," and I even made one of Jerry's combat tapes to his mom.

My only other brush with the medics in Vietnam was when I tried the local pot, or "dew." After dark one evening when Fergy and I had drunk a few beers, we found a couple of outprocessing black artillerymen behind our hooch sucking a pipeful of pot. The sweetish smell permeated the shack. They had a good supply and invited us to join them. I took several strong hits while I was still drinking beer. Later, in my bunk, I tossed around a long time, then awoke with the worst headache ever—about 0.8 on the Richter scale. I reported to work hoping to last a few hours, but I just couldn't shake it. It far surpassed any hangover I had ever experienced. Eating made it worse, and finally I ran outside to throw up everything. It felt like blood would squirt from any existing orifice in my head, if not force its way out of a new one. Carpentier let me take the rest of the day off. The stuff stayed with me for two days, and I never touched dew again. Beer remained my mainstay.

Around this time, we came up for a general inspection, one of the staples of basic training and AIT. We almost expected one, but the implications of a review made strange things happen. Inspections serve to retain some type of uniformity over such a large organization as the Army. Carpentier told us we had to tear down the inside partitions in our hooch because they were not up to Army standards. The whole interior was jury-rigged from odd pieces of plywood. The GIs who built them, like us, had no access to a lumber yard, and probably took the lumber from a dilapidated hooch. If the Vietnamese had to comply with such regulations, then half the country would be homeless. They swiped or took the odd lumber that even the GIs didn't want.

    We bitched and moaned and only convinced him to let us leave the sidewalls of the cubicles, eliminating only the walls forming the central corridor. Now anyone walking through the middle of the hooch saw open bays on either side. There went privacy, something the Army never guaranteed anyone anyway, especially enlisted men. We swept and cleaned the office spaces more than usual for the occasion and avoided using the floor for the initial stages of screening records. The much-feared event over, the first sergeant held a company blowout to celebrate. A local Vietnamese band with pretty women did the music. The festivities, I remember, continued after the organized party, when my hooch-mates headed down to the enlisted club. A mild form of rivalry persisted between us and the main records branch staff. They took it on faith that they worked harder than we did, and they never had any privacy walls in their hooches. Such attitudes took on more serious aspects during general parties that brought all of us together over free flowing beer. We were about to board a half-ton truck to take us there when some guy took a punch at Fergy. The blow only grazed him, and he recovered quickly, landing the next blow squarely on his assailant's chin. The two then exchanged punches, bobbing and weaving and looking for openings in their beer-induced haze. Another guy tackled Bradley, but no one got hurt. Then a guy suckered Charlton just because he didn't like his looks. I could sympathize with that, but not as a reason to sucker anyone. We all threw the guy down and helped Charlton onto the truck, figuring we had to leave before more guys trickled out of the barracks to take us on.

VOICES FROM THE REAR

From the back of our "hooch" we could see Bien Hoa Air Base, a favorite target of Viet Cong rockets, filled with aircraft like this A-37.

In this case we were like two high schools competing with each other. Hostility deepened with time. Indeed, both sides had no homework to keep them busy, no dances to wear off some of the raging hormones. The incident hardly raised our own team spirit. No sooner were we back than Fergy and Larry got into it. These were the two heavyweights in the hooch. I broke up the fight that evening, and a couple of others in time, using my best graduate school reasoning with them. After this, I got the reputation of hooch "peacemaker." It came from my training in a large family. My age alone also made me witness to enough wasted effort in too many bars, all of which seemed part of growing up.

Part of the beef with us from the guys up the road was that we didn't pull guard duty. Carpentier soon had to reverse his stance on this. The party-night fight raised the issue again, and we had to take a turn at protecting the perimeter of the base. On the day my turn came, I reported up the road to the headshed with my M-16 and flak jacket, helmet, and canteen and belt. From there I was assigned a bunker along with three other guys, only one of whom I barely knew. With an M-60 machine gun and our M-16s, we walked a mile to the bunker line, finding there an M-79 grenade launcher, dozens of hand grenades and flares, and direct controls to fougasse and Claymore mines. The fougasse was flammable fuel in 55-gallon drums laid parallel to our positions at various points in the wires. Set off, the barrels would spew burning fuel from both ends down the wire line to kill any sapper trying to cut his way in. Of course, we would have to spot him first.

The "hooches" at Bien Hoa with the author and Bitch the dog.

Our bunker was dug into the berm line with a two-man outpost on top and with sandbags on three sides, the back opening facing inward towards our base. A small ladder connected the two levels of the bunker. There was no latrine. We just peed outside the bunker when we felt the urge, but the breeze just brought the smell back into the interior of the bunker. The bountiful mosquitoes swarmed to the odor, since it signaled the presence of warm-blooded denizens. A bunk bed allowed the two off-duty guards to rest while the other pair watched, one in the bunker and the other on top. The bunks had very little netting, and the mosquitoes murdered sleep. Repellent helped somewhat. A recumbent troop would wear the cumbersome helmet, or at least the helmet liner, to bed, pulling up his shirt collar and holding it taut around his neck and lower head, leaving his face exposed. The humidity made everyone sweat constantly, drawing our insect friends the more.

A radio phone linked us to the command post, which we reported to every hour, starting at dark. An illusion of safety infuses the defenders of a post like this. A sapper would have a hell of a time negotiating the wire and facing all the firepower we had. An all-out assault would be costly for an attacker because in addition to our munitions, we could also direct heavy artillery close to our position.

We often saw the U-2 on the airfield from the back of our "hooch."

The village of Bien Hoa lay directly in front of us. We could see Route 1 leading off to Saigon. Chemicals had denuded the area directly in front of the bunker and wire line nearly a year before. The foliage grew back rapidly, though. Now nearly four feet high in places, it was enough to hide a squad. Time to mow the lawn again with another chemical attack.

That night we fired eleven M-79 probe rounds followed with flares. The flares really lit up the area and renewed our confidence that there was nothing out there. The range of the M-79 was about 350 meters. We tried to put the rounds behind boulders and gravesites—anything that could provide some cover to a crawling sapper. Firing the piece at high trajectory allowed the round to drop behind these obstacles. It was fairly easy to find the right angle. I felt no remorse about damaging someone's grave. We would defend the bunker and its occupants. After all, the position could become our grave.

Thundershowers and impressive bolts of lightning broke the night intermittently. The lightning acted as an instant flare, laying visible the terrain out front for a few seconds. My glasses fogged so badly I sometimes couldn't see out.

The night also enforced a sense of isolation among the defenders. You never chose or knew the people you were out there with. The policy of having two men up and two men asleep put the two on alert out of contact with each other. One stayed above while the other remained with the controls to the fougasse, the Claymores, and the phone. I suppose this was done for safety purposes. The guy on top had a better view, but he was in the more vulnerable of the posts. He had his M-16, the M-79, and some hand grenades. We didn't communicate very often, but we switched positions about halfway through our two-hour shifts. Separated, we wouldn't talk and thereby divert attention from the outside. Other bunkers were about 75 yards from us. We called the CQ (Charge of Quarters) on the hour, but we could break radio silence with our neighbors only in emergency.

Nancy periodically sent me cookies and brownies. Guys always came around when a package arrived. I willingly shared, but saved most for me because it was my package. Warbeck, the connoisseur, wanted to taste the cookies, even knowing he could not implore this manufacturer for free samples.

With such a population of young men on the scene, discussions of sex in all its forms were constant. Any conversation on the mundane tribulations of life turned to this in a heartbeat. Talk would shift from old girlfriends to wives to new girlfriends and some new Vietnamese girl at the club. Finney stopped on his way out to the club to discuss the pros and cons of extramarital affairs. He supported the idea and had admitted to many one-nighters during the course of his five-year marriage. He was away from his wife and did not really have an outlet, he declared blankly. He would never attempt to seek out a piece if his wife were living with him. I asked him if he thought that there was any correlation with his attitude and the fact that his wife was now reportedly sleeping around in his absence. Finney didn't think so because he believed his wife never knew about his affairs because they were always in another town or area.

This also set off Finney, with Bradley and Fergy listening in, about their recent trip to Saigon. A Vietnamese pimp, a short man of nearly forty, accosted them with the promise of boom-boom. They all said they bought it immediately and followed the guy down an alley though some rundown double and triple story structures. Immediately they were glad that had decided to stick together because shady looking characters inhabited the alley and peeked from behind fences. They were unarmed because no one was allowed to carry even a pistol from the division into Saigon.

In a dimly lit small three-story house, the pimp brought out some young girls in their late teens or early twenties. Bradley and Fergy picked their women immediately and went off into two cubicles covered in the front by a beaded draw curtain. Finney picked a very pretty girl. They entered a cubicle, in Finney's story, and he went on about her wonderful body with small but firm breasts. He maneuvered his dick into her and was pumping when he was grabbed from behind and lifted off the girl. He heard yells of more than one person. Fear and adrenaline surged through him. It seemed like a half a minute before he could free himself and turn on his assailants, only to find Bradley and Ferguson howling in glee. They had finished and wanted to put the fear of the Lord into Finney, now swearing loudly "You goddamned motherfuckers! I am paying for this piece of ass, and I don't need you two motherfuckers in here." Finney was now laughing at his own story, not too pissed because he believed his ass was grass in the first place, and he was sort of relieved that it was those two and he was not about to expire. He had persuaded the two to beat it so he could work on his own deflated tool and finish his business. Ever after, though, he would place the women so as to give himself a clear view of anyone sneaking in.

Finney never held that practical joke against Bradley and Fergy. The story came up repeatedly, but he never even tried to avenge himself. The story brought him endless notoriety and status as a folk hero. Macfee put it in his own way: "Ah, er, Finney, you fuckin' dip-shit, you're the only motherfucker I know who has actually taken a flying fuck."

On September 14, 1969, I got to Saigon. Carpentier called, and he wanted me and Jerry Poire to go with him if we liked. I guess it was our turn, but I also think that it was Carpentier looking out for his team. If the other guys could go, then we also should get a chance to do the same. Jerry and I got into the back of a truck with some other guys and took off for Saigon. Once off Bien Hoa base, we ran along the fence lines of Long Bien, the massive installation housing MACV headquarters, passing fields, shanties, water buffalo, and Vietnamese of all ages in packed truck buses, on motorcycles, on bicycles, or on foot. The closer we got to the city, the more crowded the roads became. Inside Saigon, people were like flies. We could barely maneuver. There were Honda motorcycles everywhere. The Japanese had invaded Saigon. At the USO in Saigon, Carpentier took off with the master sergeant and told us to meet there in three hours for the ride back. Jerry and I went into the USO and listened to a live Vietnamese band, the best I heard in Vietnam, doing pidgin English rock 'n' roll favorites. It certainly took me home.

For two hours, Jerry and I wandered the streets of Saigon. A middle-aged Vietnamese man asked me if I wanted a short time, slang for a quick ride with a whore, as opposed to a long time, when you buy the woman for the whole night, or even a week. We begged off and were soon approached by another Vietnamese man selling cigarettes stolen from the PX and marked up at least a hundred percent. He pestered us until we moved off his turf.

My first trip to Saigon (note the Chevy in the rear).

Life carried on in Saigon, war or not.

In the streets and alleys, there seemed no plan to the city layout that I could determine. Along the waterfront some freighters were unloading, and some U.S. Navy ships were in evidence. Local workers unloaded the ships as part of the U.S. deal with the South Vietnamese government. After unloading U.S. material, the Vietnamese were supposed to transfer the goods to ARVN trucks for transport to various U.S. bases. A large part of the goods never got to its destination. One estimate had one of three of the large metal Conex shipping containers just disappearing from U.S. inventories. In a convoy of ten trucks, nine might make it to a planned stop. Seeing was believing in this case. Our walk along the waterfront showed where much of the goods were. They were on sale by vendors who spread everything out on the sidewalks. Peddler after peddler lined the streets and hawked American commodities supposedly available only in our PXs: cigarettes, deodorants, toothpaste, and loads of the colored print film that I couldn't buy at Bien Hoa because they were always either out of it or awaiting another shipment. Every vendor had colored film. Among the vendors were beggars looking for money or anything thrown down. A boy of about eight was selling fresh (supposedly) donuts. Unpackaged food was poison. No one knew where it was cooked or what it was cooked in. We each posed with this kid for pictures and gave him a buck, more than he had all day.

VOICES FROM THE REAR

Streetside cafes catered to a varied clientele.

Now a South Vietnamese soldier demanded a dollar. This skinny apparition stunned me. Here was a Vietnamese soldier for whose freedom I had been drafted to fight. And he had the balls to ask me for a buck. He should be buying me a fuckin' drink. I felt like saying "get your fuckin' boy scout uniform and your mother fuckin' ass out there on line and kill a Cong or two so that I can get my fuckin' ass out of here." I pointed to my PFC stripes and told him loudly in broken English "I only PFC make *titi* (little) money, no have no dollar not even to buy your sister for bang bang." Then with a smile I proposed "You give me dollar so I send number one present to my girl." The guy smiled and went his way.

I was furious. What the hell are we doing here? Here were masses of stolen goods that our own troops a few miles away couldn't get. These "wonderfully freedom-oriented people" were stealing us blind and making profits. Simple logic implies that if you give someone your time, money, and life, you don't give him the additional privilege of robbing you.

Then we met a Vietnamese who spoke excellent English. Dressed in Western style slacks and a sport shirt, he actually led us back to the USO when we asked the way. We followed him through an area of black marketeers with their little children listlessly lying on blankets beside their parents. He bluntly confirmed that all the exposed merchandise was stolen from American ships and PXs. He agreed with me that these people were making money quickly. About three million people were in the city then, lured by the attraction of the fast dollar. It was more and more difficult to get around. Hotels along the way had numerous taxi girls and pimps standing outside. Some of these sleazy hovels advertised hot water for those who chose to stay the night. Back at the USO, Jerry and I wondered at this guy's background. He seemed to work for the U.S. or South Vietnamese government. His English was too good to be a recent acquisition, and his pro-U.S. thinking even made him vaguely suspicious. If he were a CIA plant checking on the views of various GIs, he got some unguarded opinions from us.

Saigon's streetside cafes catered to a varied clientele.

The Saigon visit was an eye opener for me. The city had one of the world's largest black markets. Was capitalism reaching its logical extreme in this haven surrounded by a war zone? I doubted we were helping to build the type of society we claimed was arising here. Even at the time it occurred to me that when the American goose ceases to deposit its golden eggs, even fast buckers of South Vietnam will be left high and dry. Famine, poverty, and defeat will be the future for these people. They will blame the United States for that. The North Vietnamese would surely take over when we leave in our attempt to turn the war over to the South Vietnamese. We as invited guests could not compete with the control the North Vietnamese and the Viet Cong exercised in their areas. They have the stronger position. We were suckers for the extent of our stay with no assurance that we are doing any good.

A couple of weeks later I got to Saigon again when Carpentier sent me with Larry, who had not been there in about three months. Larry was going in on a quick turnaround to use the phone bank in the USO to call home. At the USO, the usual pimp approached, and Larry ran down the list of prices for various services just for hell of hearing it. Short time was $15 to $20. Larry asked what he could have for $5.00. The pimp considered this.

"Which way you come into Saigon, you come in Route 1, no?"

"Yes," said Larry.

"What you see? You see people?" the man went on.

"Yes," Larry said. Lots of people.

The pimp asked him "What else you see?" Larry couldn't remember. The pimp added, "You see water buffalo, no?"

"Yes," chimed Larry, thinking a deal was coming.

"For $5.00, you get water buffalo!" He fell to laughing uproariously. We couldn't help following suit.

"Let me think about it," Larry, said, turning into the building, "Is the $5.00 for short time or long time?"

A band was playing inside, but Larry headed for the phones and I followed. The line was endless and we finally had to give up on the phone call. With no guaranteed ride back, we couldn't wait any longer. Outside the USO, it was nearly dark when we got a cab that dropped us at the outskirts of Saigon, where we were on our own. We started thumbing, hoping for some GIs. We got a ride to Long

Binh by dark. We then hiked the road in blackness, scared and out of our element. I really wished that I had my M-16. We were vulnerable, to say the least, defenseless against armed thieves and the Viet Cong. With weapons, at least we could have fought back some thugs. At night, we heard, all roads belonged to the Viet Cong. When they set up the rockets that penetrated our perimeter at night, someone had to carry the rockets out there in the dark. After nearly thirty anxious minutes the huge lights of an American five-ton appeared and three guys from the 1st Cavalry, stationed in Bien Hoa about a mile from us, picked us up. We were taking a chance being out there alone, they observed gravely. They had M-16s, and we felt a little better. They drove us right to our hooch.

During my year in Vietnam I would periodically meet old friends or people whom I had known in basic training, AIT, high school, college, and graduate school. It wasn't that much of a coincidence. People my age from Portland were being drafted, and the draftees at this juncture usually ended up in Vietnam.

On September 22, 1969, right after Jerry's orientation, I looked up from my desk and was surprised to see Stan Smith inprocessing into the 101st as a PFC. I had met him the first day at the induction center in Portland. During basic training, we had taken several trips back to Boston together. We got stuck at the YMCA in New York because of the snowstorm. He was also at Leonard Wood, but I had lost track of him during my week in the hospital. Stan had been accepted into OCS, but stuck with it after AIT. He spent two weeks at OCS and immediately applied to get out, but the Army kept him in OCS for fourteen weeks. He just didn't want to be a first lieutenant in a combat engineer company or an infantry unit. He discovered in basic, as I had, that he couldn't become an intelligence officer as he had hoped because the Army needed infantry officers. Since he announced a change while in OCS rather than in basic training, he hoped the Army would leave him stateside as a company clerk in an OCS training company instead of sending him to Vietnam. It was a good plan, but it didn't work out the way he had wished. The Army was not going to give up a body that it owed nothing to for a posh stateside assignment. Stan retained his MOS as a combat engineer. I attached a note to his 201 file indicating that he had a B.A. degree and could type 50 words a minute. He hoped that he could get a job in personnel rather than go to the 326th Engineers, the engineer unit attached to the 101st Airborne Division. I didn't want to dampen his hopes, but he could just as well be assigned to an infantry unit.

In the complicated rules of the game, even if I decided to extend my tour, Stan would have to spend almost two more months in the Army than I did. If I didn't extend, I would have to spend three more months in the Army than he would. I had lucked out. The only thing better would have been a stateside assignment or perhaps a tour in Germany. But the Army didn't usually send draftees or soldiers who were not committed to an MOS or a specific school and with less than a year and a half remaining in service to such choice places. Stan was very apprehensive about his upcoming assignment, as most of us had been at that stage. I tried to calm him by telling him that I would do all I could. That evening I walked over to the P-training area to bring Stan back to talk to the guys and have a few beers. We talked about his stint in OCS, which he really didn't like. He got along fine with some of the guys. Stan went through P-training, but on the last night he was caught taking a leak while on interior guard duty at the moment that the officer-in-charge was making his rounds checking guard points. That officer told Stan that he would have to repeat P-training. I filled Carpentier in on all this, and he went to the Black Hats to get Stan's assignment orders. Stan was the only one of 106 in his class to remain in the rear area assigned to our company. He was ecstatic when he found out Carpentier had gotten him out of another round of P-training. Of his entire group, his was the only record to which I attached a suggestive note. Stan was assigned to the enlisted records branch of the company where he was responsible for maintaining the records of several line companies. We were separated, so I saw him only occasionally at company formations and gatherings. He figured he owed me one.

A couple of weeks later, I met another guy I had known in the world in the chow hall at lunch. Someone called out my name from the officers' side of the mess hall. It was a first lieutenant who had received his commission at the graduation ceremonies at Niagara University in June 1968 after four years in ROTC. He had recognized me as one of the dorm proctors at Niagara during his junior and senior years. I didn't know him that well since he wasn't on my floor. We talked for a few moments about the people we knew at Niagara. He had an assignment to an infantry unit in the 101st and was headed north that afternoon. It just seemed like ages ago that we had been students, he an undergraduate and I a graduate student. Yet it was only 15 months since we had graduated. Another Niagara first lieutenant, Tom Vaughn, whom I had known for two years showed up shortly after that. A sensible if average student with middling motivation, he buckled down when necessary, but partied when he wanted to. He was in the company area overnight before going north to another unit. I invited him to the hooch for some beers and introduced him to the guys. Even Carpentier showed up that evening, which was unusual. I thought Tom was taking a chance by socializing with enlisted folk, but he was no snob and had no plans to stay in. Besides it wasn't his unit. He said he was in some type of intelligence work but I never knew what unit he was assigned to.

Tom was nostalgic that night. We talked about the guys we knew, and it seemed as if many of the 58 officers commissioned from the Niagara class of 1968 either had gone to Nam, were in Nam, or were going to Nam. We reminisced about beer blasts in Niagara Falls and the Buffalo area, the university, the Niagara basketball team, and its great players, Manny Leaks and Calvin Murphy who was then in his last year and breaking all the school scoring records. Tom left the following morning and I never saw him again.

Brud Higgins, another graduate student friend from Niagara, sent me a letter. I had last seen him on leave before I came to Nam. An American history major, Brud graduated from St. Anselm's the same year I left U-Maine and was a graduate assistant during the same two years that I was at Niagara. He was a grand talker with an even grander sense of humor, extremely bright, self-effacing, and possessed of tremendous conceptual abilities and a slight penchant for procrastination. He had the makings of a great college teacher. Here he was telling me that the moon rock that the astronauts had just brought back reminded him of me because of the relatively smooth surface on my head. I spent many a night in his apartment, and on weekends we would cruise the bars of Niagara Falls and even once in Toronto.

Brud's letter made me homesick again. In mid-1967, with exams over and everyone leaving Niagara, we sent Brud's roommate off by mooning him as he headed for Springfield, Massachusetts. "By the Light of the Silvery Moon," we sang cheerily, to the dismay of the old-lady busybody across the street.

One February night the previous winter we had our own encounter with willing lasses at his place. I was the designated blind date for one of these strangers. In the middle of the proceedings, Brud and I were suddenly overtaken with laughter as we stuffed ourselves into his closet bathroom to brush our teeth in preparation for larger events. I was spraying stuff into my armpits when my devilish look set him off. We were both howling when the ladies protested outside the door. We were all downing straight hard liquor, fumbling around in the dark with one couple not two feet from the other. The next thing I recall was light in the room, and any thought of resuming the play squelched by the nearness of the others. I exchanged a couple of letters with my friend of the moment, but nothing more came of it. I later became Brud's best man, and events moved too swiftly—the last year of graduate school, my fight with the draft. 1968 was too crazy a year: Martin Luther King was killed in March, and Bobby Kennedy in June. There was the Chicago convention in August. But here, in his letter, was a connection to a world thousands of miles distant and seemingly years away.

On my way to the PX one day I saw another familiar face. He was on the other side of a six-foot wire fence when I hollered at him. He knew me at once, a kid a year or two behind me at Cheverus

High School. He brought news about people from Portland. Assigned to the 1st Cavalry Division, he was nervous as hell about his assignment because he was an 11B10, or infantryman. He had graduated from Boston College in June 1968. With the draft board in Portland breathing down his neck, he couldn't find employment. After a bunch of odd jobs under his belt and an attempt to get into law school, he had received the lovely letter from "Miss Miserable," the clerk at the Portland draft board. Many others in his class at Cheverus also received their notices. By a not too odd coincidence, another mutual friend of ours, Cliff Hobbins of my Cheverus class of 1962, was also drafted. Cliff later processed through the 101st Admin Company, and I committed one of my most spectacular moves while at inprocessing. Cliff had attained his B.A. and M.A. degrees from Marquette University. He had taught for a year at a prep school in Fryeburg, Maine, until the octopus hand of that draft board got him also.

Between preparing for the East Asian history class during September and October and reading whatever I could get my hands on, I also pursued articles about the war. Nancy once sent me the text of a speech by Harvard biologist Dr. George Wald, the 1968 Nobel Prize winner in physiology and medicine. The *Boston Globe* printed his whole speech at MIT on March 4, 1969, "A Generation in Search of a Future." Essentially he claimed that the draft was the most un-American thing he knew about, but he buttressed this statement with some really limping statistics. He claimed that the bulk of the 1969 armed forces were genuine volunteers, and that among first-term enlistees, 49 percent were true volunteers. Another 30 percent were so-called reluctant volunteers, persons who volunteered before the draft got them anyhow. Only 21 percent he claimed were draftees. He must have gotten this stuff from the Pentagon. If 49 percent volunteered, it was because they knew they would be drafted and they wanted to avoid an infantry MOS. The way to do that was to sign up for three or four years for a specific MOS. Without a war, many of those people would not have signed up in the first place. In 1969 not too many draftees were being sent to Germany, the assignment that many of those drafted had put down as their place of preference, if they had not requested stateside. In addition, it takes a large amount of logistic support to back up an infantryman or a combat man—usually four or five, or some say even eight to one. Most of these slots are filled by people who sign up for three or four years. But would they have done so had there not been a draft? I kept my own careful statistics showing that the majority of the E-2 to E-5s that inprocessed into the 101st Airborne or Airmobile Division were draftees. Indeed, 99 percent of these guys were draftees, two-year draftees who were willing to take their chances to make it through a year in Nam. This was 1969, and the war had been going on heavily for at least five years, and if it weren't for the draftee, the military could never have kept producing fresh young 11B10s or infantrymen as replacements for those killed, wounded, and DEROSed annually. Without a draft, the Army would have had to pay handsomely to continue this effort, especially since so many, especially college youth, had turned against it. Wald never mentioned that the Marines were drafting at the time. Who the hell would volunteer for the infantry for Vietnam in 1969 if he didn't have to? My statistics showed about six volunteers out of six thousand thus far, 0.1 percent of the people I saw coming past my station.

Another thing never factored in here was McNamara's Project 100,000. In the late 1960s, as a social uplift program, the Army began accepting men of substandard IQ, usually rejected by the draft. Some were truly handicapped, with test scores below 70; others were bright enough, but illiterate—they simply never had the luxury of school. Mr. Mac wanted to give them the opportunity and privilege previously denied them to become viable members of the armed forces and to enter the crusade against communism in South Vietnam. These guys, because of their native intelligence, were never going to be Army rocket scientists. They ended up in the combat arms.

Besides the guy in AIT who almost blew me away on the firing range one day, the 101st Admin had at least one of Mr. Mac's aces.

He was a loose cannon. His name was Tentkeg and the guys called him "Tent Peg." He had a good personality and was trained as a driver. The first sergeant adopted him and made him a sort of company mascot while running him through the ranks very quickly to E-5 sergeant. No one dreamed of letting him push troops. I never saw him on guard duty. He could barely read but served as the first sergeant's driver. Our constant references to "down the road" to "up the road" baffled the man. He managed to deliver packages and people, although there were some good stories about his getting lost when driving off the base.

It was late September when I first heard about Woodstock. An inprocessing college man first mentioned it. Larry and I were discussing the possibilities of another pullout and whether our division would ever be earmarked for such a possibility. We talked about the changing mood on the home front against the war. This guy asked if we had heard about the "message of Woodstock"? I had no idea what he was talking about, nor did Larry or anybody else on our team. The guy explained that somewhere between 400,000 to 500,000 people attended a three-day music concert in mid-August in this small town in upstate New York. Drugs were plentiful, but violence was not. With little sanitation, insufficient food, and relentless rain, the whole thing had been a crimeless symbol of a counterculture that had the antiwar fervor at its center. People who had not supported the antiwar movement were taking a hard look at it and becoming sympathetic to it, if not joining the cause outright. The guy believed it was just the beginning of more antiwar activities that would eventually force the government to get us out of the war. He told us "at Woodstock, people were grooving on the music and themselves. There was a closeness of purpose and spirit." He was visibly moved. Of course we asked him why he bothered to come to Nam, and he replied that he had wished he hadn't but he was willing to take his chances to get the curse off his back. The fact remained that we had not heard about it or read about it in the *Stars and Stripes*. We couldn't remember reading anything about it in *Time* magazine either. Maybe the press had not picked up on its significance yet.

Neither did we know that the President planned to pull out some more troops, making a total of 60,000 withdrawn by the end of the year. But at that rate we all agreed that we would be long gone from Vietnam before he got down to the remaining force of 490,000. We did grow anxious about the pullouts, especially since we were still here with fewer guys on our side and a supposedly ever-increasing enemy.

Sports news was always a couple of days late. There was no daily newspaper, so we really lost interest. My beloved Red Sox had finished third in their division with "Yaz," Carl Yastrzemski, having a credible year with 40 home runs and 110 RBIs but batting only .258. Once again their pitching sucked. The Mets had beaten all odds and won the World Series, but we really couldn't get into that. It seemed a million miles away. All Yaz's performance could do was recall the dream year of 1967 when he won the triple crown. When I returned to Niagara that year, a group of us Boston fans drove to Cleveland to see them play the Indians, who were awful again that year. But the race was close, and the Sox needed every win they could get. The Cleveland stadium was huge, probably three times the size of Fenway Park. We took our general admission seats on a cold and damp and rainy night when hardly anyone was there. We ended up in box seats near the Red Sox dugout, as close to actual major league players as I've ever been. The Sox scratched out a 4-3 victory. Then they made the World Series. For every series game, seven Sox fans crowded Brud Higgins's apartment cheering and sucking suds. Maybe this was the year; yes, we thought they could come through. I remember walking out of his apartment after the seventh game feeling so distraught. It was the lesson of Puritan Catholic New England, as the Celtics build you up in victory, you must not feel too good, for in time so shall the Sox bring you down to defeat and despair.

While the Sox dashed our hopes again, our lives went on. Finney returned from Saigon one day with a parrot in a cage. He spent about $50 for it. He hung the cage in the bar and repeated proper English phrases to the bird: "Fuck you, asshole!" or "Chairborn! Sir!" Finney and Ferguson often repeated these can-do chants before an officer as they tossed off the mandatory salute. The object was to swallow the words so the officer couldn't tell what you were saying. Another common salute was "Up to Here, Sir!" while snapping the extended fingers of the right hand to the level of the right eyebrow. Like so many of these Army rituals, this one was open to interpretation. It could mean the officer was full of shit up to that point on his head, or the shit you were taking was now up that point on your own forehead.

Finney tried endlessly to make the parrot talk. He came back to the hooch at noon to work on him and continued in the evenings, to no avail. Fergy and Bradley tried their hands, too. One night we were about to turn in, when Bitch started barking at something outside, as she often did. Someone rousted out to see what was disturbing her when the parrot cut in, "Shut the fuck up, Bitch! Shut up, Bitch!" A few days later, the still ecstatic Finney let the parrot walk around the hooch and caught it by the talons to return it to the cage. We didn't think it was a good idea because the bird would hide out in the rafters, then fly out the screen door when someone opened it to come in. Finney said, "No way, the parrot likes it here," Finney assured us. One day, as predicted, the bird flew out the door, circled the hooch a couple of times like the Wicked Witch of the East, and made off, never to be seen again. If it went back to its former owner in Saigon, there was the possibility he would sell it again to some ding-dong GI with a hankering for a parrot. Macfee had the last word: "Er, ah, you know, Finney, as the fuckin' bird flew out the door, I definitely heard him say, 'Fuck you, asshole!'"

It was just another morning at inprocessing when Bradley came over to harass Macfee and talk to Finney and the rest of us. Bradley asked us if there were some of the guys that didn't have their toe prints. Finney who was screening a young kids records said "Hey, this guy doesn't have either fingerprints nor toe prints." The kid was a small eighteen-year-old with a tenth-grade education. Finney walked him across the room to the fingerprint table and made out the cards for the fingerprints, an essential part of the inprocessing procedure. Most had fingerprint cards completed in the states, but every once in a while we would get a man who had lost his records and the clerk in Oakland or some other installation was too lazy to do the prints again and opted to pass the chore on to the next and final station, which was us. While Finney did the fingerprints Bradley used the same cards and typed out toe prints, right and left foot. The kid, innocently cooperative, took off his shoes and socks and rolled each toe across the card in the proper finger space. What was really funny was when he had to roll all four together, it was really difficult, and Bradley suggested that he do it several times so that it was done right and he wouldn't have to come back and do it again. The entire inprocessing line was rolling. Finney and Bradley never cracked a smile during the entire proceedings.

The kid never really knew that anything was amiss until Bradley helped him put his shoes back on and put his arm around him and told him. Bradley walked the kid to the front of the finance line and told him to come back and see him when he finished. Then Bradley went with him to the Black Hats to tell them that the kid was on clean up detail at inprocessing for the rest of the afternoon. We could do that with the cherries. Then Bradley gave him the rest of day off, freeing him from any Black Hat detail.

But Finney was not quite finished. He filled in all the squares of the toe print/fingerprint card and placed it in the guy's records behind his fingerprint card. Finney signed the official's name as Ho Chi Minh from Saigon. For all we knew, it could have stayed in the man's records until he left the service. Little things occupy little minds.

Every once in a while, usually in the evening, an egregiously drunk troop would wander into our hooch from another company. Mostly they were older men, lifers as we called them, men in their late thirties or early forties who had been up and down the ranks, busted for drink or sassing some asshole officer. After eighteen years, one of these guys would be lucky to be an E-6, a staff sergeant. And probably his E-6 was reinstated because of the Vietnam war. These fellows never meant any harm even though they were almost always drunk. They usually were lost and had gotten fucked up somewhere on booze and saw our light and refrigerator, and probably wanted another taste before they headed back to wherever their hooch was. Some came in fairly beaten up, victims of a brawl, their faces showing swelling and recent cuts.

One evening our door burst open and this huge mother came in shooting his mouth off that he was going to take on all comers and was going to beat the piss out of them. He was about 6 feet 4 inches and 225 lbs. He looked about forty, a lot older than we were, and he didn't look too quick. I was sitting there with Larry and Jerry. So we asked him to sit down and take a load off his feet, which he did. But he kept mouthing off and yelling about beating the shit out of someone. Presently, Fergy and Finney came back from the club and caught the tail end of this conversation. Fergy told the guy to shut the fuck up or he might get hurt. Fergy and Finney had their own share of the juice.

"So you been in the fuckin' Army for nearly twenty years and you're already an E-6? Wow!" Fergy didn't give a shit what he said to the guy, and neither did we after the guy kept mouthing off that he was going to kick Fergy's ass.

"You ain't going to kick anybody's ass, you're too fuckin' drunk and too fuckin' ugly for anyone to fight you." Well, the guy kept on about taking on any three of us at the same time. Fergy had enough and told the guy to leave, as did Larry. Finally, the guy said to Fergy, "You couldn't touch me because your too fuckin' skinny and I would whip your ass in an instant."

Fergy told the guy to get outside and he would oblige him with the fight he wanted. They stepped outside the door and they started to measure each other. Fergy was much faster. He punched his man twice in quick succession, and the guy was on the ground. But he bounced right back up. After dropping him for the third time, Fergy worried that he would have to hurt this guy. He sought some inspi-

VOICES FROM THE REAR

ration from us. Finally, Larry started to settle the stranger down. He had fought a great fight, he told the reeling combatant, but now it was time to go. Finally the guy agreed, and Larry pointed him in the presumed direction of his own hooch. We never saw him again.

We roamed the base in the evenings. For me, the drawing card was food. After a day at inprocessing we most often went back to the hooch to rest, read, or have a beer. We often didn't bother to walk the 400 hundred yards up a hill to go to chow, and at 8:00 in the evening we got hungry. We hoarded snacks, cookies, and other goodies from home, and could always pull those out if necessary. But we were always looking for something more, and Johnny Bradley invented another play-action game.

For this, JB got into wearing officers' insignia as a ploy to cadge food. He would walk up the road with captain's bars pinned to his hat. About six o'clock one evening, I watched an old E-6 from the 101st Admin Company come rumbling down the road in a half-ton and happen to see JB walking up the road with his captain's bars. Now this sergeant wasn't the brightest, but he knew the consequences of impersonating officers. He was a straight troop, always in starched fatigues and trouser cuffs properly bloused outside the boots. This twenty-year veteran's white hair made him look like he was fifty. He never pulled his weight around the troops. He was one of us, but just too much older to figure that this was safe. "Captain" JB strolled the side of the road as the old sarge braked the half-ton to a sudden halt, stirring up a dust cloud that took a moment to clear.

"Johnny, what the fuck are you doing?" he yelled. JB just turned to him, put on an enigmatic smile and put his finger up to his lips. "Shh," he breathed back at the incredulous noncom. The old sarge just shrugged, slowly shook his head, and got back into the truck and headed off. JB could pull this stunt off. The sarge seemed to believe he had just encountered another of the Army's mysterious ways. JB was clearly on an important mission and couldn't talk.

The reason for JB's disguise was that it helped him suck up to an enlisted E-6 cook in another company, who was doling out some free food. He cultivated the cook, who never questioned JB's rank.

Johnny would bring home some meatloafs and fried potatoes, enough for everyone. He ran this scam once a week for about a month. He came back one night to tell us that the cook was doubting he was an officer. Now he needed additional proof. He told the mess sergeant he would bring by one of his officer friends who lived in his hooch. He promised to do this the next evening. Johnny didn't have an officer friend and solicited volunteers. No one came forward. The food was great, but no one wanted to risk a violation of the military code. Johnny pleaded his case, explaining it would be almost dark when we went and the trek was only about three-quarters of a mile. He wanted me to go with him, since I looked like an officer, and I was older. The other guys agreed and urged me to help the cause. Bradley added that he would do all the talking, I just had to be there as proof that he was truly an officer in the United States Army.

With all the cajolery, I reluctantly decided to go as Captain Bradley's lieutenant friend. Two hours earlier we could have had the same food at our own mess hall. We were really like my dog Sandy, a well-fed hound who still scrounged around other people's garbage cans and the local ice cream hangout to steal a melted ice cream soda from the trash. For the dog it seemed that food always tasted better when he stole it or foraged for it himself. I was ready for the hunt.

The next evening Bradley gave me silver bars for my cap. We walked side by side up the road. Fortunately few vehicles passed us. I thought about the repercussions of getting caught. Then I thought, what are they going to do me, send me to Vietnam? There was always the threat from the first sergeant the day I walked into the company, "If you fuck up I will send you to the line." That statement weighed heavily on me, and I knew perfectly well that the first sergeant could make good on this. Bradley didn't give a shit; he just wanted to continue the scheme. Here I was, playing second fiddle to a guy nearly my direct opposite. He was just come back from R&R in Hawaii, where he dropped over $2,000, not including his wife's airfare. He had ordered two hamburgers and beer from room service at 2:00 a.m. and paid $37.50, plus a tip! I would have had beer in the refrigerator and gone out and got some burgers for $5.00. I was too used to being a poor student. Bradley would go for it while I remained a tightass. I admired him for his daring and wished I could pull that off. As we arrived at the 1st Cavalry chow hall, I hoped we wouldn't run into the guys who had picked up Larry and me that dark night we thumbed in from Saigon. I would tell them that I just received my direct commission and was assigned to the same company for the rest of my tour. Bradley introduced me to the E-6 as Lieutenant Watson. I shook hands and asked him where he was from. He wasn't that much older than I was and had been in the Army for nine years. This was his first combat assignment, the others were stateside and Germany. Bradley asked him outright for some meatloafs and potatoes. He offered up four huge loafs. Bradley in return handed him a bottle of bourbon, the first time he gave up anything in exchange. We weren't there fifteen minutes for all this, shook hands, and left with our prizes. Bradley congratulated me for a great job, figuring we could pull this off weekly at least. The guys were like baby birds in the nest when we returned. There was plenty for all of us. Bradley sang my praises for weeks. I was relieved that it was over and no harm had been done. There were no explanations to make. Bradley would get into his disguise several more times before we had to leave to go north.

Tom Tate wasn't the swiftest of people, but he was a hardworking, decent sort from northern Alabama with a distinctive southern accent. He was a young E-5 lifer about twenty-three years old. He had four years in service, and if he continued to like it he would stay in the Army. He was a married Spec-4 with four children. He said that he and his wife started right away using different methods of birth control, but he just blew through everything. He had worked in personnel his entire Army career, with the exception of basic training and AIT. He wasn't quick to pick up things, but once he did, he usually recalled them. Carpentier brought him in one day and asked me to break him in. He had worked with personnel files, so he could grasp our routine very easily.

He was enormously serious, too old for his age. Maybe it was the responsibility of having so many kids. He never made the trek to the 1st Calvary chow hall with Bradley. He had one memorable expression that stuck with me. If someone said something he didn't think was too bright, he would say, "That guy is dumber than a government mule." Tate just didn't think around corners. He was always too busy or always working. He seemed to live by regulations. If he could finally comprehend the regulation, it would become his bible. He couldn't survive without regulatory codes. A guy like this uses the regulation as a sword against the world, but it's really a crutch for his own inadequacies. He often dampens creativity and thwarts new ideas. So we didn't quite match up. He worked well on the inprocessing line, and he didn't give anyone much heat.

Like Tate, Sonny Gatchell was from Alabama. I remember when Sonny inprocessed into the 101st as a PFC. His file revealed a physical disability profile resulting from a fall from a telephone pole while training as a lineman. He had broken his leg and had two more months before he could be given any strenuous duty. I put a note on his 201 file and sent it up the road. He was assigned into the 101st Admin Company and to inprocessing. He believed I had saved his ass from a line assignment. Sonny was nineteen, good looking, and somewhat subdued, yet he was not to be fucked with either. He had signed up for three years and had about two more to go. Larry and I showed him the ropes of inprocessing, and he picked it up immediately. Sonny typed a blazing sixty words a minute, which made the line move. Sonny availed himself of the PX system to load up with stereo equipment. Prices were much cheaper than stateside, so many guys bought equipment, receivers, and huge speakers. I bought a camera with some extra lenses that I practiced with once in a while.

Sonny made what we all thought was a huge mistake while we knew him. He re-upped just so he would get the leave to go back to see a girl he had recently met at home. Reenlisting for three years gave a man a month stateside, which would count towards your year in Vietnam. It was the craziest idea ever. We all tried to talk him out of it. Finney practically went nuts when he heard it and tried to talk some sense into him. Sonny would owe three total years from the time he signed the papers, whereas he had less than two when he signed up.

Macfee, in usual form, observed, "It's the fuckin'est stupid thing I ever heard of. Goddamn it, Sonny no piece of fuckin' ass is worth another year in this motherfuckin' Army. Hell! I can get you a piece of motherfuckin' ass if you need it that bad." Macfee was so upset he even cleaned up his language. Sonny's intentions upset the whole hooch; it was as though he had broken an unwritten moral code. Sonny would have made sense if he intended to stay in and make the Army a career, but those were not his plans. Indeed, many were the senior lifers who timed their reenlistment time for six months in Vietnam so that they could take a month's leave which counted on their year in Nam. When they got back, they only had five months left in their Vietnam tour, a loophole in the rules that many a guy made use of. Sonny had a safe job in Nam, and if he completed the tour, he would have but a year left. Now, when he left Nam, he would have more than two. Christ! The Army could even send him back for another tour although, that was highly unlikely. But Sonny had heard enough, and all pleas fell on his deaf ears. He reenlisted and went home to Alabama. This famous girl, in his two-and-a-half-month absence, had found someone else, just as we predicted. Sonny at least found that his mother was glad to see him, but quite disappointed that he would have to return to Vietnam. His more suspicious father wanted to know how and why he was home. Sonny told him that he had reenlisted, and his father said, "Well, don't do it again." *Some people have to learn for themselves.*

Something I resented was having a recruiter posted so near the whole inprocessing system. These cherries were sweating their assignments, scared about the possibilities of getting wounded and possibly killed. With the antiwar sentiment at home, attracting bright young enlisted men to the ranks was becoming increasingly difficult. If the Army could get a recruit to add a year or two to an existing enlistment, a future recruiting year quota was filled, good business for the Army. For me, it was like cardsharps preying on the

163

vulnerable. Still, it was surprising that so few did reenlist. Even Sonny thought about it for two months. It was as though these kids were bullheaded Americans who said "Fuck you, I'm going to take this fuckin' ordeal and get the fuck out of here in one fuckin' piece, despite this fuckin' Army and its fuckin' war." I was proud of that. If our country were ever involved in a war for real national interests, we would have the stamina and guts to fight it. Here we were, a bunch of patsies, telling our vaunted and corrupt ally and the ARVN weekday warriors to take from us all they wanted.

Two Korean women set themselves up in the compound to sell Bibles to the cherries coming out of the finance line with their back pay. Again, these were apprehensive guys, vulnerable to thinking about God at this time. These people were making a profit off God by selling their Bibles to worried GIs about to go out to the field to commit the most inhuman acts. The Vietnamese population was much more heavily Christian than the Koreans, but the presence of Korean civilians on our bases to run camera shops and other quick-profit concessions was part of the compensation for the Koreans who so willingly supported us by contributing to the cause with 50,000 troops in Vietnam. Why the Korean women did not stand outside the "steam and cream" during the afternoon selling Bibles is a moot question. Some of these guys could take their Bibles in with them to ponder certain entertaining passages while receiving services. No, it was the carpetbagger and the scalawag all over again. Where there is a chance to make a buck, someone will go for it.

Rumors of an impending move north that circulated around the 101st Administration Company reached a crescendo in October 1969. I thought nothing of it at first, but on October 9th Carpentier ordered me to measure the cubic footage of all the furniture and office equipment. A move was logical at this point. The headquarters of the 101st Airborne Division (Airmobile) was at Camp Evans, near the old capital city of Hue. Leaving the division's administration company in Bien Hoa separated our function from the main divisional activity. Space at Camp Evans was short, and we figured if the line guys compared our existence to theirs, there would be trouble. But President Nixon had also withdrawn 25,000 American troops in August and planned to remove another 35,000 by December. We would be taking over some of the space they left.

By early November, rumor had us moving to Phu Bai, near Hue. The Navy Seabees in the area were pulling out. We also found out that "in-and-out-processing" would be the last to be sent north. The "up the road" portion of the company would be sent first and we would follow. The company vehicles started to disappear north, and we now had to hitchhike the records up the road daily and hope for a return ride. November would be one of the largest inprocessing months because in that month of 1967, several of the division's brigades went to Vietnam with an initial infusion of some 4,000 new troops. Large numbers of men would now outprocess, meaning that their replacements would also inprocess. We anticipated nearly 3,000 people through our lines instead of a peak of 2,000. Of course, there were plenty who left sooner than a year, the wounded and those killed.

Going North would put us in Phu Bai in the middle of the rainy season, which was much more severe there than in the South. The monsoon in Bien Hoa had some rainy days, but it was never that cold or damp.

Some of the company elements already there reported that quarters were fine, but they were working long hours. It was also rumored that we would have to pull KP and a lot more guard duty. The guard duty I didn't mind, but KP was a pain. I would rather pull guard duty three times a week than KP once a month.

During November we had to pull office CQ until about 10:00 p.m. to keep in contact with the elements of the company in the North. I often sat by the phone with Bitch on my lap, stroking her ears while reading a book. Bitch was almost too big for my lap, but she wanted to be there, curled up and asleep. Often times Larry would keep me company, and I would do the same for him. Late one afternoon some Vietnamese kids wandered in and remarked on eating Bitch for supper. Larry sent them off with "How about me feed you to her for supper? You like that, no?" They just sort of laughed and gave us the usual nonsense about the Screaming Eagle division patch on our shoulders: "You fuck a chicken, no?" I think they got that from the 1st Calvary or some other Army unit paying us a complement.

This was a depressing time, not knowing where or when we would be going, but we knew we would be going North. I had read in the November 10th *Newsweek* that the 101st Airborne Division and the 1st Cavalry would remain in Vietnam even if others pulled out. According to the piece, the 1st Calvary would remain in the south around Saigon while the 101st would cover Hue. That coincided exactly with events. No one I ever dealt with in the Army could give a clear view of events. Enlisted folk weren't supposed to think; an old Army cliché holds that they are only cleared for rumor. Someone was always generating news, based on the latest intelligence, about a huge company of Viet Cong and North Vietnamese regulars around Bien Hoa. What was the source? Where had they been seen? Were they heavily armed? Were they carrying many rockets? What was their purpose? Who had seen them? How long ago had they been seen? Was that Tet '68? We got only rumors. We dismissed so many that if a huge enemy contingent was nearby, no one would believe it until we were overrun.

Our last Saigon outing and the possibility of a phone call to Nancy before the move made me want to try to get there one more time. Carpentier let Larry and me go one lazy afternoon. A warrant officer named Bennett had actually taken over. Carpentier had known him as an E-7. Carpentier would assume full control again up North.

We knew we could get to Saigon, but could we get back before dark? We got a ride to the USO and waited for our turn at the phone bank. I got Nancy to send me her phone number in case I got to Saigon again. My wait in line seemed endless, and I was nervous. She answered on the second ring, as though she had been expecting my call. I told her how great it was to hear her voice and how much I had missed her. It was sometime in the middle of the night, but I didn't care and neither did she. She was working hard in school and was really swamped with papers. In our long-distance correspondence, this angel had accepted my proposal. We had agreed to get married the next time we were together, but I had no real fix on an R&R until we moved North. We had also had to work out a good time for her, since she was a full-time student. At my rank and pay, I had to call collect, and when ten minutes had passed, we had to stop. I signed off telling her how much I missed her and loved her. It made me feel empty having to hang up. I just hoped that we could pull off the R&R together.

Larry was still on the phone when I hung up. Talking with his daughter brought tears down his cheeks. When he finished, he said nothing for fifteen minutes. "I'll be home in December," he finally declared quietly. December 9th was his last day. He had extended for a month. He would be home for Christmas.

A comforting nighttime occurrence was the sound of the B-52s working out. With the troop withdrawals, the thumping of distant bombs provided relief that the enemy was not roaming totally free at night.

Now we had to get back to Bien Hoa before dark. This time, Larry suggested that we negotiate with a cab driver to get us to the outskirts of Bien Hoa. We got one and asked how many "P" to get to Bien Hoa. When we pulled out the exact money and agreed upon the price, we took off. When he let us off five miles short of Bien Hoa it was almost dark. We paid the fare and started walking. We figured that any vehicle coming at this time would be U.S. military going where we wanted to be. Sure enough, in about ten minutes a half-ton driven by the guys from the 1st Calvary picked us up and delivered us to the door again. I had been fortunate to see Saigon three afternoons in five months.

The November rush rolled over us as expected. We inprocessed 130 in a single day, and by November 22, we had exceeded 1,700, with eight days remaining in the month. Our post office moved north, which screwed up our mail. I had only one letter from Nancy in fifteen days. I knew she was writing to me, and other guys weren't getting mail either. All this confusion led to increased drinking and fights in our hooch. This was the time that Finney bruised the guy's ribs so badly that he had to be taken to the medics and had to wear a brace or bandage for some time. Finney was also concerned how he was going to get Bitch up north. He would stay up late, half drunk, playing with his M-16, making the rest of us fear an accident. As the bulk of the company was already up at Phu Bai, it occurred to us that we would get the last pick of the hooches.

One November night about twenty of us polished off eight cases of beer in three hours, or about 9.6 beers apiece. Funny, but no fights occurred that night. Another night I had about five beers in three hours, then took several aspirin tablets before going to bed. I read a couple of chapters before turning out the light. In the night, I went outside to take a leak. A late rain left the grass outside slippery, and I pitched down, cut my head, and came back inside dazed and bloodied in several places. The beer and the shock must have confused me. Charlton woke up with a start to see me looking down at him—I thought he was sleeping in my bunk. He shoved me into my place next door. I had scabs on my head from the fall, and some of the guys said someone had hit me on the head. I didn't want to ponder that thought, because I probably wouldn't sleep for several nights.

Finney, Fergy, Bradley, and Larry attempted to lift our spirits by stealing more food for a barbecue. "Captain" JB got the 1st Calvary cook to give us some trays of chicken, and Finney made his own sauce which was fantastic. More beer washed it all down.

The cherries kept coming, 177 in the largest single group, followed the next day by another 130. But the future looked promising: only 20 were expected on Thanksgiving Day. The only thing that made that day any different was the feast of turkey and all the trimmings in the chow hall. The cooks outdid themselves. Tables were decorated, and the division cooks made the day memorable. We sort of drank our way through our remaining stay in Bien Hoa. With one last rocket attack, Charlie Cong said good-bye to us. The sirens sounded, explosions reverberated in the distance, but nothing came near our hooch.

Finally we stopped all processing. Pallets showed up outside our hooches, and we piled our office furniture, wall and foot lockers, and duffle bags packed with our clothes on them. Specialists wrapped plastic around the goods and strapped them tightly to stabilize the whole load. Forklifts hoisted the pallets to flatbed trucks headed for the airport. I sent home the many books I had collected, in part to avoid unloading them at Phu Bai. We followed the flatbeds to the airport where everything wound up inside a C-130 transport. The pallets were strapped down on the aircraft centerline in an amazingly efficient use of space, and we sat on the side of the aircraft. We could be back to inprocessing in less than a day.

The crew chief wouldn't let Bitch on board. Finney stayed behind with the dog, later joining us after persuading another crew chief to fly the dog. As the plane took off, all of us were together—Larry, Fergy, Bradley, Jerry, Warbeck, Tate, Sonny, Charlton, Macfee, Carpentier, and a few others. Most of us had been together for nearly five months, some longer than that, time that seemed to move by quickly now. Larry and I shared a rare porthole window. The aircraft dipped over the fields around Bien Hoa and Long Binh.

Larry's eyes clouded up; he had spent a year there. He would never see this place again, home to him from October 1968 to November 1969. He would be gone in two weeks. I never got attached to Bien Hoa, but I knew a place in my life was gone forever. It was November 28, 1969. I had seen the best of Bien Hoa.

CHAPTER 5

PHU BAI

Within two hours, the C-130 put us down in a rainstorm at Phu Bai, a small town south of Hue about fifty miles from the demilitarized zone (DMZ). It had rained for nine straight days. A damp chill, unknown in Bien Hoa, penetrated to my marrow to emphasize our change of station. At the new company area, not far from the airfield, I got into the same hooch as Larry and Jerry. The others settled in where room permitted around the area. The truck stopped a hundred and fifty yards from the new quarters, and we tracked the mire up the stairs and into the place as we unloaded duffels and footlockers.

Hooches in Phu Bai were up on stilts instead of being anchored to concrete slabs. The air circulation made them colder in the rainy season, but breezy and cooler in the summer. With ground floors starting two to three feet above the ground, depending on the contour of the land, they lacked the waist-high sandbag protection as at Bien Hoa. The good news was that this base hadn't endured a rocket attack in over a year. On the down side, everything was much smaller than Bien Hoa's quarters. About eight guys squeezed tightly into one of these hooches, separated only by a row of wall lockers, leaving no room for our cherished bar and refrigerator. The Navy, in charge of most of the base construction in Vietnam, seemed to have it better. I would bet the Navy had four men to a hooch.

C-130s, whether in flight or on the ground, were as prevalent as UH-1s. There was little doubt that the Hercules was a workhorse.

Since we were the last to arrive, we got the hooch farthest away from the main company area. A six-foot chainlink fence separated us from the XXIV Corps headquarters compound. The corps controlled the 101st Airborne Division and several other units in the region. The fence made some sense when the Seabees occupied the area, but since we were all army troops there now, the divider was artificial. Some of our guys soon cut a man-size arc out of the chainlink, giving access to the XXIV Corps club on the other side, larger than anything we had and featuring live entertainment twice a week. Fergy was in his glory with an easy stroll to a source of beer and a wider pool of talent for better fights.

We were at the bottom end of a hollow, so we had to walk up through asymmetrical rows of hooches to get to the bathroom. The Navy had built here the best bathhouse I saw in Vietnam, a real convenience with flush toilets and a huge open shower room, like something in a high school gym. Every sink faucet actually worked. Every day, mamma sans dutifully trooped in to make it spotless. Vietnamese soils and the vast overload on sanitation strained the drainage system, though. The toilets often backed up, and it would take days to locate the proper equipment to repair them. The company engineers or general handymen always seemed to be old lifers with a liking for the sauce. With their perpetually red faces and slow movements, they relied on a few younger but equally slow guys who came along to do the work, but there were never enough to keep our compound going.

The chainlink fence separated the 101st from the XXIV Corps HQ.

Near the latrine was the small enlisted club. A long L-shaped bar covered one wall, and several slot machines and other bar gimmicks, such as miniature bowling, stood opposite that. Off the end of the bar were tables and chairs. At the far side of the tables was a small stage. We never had a performance there until one of the company captains thought he would try out some magic tricks on us. It was awful, but we gave him a round of applause.

The chow hall was up a hill and across a road some distance from the club and my hooch. It accommodated about two hundred at a time inside and had a long, screened entry porch to shelter another sixty waiting people during torrential downpours common during the rainy season. Navy construction seemed to incorporate things the Army would never think of. We occasionally skipped evening meals at Bien Hoa to avoid standing in the rain, among other less compelling reasons. In six months at Phu Bai I never had to wait beyond the entryway. Behind the mess hall were the cooks' hooches. The cooks served up three meals a day for all the 101st Admin Company personnel, more than 200 people; the Black Hat cadre, another twenty-five; and all the in-and-out-processing personnel—another couple of hundred people. I never had a bad meal there.

Other news was mixed. We never pulled KP at Phu Bai. The company hired mamma sans, probably holdovers from the Navy. Offsetting this guarantee, we pulled guard duty more often than at Bien Hoa—every six days, with no sleep in the morning. Guard duty five times a week was preferable to KP once a month. I had enough of that in basic training and AIT.

VOICES FROM THE REAR

The back door of the "hooch" provided a clear view of the mountains. The mess hall is to the left. Off in the distance is the guard tower (right).

Beyond the mess hall, a gradual hill rose about a hundred yards to the right and ran to the 101st Admin Company headquarters building, a massive tin structure with multiple entrances. It had been a Seabee warehouse for heavy equipment and supplies. The entire admin company fit under this single roof, with my in-and-out-processing separated from the rest of the branches by only a wall instead of a distance of a mile and a half, as at Bien Hoa. We could deliver our 201 personnel files to the assignment branch located on the other side of the wall. Other branches, such as senior enlisted, officer records, and all the various company record clerks, were located on either side of a wide center corridor, all spread out beneath the thirty-foot-high rafters. In a set of enclosed offices raised a story above the warehouse floor were the "cheeses," the commanding officer, a major, and some captains who ran the company. They surveyed the entire record-keeping area from their glassed-in perch, but our in-and-out-processing branch was directly under them and out of their sight. Those people had one important advantage over the scumbags below—they were air-conditioned! In the usual

Army two-class system, the shitbum enlisted almost literally fried. On overcast days, the building was livable, but when the sun hit that tin roof, it was, in Macfee's inimitable words, "one motherfucker of a motherfuckin' oven." With no screens and no windows, all we could do was open all the doors for cross ventilation. As a warehouse, the place was all right, and people retrieving goods and equipment could step into the air-conditioned office or go back outside. I never sweated like that before or since. I actually watched my fingers perspire. We all sat around in soaked camouflage T-shirts all day.

Centralizing the division's administrative functions in this way was a piece of genius, but the new location was murder. There was probably little choice. Our unit needed so much square footage, and in the Army way, that's what we got. Officer, senior enlisted, and E-6 and below from all over the division could come to that building and annotate their personnel and finance records. The place was so cavernous that eventually the command installed an information booth in the center of it to direct GIs coming from their units with some matter their company clerk couldn't handle. Again, all the records of every single individual in the 101st Airborne Division were maintained in that building. When an individual was killed, a company clerk had to inform the personnel specialist who maintained that company's records and who would in turn forward the deceased's files to the proper stateside address. The system worked the same for those wounded. Records had to be kept when the individual was airlifted or medically evacuated from Vietnam to Japan or some other location. The clerk had to make sure that the wounded man's records followed him. If the casualty returned to his unit, he would inprocess all over again. Award and promotion records and, most important, DEROSes had to be scheduled and recorded by specialists in the company. One specialist often handled several companies. The 101st Admin Company also kept statistics on wounded and killed and the unit location and other specifics of where the casualty occurred.

The mechanics of the system were many and varied. In my own

case, I was unaware that I had been promoted on November 9, 1969, to Spec-4. This was an almost automatic promotion when serving in Vietnam. But I was unaware of it until the clerk who maintained my records informed me about it. My monthly pay increased some $72, and when adjusted to the date of the promotion, it stood at $292. Being among the last elements of the admin company to leave Bien Hoa, I had lost touch. and might have known about my promotion much sooner.

About seventy-five yards from our tin warehouse, on a slight rise, was the officers club, surrounded by trees. On the other side of the officers club were various supply buildings where we drew supplies such as sheets, ammo, and clothing.

Past my hooch and the huge chow hall was the company headquarters, the first sergeant's abode. This was a small hooch similar to the one at Bien Hoa, facing a sort of mud path running between the dwellings. Across the street and to the right of the headshed was the equipment barn, where those red-faced lifers held forth with their supplies and filled requisitions for anything broken. It was a good thing the guys in my hooch were fairly handy and could repair things like broken screens because low-rankers like us would get no service no matter how long we waited. Beyond that area were marshes and the berm line as well as the guard-duty posting hooch. This is where we would all meet for guard mount and line up for bunker assignment before trekking out there.

To the right of the CQ hooch were more hovels housing guys of the 101st Admin Company. On the other side of the road there were ten more hooches that included another flush toilet and shower. Farther down the street on the company side were some shops, a seamstress, and a photographer where the GIs could have portraits made to send home. Continuing down to the right of those shops on that side of the road were senior enlisted hooches and the dispensary, or clinic, and beyond the senior enlisted quarters was an excellent cement basketball court.

The road then turned to the right and dipped a bit down a hill. On the right was the Black Hat Headquarters and the barracks area where all the inprocessing cherries and outprocessing veterans stayed. The road ended in a large circle. At the edge and left center of the circle, a large amphitheater able to hold 250 to 300 GIs on benches sloped down to a stage twenty-feet deep backed up by a large screen across the width of the stage. It looked like a drive-in theater. We could see movies there as well as an occasional live show such as a Vietnamese band that included girls. From the middle of the circle, a path headed out to a large enlisted club on a bluff overlooking some marshes. This was a much larger watering hole than the one in our own area. Besides the normal amenities, it also had outside tables and chairs where the GIs could get away from the music and noise inside. It was always crowded, mostly with guys going home, as the cherries were perhaps too apprehensive to use it. The guys who were outprocessing had something to celebrate. We used that club periodically, and more so as we became shorter. Down the slope and to the right of this club was a built-up two-foot-wide path of PSP meandering about 500 yards through the marsh and bog to an Air Force communication installation. We generally stayed away from the Air Force community, mostly because we had our own bars, but we took several memorable treks out there and back. Beyond that was the bunker and berm line.

Starting from the back door of my hooch, a distance of about 100 yards, past some graves to the left, was the compound's main artery. Turning left would take you back to the area of the mess hall, but turning right took you past the vehicle maintenance shed. A few guys always hung out there, supposedly working on company jeeps and half-ton trucks. The road then went up a steep hill to the main gate of the 101st admin area. All the Vietnamese who worked in our compound were individually checked in here. About fifty yards before the gate and on the left side of the road was a series of shops, the largest belonging to a tailor. He made a small fortune fashioning suits, including mine, and other articles of clothing for guys going on R&R. This defined area was my home from November 28, 1969, to June 9, 1970. Not counting several trips to the main PX about a mile from our compound, I ventured off this area only a half a dozen times during my stay.

My first two days were very depressing. We had gotten the shit end of the stick as far as hooch location was concerned because we were the last to arrive. In-and-out-processing was now directly attached to the rest of the company. This meant we were subject to new controls. At Bien Hoa we had pretty well managed our own affairs. We did everything by and for ourselves. Sure, SFC Carpentier was there, but many days he didn't show up until late afternoon; we often just handed him the day's intake and he was off. He had other responsibilities besides us. We would close up shop and go back to our hooch, far removed from our regular company. In fact, the master sergeant who gave me my initial lecture about "working hard and don't fuck around or I will send your fuckin' ass to the line" had completed his tour and had left for the states in early November. We never saw him go. The Black Hats—a contingent of which were now stationed with us—as at Bien Hoa answered to their own first sergeant and chain of command structure.

On tighter orders, we worked until 9:30 every night, whether we had cherries or not, with no half-day off. It was seven days a week straight through, broken only by infrequent company formations. Our company officers and senior enlisted seemed to be conspiring at toeing the line immediately to show the division command how hard we worked. After all, they were within a few miles of headquarters now, rather than about 400 miles, much closer to the flagpole. I sensed a bit of guilt or paranoia as the rationale for the increased harassment. Maybe they just didn't want to give us time to think clearly about the war.

Within a few days, the weather broke, and it warmed up considerably. I felt better with the sunshine. Scenic countryside appeared out of the mist. The Annam mountain chain lay in the distance, and some of the peaks rose above the clouds. The landscape was very green and lush, especially after a downpour. Under other circumstances I would have liked to hike to those peaks. I knew our infantry was out there in their shadow, risking life and limb. No matter how bad Phu Bai was, those grunts had it much worse. Trekking through that jungle area in deluges and penetrating dampness was sheer misery. Imagine having to bed down in those conditions and trying to keep a weapon dry and living for weeks on C-rations. Besides the rotten weather, enemy ambushes, mines, and booby traps made life wretched. Those bush-humping grunts, with their 11B10 MOSs, deserved a lot more honor than they got when they returned to the states.

On the second day at Phu Bai, as Larry and I were walking to the PX during lunch, a lieutenant riding in a jeep yelled my name. It was Bob Small. He had been drafted right out of the University of Maine in 1967 and went to OCS. He spent a year in Germany with his beautiful wife Sharon and became quite fluent in German. Now the Army decided to use his German in the Republic of Vietnam. He came over to the inprocessing hooch for about forty-five minutes next day. Bob had been a renowned athlete in high school at Freeport, the home of the famous L. L. Bean company. He and his friend Tommy Trufant hit it off immediately with our crowd from the Portland campus. He was an excellent basketball player and a good student, and we frequently partied together. I got Bob a part-time job in the requisition files at the Union Mutual Life Insurance Company. He married Sharon after his junior year, and his partying days were over. The grasping hand of the Portland draft board had plucked him up, too. Listening to Bob again made my blood boil over the way the draft worked throughout the country. From what he said, he seemed to be in some type of Army intelligence because of his language training. He was stationed at Da Nang but did a lot of traveling in the area. This was his final tour, and he couldn't wait to get out. Even this pleasant interlude couldn't pass without our recounting a legend attaching to him and his high-school girlfriend.

One evening he went to her house to watch TV. Her parents went out to do some shopping and Bob and his girl did the normal thing—they got into it heavily, and soon Bob had his fly open and his shortest leg at full sail. Suddenly, the door opened and the parents surged back in with polite inquiries about the movie and what they had eaten. Bob quickly sat up on the couch and hugged a pillow to his extended member. It took an eternity before the parents finally left the room. His girlfriend remained calm, fully clothed, and aware of his predicament, but seemed to encourage more conversation with her mother while Bob struggled with his situation.

We pulled guard duty every six days. Here we could choose our guard duty partners, but we covered a much larger sector than at Bien Hoa. About 5:30 in the evening we approached the security hooch with our M-16s and wearing helmets and flak jackets. Lining up four deep behind a row of signs, the number of which represented a specific bunker, we reported for guard mount. At the front of each line was an M-60 machine gun. The captain ran through a pep talk relaying the suspicious events in the area passed on by intelligence sources. Of course, we always felt that whatever he reported to us was always slightly enhanced by rumor or just plain hyperbole. We were told that we should always be aware of sappers.

We knew that the ARVN 1st Infantry Division was in the area, perhaps a mile and a half from us. This division was considered the equal to any U.S. unit. Their reputation as a crack fighting outfit breathed hope into U.S. efforts at Vietnamization. No other Vietnamese unit ever attained equal stature. Besides the 101st, other American units in the Quang Tri–Phu Bai area at the time were the 3d Marine Division and the 1st Brigade of the 5th Infantry Division (Mechanized). Our piece of the action on guard duty was no more grand than providing local security.

We picked up our gear, one guy lugging the M-60, and another of us carrying the M-16 of the guy toting the M-60. We headed for a bunker line different from those at Bien Hoa. There was no real berm line. About thirty yards of wire with all the fixings ran in front of all the emplacements and the spaces between them. The bunkers themselves had at their center a Conex, the large metal containers for shipping all type of goods, such as furniture and ammunition, and derived from the name of Continental Exchange, the company that manufactured them. Huge swinging doors opened in the back of this box. These for the most part were kept open to allow air circulation. A window was cut into the front top of the Conex just under the roofline to allow the M-60 a field of fire of about 140 degrees. Sandbags surrounding the outside of the box sloped down from the window at a 45-degree angle, giving the whole thing the appearance of a pyramid. The top of the conex was sandbagged on three sides, making a U-shaped wall about 3½ feet high. As at Bien Hoa, the M-60 was mounted in the opening in the bunker section while the man on the sandbagged topside handled the M-79 grenade launcher. Wire controls for the Claymores and the fougasses ran into the Conex amid the supply of hand grenades, flares, M-60 belts, and a myriad of M-16 20-round clips. A couple of double bunks inside also allowed two men the chance to sleep while two watched. At least these didn't have the same smell of urine I remembered in the Bien Hoa bunkers. Perhaps the better circulation within the bunker had helped, or the heavy rains took off the stench. Whether you were Army or Navy, you still had to pee.

A major gate into Phu Bai as seen from the guard tower.
Note the bunker in the right foreground.

VOICES FROM THE REAR

But there was a real difference in the perimeter at Bien Hoa and our sector at Phu Bai. Beyond the wire line, the Navy had erected huge baseball-type backstops of chainlink steel fencing about twenty feet high. These were to intercept incoming rocket-propelled grenade rounds on their way to a bunker. Guard duty on the Phu Bai perimeter was a piece of cake with the huge stadium-quality lights that lit an area nearly 200 hundred yards in front of the wire line, like lights on a driving range at night. Everything in front of us appeared in stark relief. It would be suicide for any sapper to attempt to penetrate our wires. This was enormously expensive, but the Navy could provide for its land-locked people the lights, generators, and other extras now inherited by the cannon-fodder Army draftees not eligible for such protection. We had lucked out by taking over that Navy compound. The Navy had also built 50-foot towers looming over every fifth or sixth bunker. Our sector had at least three of them, one at each end and one in the middle. These structures were roofed and had windows to the front and sides overlooking the bunker line. Two men usually manned the tower, one asleep in a comfortable bunk while the other stood watch. The men in these perches usually had only their M-16s, but the towers had infrared night scopes that could pick out objects even beyond the range of the lights. A phone system connected everything, and every hour we had to dial into a central security system or a level higher than our own company. As at Bien Hoa, we were not to use the phone for other than official reports or emergencies. For me, the infrared system was a real comfort. We could see so much. And since we pulled guard duty so often, I became used to it.

The bunker line offered some humor, too. In a routine nightly exercise, one guy fired an M-79 round out into the darkness, but he didn't quite get the proper elevation. The round clipped the backstop and exploded there, shooting fragments back at the guy who fired it. He took a piece in the arm and had to be taken off guard duty for that evening. We laughed at the news that he had been awarded the Purple Heart for being wounded in action. Although his wound was self-inflicted, it had not been a purposeful act, but a self-administered accident.

A view of our area in Phu Bai taken from the guard tower—the 101st admin area. Note the marsh area we defended at night.

Guard tower view. The helicopter (Huey) is nearly at eye level.

The graves at Phu Bai.

Closer view of the graves at Phu Bai.

Sitting inside such a defensive barrier lulls troops into a false sense of security. Rows of concertina wire peppered with tin cans and glass as alarm systems sat out there in front of a small arsenal of Claymores and gas. One evening before nightfall, one of the pet dogs named Brutus made his rounds along the bunker lines, meandering from bunker to bunker to see what goodies he could scoff up. The seventy-five pound Brutus on this occasion spotted a rabbit in the wire and proceeded to perform the best piece of broken field running that I had ever seen. He tore around the labyrinth of broken glass, tin cans, and triple concertina wire, and raced in front of the Claymores without a scratch. By dint of his smaller size, the rabbit stayed ahead of him, running through small spaces in the wire. Brutus came in with a mouthful of rabbit fur. Despite the comedy, I thought if a dog of that size could do this, then a well-trained slight human could slither through the wire also. No matter what type of security system we had, it could be breached. It left me more watchful that night.

Brutus developed another habit acquired from his proximity to GI life. Guys smoking pot would share a joint with the dog, and he seemed not to mind it. They would blow smoke into a paper bag and put it around his snoot. He took in some and got a little woozy, but he did not leave the scene or refuse the bag when offered. I don't know if he smoked it on guard duty, but his mind was certainly clear when he went after that rabbit.

Brutus was not the only camp dog with particular habits. When we lost our dog Bitch under the wheels of a half-ton shortly after Finney rescued her from Bien Hoa, Finney never replaced her. It was too much pain. We soon became attached to another little black dog named Pig Pen because she always appeared dirty and slept in the mud under the hooch. Pig Pen always went to the amphitheater for shows and movies, and she always sat on the edge of the bench. She was not watching the movie; she just peered out toward the perimeter, looking for anything suspicious. I felt these dogs had a sense of duty to the GIs who fed them and took them to the vets for proper shots. Time after time, I would see them bark at the Vietnamese people, even the ones that came daily to the base. Maybe they liked the GIs because of some sense that Americans did not eat them, as the Vietnamese did. Or perhaps they just liked the hand that fed them.

All this aside, there was one more thing associated with the perimeter line that kept me a bit on edge. At about daybreak each day, the officer in charge would send three or four guys outside the bunker line to inspect the wire for cuts or attempts made to damage it during the night. We would have to go out about fifty meters from the wire to spot any fresh holes in the ground that might be a sign of booby traps and recently buried mines. During the day, water buffalo ranged freely in front of the wires, and their hoof prints were common in the waterlogged ground. It was next to impossible to distinguish a man-made hole from one made by a large animal. In this rather futile exercise, I went last in line and carefully stepped where other guys had already walked. The idea was if they stepped hard on a spot and nothing happened, then there was no mine or booby trap. I never volunteered to be point man on the wire search.

Another thing that one wanted to avoid were the water buffalo pies spread randomly about our trek. If I were the enemy and wanted to fuck up the GIs, I would bury a mine in a clear spot next to a buffalo pie. You could drive yourself crazy thinking about it. So the trek in front of the wire became just a crapshoot.

Early on, the depressing thing about the guard duty was that we couldn't get any sleep afterward. We could shower and eat breakfast, but we had to report for normal work immediately. In Bien Hoa, we had the morning off and did not have to appear until 1:00 p.m. Besides the harassment, I believe the reason for this policy was that the company had to supply about forty bodies a night for guard duty. With that many hands gone in the morning, the effectiveness of the work force would have suffered. Our cadre and leadership never gave us a kind word or an explanation for this policy. The major in command might have taken ten minutes at a company formation to do so. He usually delivered news of any kind from the balcony of his windowed, air-conditioned perch. It was this lack of communication that we hated, for it implied a relentlessly mindless existence for the troops.

The weather on guard duty didn't help much either. Rain always meant penetrating dampness or cold, and the lack of sleep didn't work well with my constitution. I got a head cold and was constantly taking some type of pill or going to sleep early every night possible. I never missed work, but when I suffered from a cold I was fairly miserable. I know that not being able to sleep those few extra hours contributed to the contagiousness of the disease. Indeed, about every third man was snorting and wheezing from something those first few weeks in the North.

One of the saddest things that I had to do during those first few days in Phu Bai was say goodbye to Larry. He left as scheduled. He was so short when he got to Phu Bai, with less than two weeks left, that he never pulled guard duty. One of the last things we did together happened on the way to the main PX. A train was moving slowly, about seventy-five yards parallel to the road that we were walking. It looked like an ordinary freight, but we noticed it was laden with ARVN troops. They all carried weapons. The cars looked like cattle cars. We couldn't tell what unit they belonged to, nor did we really care. We could barely distinguish some of our own units. As the various cars passed, two ARVNs threw us the bird, and as quick as a fast-draw, Larry and I almost simultaneously returned the salute, first with our right hands, then the left, then we held up four hands together. They were within rifle range, but we figured they couldn't shoot that well anyhow, even if they were members of the crack 1st Division. We also figured that we could have made it back to our own area before they could get near us. That pretty well expressed how we felt. We were over here helping them ward off their "Colossus to the North" and this is how we were treated.

Larry left a few days later. Jerry and I walked him to the Black Hat headshed area where a half-ton truck took him to the Phu Bai airport. We shook hands and wished each other good luck. Both Jerry and I would miss Larry, but we didn't tell him that.

Almost immediately upon arriving at Phu Bai I wrote a letter to the education officer and USARV (United States Army in the Republic of Vietnam) headquarters asking if there were any openings in his education center. I listed my credentials to include the courses that I had previously taught. I even said that I would be willing to transfer if he could swing it. I knew my chances were slim, but it didn't hurt to try. Under the present duty hours, I could never teach a course—there just was no time. Larry's absence left only Jerry in my hooch from the Bien Hoa gang. Macfee, Fergy, and Bradley were not that far, nor were Sonny and Eddie Warbeck. I think I saw Charlton about three more times, and he was always scheming some deal for some article of clothing from someone. I never visited Tate in his hooch, but I saw him every day, which was enough.

Macfee acquired a new friend whom I liked almost from the start. Pat Kelly was from Pittsburgh, Pennsylvania. He was a twenty-year-old redhead, close to 5 feet, 11 inches, and probably about 150 pounds. He claimed to have been a former Golden Gloves champ in his weight class, the 120-pound range. Like Macfee, Kelly had signed up for three years, and his Vietnam tour was his second. Patrick was nearly a clone of Macfee, though his language was better, which is not saying much, because Macfee's verbiage was about the worst (or the best depending on your perspective) that I had ever encountered. Kelly arrived in the division in mid-October and was assigned up the road at Bien Hoa, so I never actually met him until we got to Phu Bai. He loved his beer much more than Macfee did and was always talking a blue streak when he was in his cups. Kelly was assigned to the Identification Card Section, or ID Section—he issued new IDs to troops who had lost theirs. He also had airborne cards that indicated a person had qualified as a master parachutist by actually completing the required jumps. Most of the 101st troops had by this time not gone to jump school, but Patrick rewarded his friends with their own master parachutist cards, whether they wanted one or not. Usually Patrick would get drunk in his hooch, and he and Macfee would have an official standup ceremony awarding some unsuspecting fellow-drinker with the honor. Of course, Kelly would add, "Your first duty if you accept this gift or honor will be to take my assignment on guard duty for the next two weeks." So the guy receiving the award didn't really know whether to accept it or not. Pat also volunteered for chopper rides to various fire bases, where he issued new IDs to troops that might have lost theirs in the boonies. He assisted them in another personal matter. He often packed a sack full of ice-cold beer. While he was distributing his wares, he was not averse to testing the substance in the process. "It would be a goddamn shame to insult Macfee" said Kelly after one of his trips, "if I let these guys drink a cold one without joining them." Like Macfee, Kelly also had a big heart. He had one nemesis in Vietnam: our company's new first sergeant, Master Sergeant Plummer. Plummer seemed about thirty-five years old. His black-rimmed glasses made him look more like a college professor than a noncommissioned officer. His overly paternalistic way rubbed Kelly wrong from the start. Plummer was constantly issuing company directives about mundane topics. His written injunction requiring shined boots at all times in the office set everyone off. Kelly led the others in opposing this. We had to traverse through mud, muck, and mire above our ankles before we arrived at the office. You could beat this by carrying a clean, polished pair of boots and then take off the filthy ones at work, or stash a clean pair in the office. Certainly the guys with desks could do this; we couldn't because we sat at long tables. But Kelly took loud and continuous issue with the legitimacy of the edict for having clean boots during the monsoon season in a combat zone.

Kelly volunteered for overnights to the fire bases to get a forty-eight hour break from Plummer. A couple of times Kelly saw action and was fired upon while in the chopper. He mentioned this to Plummer to see if he could be awarded an Air Medal. Kelly did this mostly to piss off Plummer, and when the master sergeant refused, Kelly countered with, "I don't see why not, the major and his cronies get air medals for flying their laundry to Japan."

Soon the troops began calling Plummer's directives "another bummer from Plummer." Plummer became the lightning rod for the discontents against the whole system as the month of December wore on. Working seven days a week until 9:30 at night, and starting again at 7:30 next morning, no half-days off, no sleep after guard duty, lousy weather, and no one to shoot at caused tension to build. The news that more than 60,000 troops would be pulled out by the end of December didn't help morale. Finally, company leaders called for a party. For $2.00 you could eat all the steak and drink all the beer you wanted.

It started at noon on a Sunday. Clouds hung low for a while, but it was exciting to have an afternoon off. The day represented a change. I had a couple of steaks and a lot of beer, so Jerry and I decided to go play some basketball. We played half-court ball, five on five. I was hitting seventeen- or eighteen-foot jump shots with ease. Jerry was no slouch, either. Like me he had played guard. We moved the ball around, trying to punch it inside to the bigger players, but many times the ball came back out for me to drill a wide-open short jumper. I was shooting with GI-issue boots on. It was an hour before dark, nearly seven in the evening, when Jerry and I headed back to our hooch.

I was in bed reading when an explosion rocked the compound. It didn't sound like a rocket attack. I waited anxiously for another explosion, but none came. Ten minutes later, Freddie, a young Puerto Rican kid from New York who lived in the hooch, reported that someone had thrown a live grenade into a group at the party I had just left. A couple of guys were hurt, one seriously. He had to be evacuated to Japan. The word was that the grenade was meant for Plummer, and the idiot who threw it mistook a Spec-4 who was the most seriously hurt for the sergeant. There was a marked resemblance between the two: same height, same dark-rimmed glasses. In the dark, rank is difficult to discern, especially with camouflaged insignia. Rumors flew around about the identity of the grenadier, but no one was ever charged.

Where did the culprit get the hand grenade? Every hooch had a footlocker full of hand grenades, with one person being selected to hold the key. I had that charge in my hooch, perhaps because I was older—I never knew why. But I gladly accepted the position because I recalled Finney at Bien Hoa being drunk and cleaning his M-16. I shuddered to think of him or anyone else sitting on the edge of his bed polishing hand grenades when in a similar condition. No one ever kept a count of those grenades. I never knew how many were in the locker. I never kept an inventory. All I was supposed to do was pass them out to my hooch-mates in case of an attack. Another possible source was the bunkers. They were full of grenades. Every man in the company could take one back to his hooch after guard duty, and no one would ever know. No one ever complained that there was a grenade missing. This was a combat zone, and we were soldiers.

What I had nearly witnessed was my first fragging. Attitudes were changing. I don't believe this would have happened during the Tet offensive of 1968. The attitudes on the home front were more common in Vietnam by now. Master Sergeant Plummer never bothered me, and if he did I don't think he deserved to have a grenade thrown at him. The guy that was seriously wounded returned to the company after three months. He was fine, yet he was marked for life. He showed me the shrapnel wounds on his arms and leg.

The screws started to turn, however. All alien or unauthorized ammunition was ordered turned in. I had 90 AK-47 rounds in my locker along with an AK-47. Both were given to me by Larry because he couldn't bring them back to the States. I had to turn in the rounds but was allowed to keep the rifle and the empty clips. A law of physics holds that for every action there is a reaction. The fragging incident caused some sneak early morning standdowns, or searches for weapons and ammunition. Sergeants would come in, have everyone stand and open his wall locker and footlocker, and search for ammunition. I really didn't know what they were looking for, since it was a hand grenade that the guy threw that evening. I had the key to my footlocker if anyone asked me about this cache of ordnance, but no one knew how many grenades there were.

The inspections pulled the cover off another developing activity in the company. A search party in a nearby hooch detected something unlike the average cigarette aroma. Marijuana was now commonplace and easy to get. A two-party system was even emerging, the alcoholics and the heads, those who preferred beer and other alcohol and those who opted for pot. Well, the headshed got wind of the preponderance of pot, or dew, and called for a company formation at which the major expressed his dismay at the number of potheads under his command. He chastised the company and suggested that for expedient reasons we had better refrain from such an outrageous practice.

It wasn't long before stricter policy was instituted and a crash program established with the introduction of informants or CIDs, named for the Criminal Investigation Division that investigated drug incidents. The CIDs actually placed stoolies in the company area to inform on who was blowing dew. Fergy got wind of this, perhaps because he was puffing a few himself. So he and Bradley and a couple of other guys worked out an elaborate sting to have themselves caught smoking the stuff. When the supposed supply of pot was examined by a lab at Long Bien, the report specified that the seized contraband was pure, good old green grass. Fergy and Bradley had worked hard chopping up and drying pieces of grass, and I think even touching it up to give it the look of dew. After a time, this inside investigation method was dropped, especially since the supposed CID was having trouble sleeping at night. He kept finding lizards and other delicacies in his bed. He was lucky he didn't find a Claymore attached to his head.

It seemed that the point of concentration ought to have been on finding the man who threw the grenade. Combining that search with pot raids diluted the initial purpose. The guys on pot were the least likely to throw a grenade. When I engaged them in conversation, they were all fairly mellow. I couldn't immerse them in a thought-provoking argument on a political or military issue when they were high on the weed. They were really serene fellows. It did appear that the troops were much more willing to take chances than ever before. It was as if the GIs were much more comfortable in openly defying Army regulations. Discipline was cracking. A lot of people just didn't give a shit. Some of this new attitude could be directly attributed to the ideas of the cherries. Back in the world there were antiwar demonstrations in October and November that we eventually heard about. Then came the revelations about the My Lai massacre, then the first draft lottery in December 1969. None of this had an instantaneous affect on our psyches, but taken together, they hit like snowballs—you eventually get tired of ducking them and find them irritating. The lottery did us no good. We were here, but we wondered what our chances would have been had a lottery been in effect a year earlier. The moratoriums on the war didn't help us think that we were truly defending the goals of a united America. The My Lai massacre certainly detracted from the prestige of being in the USARV in December 1969. As the Christmas season drew near, there wasn't much of a change in spirit. It was life as usual, with one exception: the anticipation of attending the Bob Hope show. Some of the guys were fired up for the performance which was supposed to be at Camp Evans. However, in-and-out-processing had to stay, which really pissed the guys off, especially Macfee, who had planned a good time with Kelly. I think Kelly had intentions of freely distributing or even selling some expert jump badges. Finally, the resentment became so bad that SFC Carpentier set duty hours for the morning, and then closed at 11:00. He added that he wanted some coverage and that Master Sergeant Plummer had designated me as the guy. He also wanted me to get a detail together and police the area outside the Administration Company area and then stay around in case we had got any phone calls.

"What? Why me?"

Carpentier repeated that Plummer wanted me personally. It would have been great to see the show. At home, we had watched so many of Hope's shows performed for the troops overseas. I now knew why the guys went so wild at seeing some beautiful American women. We hadn't seen any in months, so seeing them live would be very special. However, I was never attracted to a huge crowd, and I believed that unless you got up front you weren't really going to see that much anyhow. I still wanted to get away from the paperwork for an evening.

VOICES FROM THE REAR

The guys boarded the various trucks, and I watched them go. I went to the Black Hat area to ask a couple of the sergeants I knew for some bodies for police call and was told there weren't any available. They sent the cherries to the show. I said okay and went back to the admin warehouse. The area Plummer wanted cleaned up was a large open space outside the warehouse. I surveyed it quickly and could see about fifteen pieces of paper strewn about. It took me five minutes, and the place was spotless and would remain that way at least until Plummer and the rest of the company returned. I wondered again why the hell I was given the opportunity to stay behind and conduct such a trivial business. I went inside and read a book for the entire afternoon. The phone was silent the whole time.

Christmas itself was depressing, the time taken up with torrential rain. The day sucked. On Christmas Eve, some of the guys in Kelly's area were acting rowdy until the wee hours of Christmas morning. Kelly was leading a group singing Christmas carols, and the more they drank, the more off-key they became until they were just plain loud. Finally, after several warnings, the commanding officer called for a formation of all participating hooches. By this time, Kelly had prepared for bed in his usual fashion by wearing nothing. The formation was immediate, so all Kelly put on were his untied boots. He and several others stumbled out to stand in formation wearing their birthday best. Some had only towels on; others donned their helmets and flak jackets and nothing else. It was some sight as Kelly explained the scene to Macfee and me next day. It was misty and damp, but all the booze kept the chill down. There was a dim light flowing from several of the hooches, and the commander told everyone to go back to their hooches and to bed or there would be serious repercussions.

"Are there any questions?" he added, a bad mistake. Kelly demanded to know why they couldn't celebrate on Christmas Eve; was he against the spirit of Christmas? Plummer, who was standing up front with some of the other higher enlisted, spun on him and hissed, "Enough of your bullshit, Kelly! You heard the commander, get your butt back to your hooch." The animosity between these two was open and unrestrained by now.

"And a Merry Christmas to you, Uncle Scrooge," Kelly intoned.

"A Merry Christmas to you, Scrooge," sang the rest of the formation in mocking monotone. A ragged chorus of "Up to here, sir!" followed. A livid Plummer shouted, "All of you get to bed!" If there was ever a perfect time for a fragging, it was then. The bosses were standing in front of the troops, who were dispersing backwards. From the darkness as the guys left came a loud "Fuck you, asshole!"

Throughout Christmas week, Kelly tried to keep the spirit alive by drinking. There was a hooch curfew in effect—no drinking after 9:00 p.m. This policy carried through to New Year's Eve. The company bosses ran inspection patrols on New Year's Eve to see if there was either booze or other substances about. Of course, the dogs played a good role as lookouts for the approaching "lifer walk-throughs." And there was drinking going on, but the noise level was greatly abated. I read a book and was writing a letter home when the walk-through team came by. I talked with the sergeant E-6, an old friend of Carpentier's. I could see that he had been drinking and that he really didn't appreciate this extra duty that interfered with his own good time. He really didn't want the duty any more than Kelly wanted to stop partying.

The curfew week broke for one night anyway. The Filipino band that was supposed to entertain us on Christmas night made it on December 26th, and restrictions were off, at least that night. There would have been a riot otherwise. We all wanted to see the girls jump around and to hear the band play some of our favorite tunes. And for me, that day represented a personal milestone—it was my 200th day in Vietnam. Only 165 days left.

January 1970 saw the same old shit—long hours, no half-days off, and guard duty every five or six days. I made it a practice of knowing the date, but I couldn't tell whether it was Tuesday or Saturday. The only day that was different was Monday because we had to take our weekly malaria pill given to us at breakfast in the mess hall.

The workday got even worse. We had to work until 11:30 and be back at 7:30 next day. There was barely time to write a letter home. The only real excitement was a letter and a care package from home. Nancy sent brownies, which were so welcomed by the guys at midnight. A real down-home snack, as one man described it.

Our cadre were getting nervous about a Tet offensive in 1970 and told us that an attack would most likely occur between January 22 and February 20. They considered making some of us permanent guards for two weeks at a time. All the guards would do was pull watch every night and have the next day off. So it would be literally 5:30 p.m. to 6:30 or 7:00 a.m., a 13-hour day with 5 hours during that time allotted for sleep, as compared to the 16-hour days we were putting in. The guards would have the entire day off to sleep or do whatever. I volunteered immediately for what seemed a welcome reprieve from the everyday drudgery of inprocessing, but it would also mean getting a half-day off every day. I figured I would sleep to noon, go to lunch, and have until 5:30 in the afternoon for myself. SFC Carpentier took my plan to the Warrant Officer, who rejected all of it because of the need to keep me at inprocessing. So we still had to pull our regular guard duty with the hope of getting the morning off the next day. It all depended upon how many cherries we had to inprocess. We definitely had the cherries. There were well over a hundred every day for long stretches in January and February.

Yet I had the feeling that our leadership was keeping us busy because we could turn our anger toward them rather than fight among ourselves. But they were taking a chance on having another unknown assailant throwing a hand grenade at them on some dark evening.

Another thing that pissed us off on the inprocessing line was the type of replacement we were getting. The front office was giving us the shit end of the stick. Macfee, Tate, Finney, Sonny, and I were the bulk of the force. Larry had left; Jerry was short. The guy they sent in was a professional bullshitter. He had jet-black hair and Hollywood good looks, but not much between the ears. I don't remember his name today, and I don't want to. He wouldn't do anything in the records branch, and he was getting too short to send him to a line unit, or at least that was what Carpentier told us. But in our system of inprocessing, you had to work. Everyone had to screen an individual's file. The cherries kept coming, and for any of us to finish at a decent interval, all had to work. This lazy ass said he could do fingerprinting and screen records as well. He had attended personnel specialist school, so I should think he could do the job. He stayed at his seat for about an hour and then got up and ghosted for two hours and didn't say anything to us when he returned. We let it go the first time. Then the jerk left again for two hours the next day. I discussed the situation with the guys who wanted to take this guy outside and simply beat the fuck out of him. They thought that a couple of blows to the head would improve his mental capacity. I said beating him up wouldn't accomplish much. I suggested that we ask the headshed to remove him. Macfee insisted that I be the person to confront the bosses, and the rest unanimously agreed. I went to Carpentier, the Warrant Officer, and then Plummer and asked them to give us someone else, but whatever they did, get that asshole out of here. I felt that we could do better without him. I told Carpentier that this guy was bad for morale. We had to function as a team at inprocessing or it simply wouldn't work. Carpentier agreed and removed the guy and put him on some type of detail like checking for headwinds with his asshole. This guy was married and I pitied his wife. He had flunked out of college, yet he was supposedly getting an early-out to return to college, or so he said. I didn't believe it, because you did either year or whatever time you had left in Vietnam and then you got out. I never heard of anyone getting an early-out for school from Vietnam. You could do that type of thing stateside. He was a despicable character. I probably saved him from a severe beating. I never felt good about that. I was more pissed off at myself for not agreeing with the guys to beat the shit out of him. Hey, I didn't like the Army any more than they did, but everyone had to pull his weight. Whether you liked your situation or not, other people depended on you.

VOICES FROM THE REAR

Roger was the next guy we got from the records branch. He was an excellent worker and would pull his weight like the rest of us. He was a short, bespectacled, wiry guy, about twenty-one. He was one of the guys essentially. He had one habit that I didn't like: he enjoyed harassing the cherries. I despised that as did the other guys.

"All right, you cherries, step up here and see if we can get you to a line unit quickly," he would constantly comment. Roger, the little guy, had finally gotten a chance to push other people around, and he took the opportunity. I had been scared when I walked in here and didn't need any undue harassment. I asked Roger to kindly stop harassing the new guys. He complied for a time, but then he started up again. I told him to stop, and he just continued. The next time I heard his patter, I got out of my seat, walked over, and grabbed his arm, and locked his eyes with mine.

"Please stop it, Roger," I gave him with as much exaggeration as I could with my teeth clenched. Roger got the point. Sonny told me later that he didn't like Roger's doing that either and was glad I had told him to stop. Sonny thought that when I got up I was going to tear his head off. I didn't think I gave that impression. I just wanted the harassment to cease. We were rudderless; no one was in immediate charge. I had no real authority to do anything, but I was older, so maybe that is why Roger took my advice.

When Roger left, Carpentier sent us a couple of guys from the records branches, especially when we had a lot of cherries. The system worked fairly well. Some of them welcomed the change of pace from record keeping to inprocessing. Then Carpentier pulled a boneheaded play. He made Finney a hard five, an E-5, and put him in charge of inprocessing. Finney deserved the position, no one denied him that, but he didn't do any work. All he did was sit in the middle of the now U-shaped inprocessing tables and supervise. This was the order that Carpentier had given him. He was there to handle any problems, but there were none since the jerks were removed from the line. It was difficult for us to do our work, facing twenty-five more cherries to finish by 10:00 p.m., with Finney just sitting there twiddling his thumbs. He knew the system and could

199

process a person very quickly. Why waste his hands? If a problem arose, he could stop screening records until it was resolved. We needed him too, and this made for some resentment. I really don't know why Finney didn't pitch in. He had to stay there as long as we did, and if he did help out he could have gone back to his hooch as soon as the rest of us. Carpentier got wind of this and brought in an E-6 to replace Finney. Finney kept his hard E-5 status, but he went back to the line. The E-6 didn't know shit from Shinola, and he didn't care to, for he spent most of the day up at Personnel Records trying to suck up to Carpentier and Plummer. So technically we were leaderless because our designated E-6 was absent much of the time. At least he stayed out of our hair.

I really despised people fucking off on the job. But what really raised my ire was when someone did it on guard duty. We had to be alert on guard duty. There was no drinking or pot smoking. Even lighting a cigarette while on the top of the bunker was dangerous because it gave a potential sniper an area target to shoot at even though our position was partially exposed by the huge flood lights of Phu Bai. Commonsense rules helped keep you and your comrades alive. Drunkenness and falling asleep on guard duty exposed the company to attack. There was one asshole who flagrantly violated this code of respect for his fellow soldier. Called "Boston," since he was from this hub of the universe, he was still a disgrace to New England. He had a real shit attitude and was negative about everything. We at inprocessing heard he wasn't doing his daily job. I shared guard duty with him once. While two men slept, I had the roof position and he had the lower spot. Instead of standing next to the phone and in front of the M-60 machine gun and near the controls of the Claymores, he sat outside the bunker reading a book by the stadium lights. I asked him what he was doing and if he planned to pull his duty. He replied, "Don't fuckin' worry, man, I'll hear anything that comes by, and so will you." I had no authority to order him back into the bunker. I was essentially pulling guard duty alone. I despised his fuck-off attitude. But I also didn't tell him when the captain came by and found him asleep outside the bunker. The captain took his name and told him that he had seen him asleep from the next bunker. The same lights that allowed Boston to read enabled the officer to see this dummy from a distance. If he wanted to sleep, he could have done so inside the bunker, without me or anyone else seeing him. I would have never known if he was sleeping because I wasn't talking to him anyhow. We were not supposed to talk. I didn't even know the guy except by his reputation as a slough-off. He was caught in his own shit.

I am sure that officer reported Boston to Plummer, who had a list of infractions on him. The threats of an assignment to the line didn't strike the fear of God in him, nor did his reward of the same within two weeks after the incident. Many of us were glad to see him go and could have cared less if he went back to the land of the Pilgrims in a body bag. He didn't even deserve that service. If he acted like that as an infantryman in his new line unit, I am sure his colleagues would have something for him in the guise of a well-placed M-16 bullet between his ears and report him KIA by enemy fire.

I wondered about myself and whether I was taking this game too seriously. Some of the other guys were not serious enough. They came to the bunker line after having had several beers or a few bowls of dew. We should never underestimate the enemy. They had proved time and again that they could strike where and when they wanted. Tet '68 had certainly proved that. I recalled seeing all those films about Khe Sanh, and no matter how our aircraft had pounded their positions, the enemy continued to surround the base. It was all so incredible to me how an enemy with no air power could continue to hold the hills surrounding Khe Sanh. I reasoned that if they could do that, they could certainly on any given night attempt to penetrate our perimeter with a dozen or so sappers. My experience at Bien Hoa had showed how easily an enemy could throw a couple of rockets at us at will. So why not play the game seriously and show up on guard duty awake and with all your faculties?

I had guard duty with Kelly and Macfee and another guy one evening. Kelly had been drinking for several hours and showed up at the bunker with a good buzz on and with a couple of extra beers in his sack. We got off work at about 4:00 p.m. for guard duty and didn't have to be at guard mount until 5:30 p.m., enough time to prepare. I am sure that Kelly left at 2:00 p.m. to run some supposed errands but went to his hooch to have a few. Macfee had toasted a few with him but was not in the same state. I suggested to Kelly that he should take the late shift and hit the sack now at 6:30 p.m. in order to sleep it off. Then he started running his mouth.

"Hey, George, the mobile re-up truck is coming out to the bunker so why the fuck don't you re-up." That the Army actually had a mobile re-up truck momentarily struck me terribly funny. I started laughing at the thought of a four-wheeled van or bus bouncing out to the bunker line, loud speaker chanting "Re-up time, get your bonus now." I couldn't stop laughing. I had been in the Army a bit over a year and I had never heard of a mobile re-up truck. Later I learned they actually existed, but I thought that Kelly had just invented one. Kelly accused me of becoming a lifer because I was on him for drinking on the bunker line. I was insulted, but I just thought it was so funny that I overlooked his comment. Kelly wound up doing exactly what I suggested, taking the second shift after sleeping it off.

We never saw a re-up truck in Vietnam, but the Army sure tried everything to get people to reenlist. The cherries now had an immediate opportunity to sign on for more time right in our inprocessing line. A ten-year E-6 sat across from me with the sole purpose of ambushing the cherries into re-upping. The E-6 had nothing to do with our inprocessing efforts. He was completely independent of our command. His tall presence emphasized by a short lifer haircut, he looked nearly bald and spent nearly four months without comment about our antics or arguments. He was looking for potential reenlistments. At times he even laughed at Macfee. I don't remember any cherry asking me about reenlisting.

We were also exhorted to re-up by a major who talked to us in groups of about twenty-five at time. This forty-year-old told us his life story: service during the Korean War and back out into civilian life and a college degree... bored with life. He knew what his existence was going to be every day for years on end. He was married and had children. He said he wanted some excitement in his life and didn't want to be tied down to a single area. The Army had given him opportunity for change and excitement. We should consider our futures, too. What were our opportunities back at home? Were we going back to some boring job? Would we remain in that place for the rest of our lives? Did we anticipate a dull and mundane future?

It was a cold and rainy day when the re-up major gave his presentation. There was nothing attractive about this assignment. It was the shits. I had been in the Army a bit over a year and had been in difficult situations for most of the time. I didn't find basic training and AIT entertaining; in fact I hated them. I had a job that was boring, and I knew what I would be doing the next day if we weren't suddenly under some type of attack. I lacked the freedom to go to a different place after dark. We were confined to our compound. We had virtually no freedom to do what we wanted, or for that matter to say what we wanted. We had one thing in common, best expressed in the song, "We got to get out of this place." To be fair, all of us had seen only the worst of what the Army had to offer. I was a historian by training and didn't mind sitting in one place and learning and researching things. I looked at my tattered acceptance ticket from The Catholic University of America that I had kept with me since the fall of 1968. That was my goal: I was going back to school.

I was glad to have heard the man talk, because it got me out of my boring job for an hour. The major didn't get any takers from this group or, I suspect, from many others. In fact, one of the jokes about reenlisting concerned the E-6 who was on the re-up poster hanging in the records branch area. He had been killed in action on his second tour in Vietnam. One of the guys wrote on the poster the date the guy was killed. The poster was soon removed and not replaced.

Another change in the inprocessing was the addition of an E-6, Bill Grant, who had convinced headquarters leadership at Camp

Evans that he could better use the talents of the new troops. This was something that I had seen from the start. There were people who had FAA licenses to repair airplanes. Couldn't this talent be transferred to helicopters? The 101st was an airmobile division that used a lot of helicopters which all required repair. The problem was that the Army needed infantry, and once again many draftees, no matter what their civilian skills, were assigned to the infantry. If a guy had signed up for helicopter repair schooling he would have made it, but like many of the guys, they wanted to take their chances with two years, including one year on line in "the Nam."

Bill Grant was a twenty-two-year-old black, standing about 6 feet, trim, and a genuinely nice guy. He was in the last year of a four-year enlistment. I could see how he could convince people at headquarters to allow him to pick out soldiers with various civilian skills and use their talents. He definitely had a pleasing personality. He looked for heavy equipment operators, people with construction backgrounds, to attempt to reclassify them into some more suitable MOS within the division. He was essentially doing a similar thing that I had been doing with college graduates with infantry MOSs—attempting to use their talents as personnel specialists or some other clerical duties. I had found that the college guys were much better at pencil pushing than people with less education. Some of the younger men had never come to terms with their own mortality. For them it was an adventure. I recommended one high school kid with superb scores for assignment to the admin company. He did a fine job in the causality branch for about a month, but took an assignment to an infantry unit because he just couldn't take the boredom anymore.

I got on well with Bill Grant. Although he selected people and looked at their records, he had nothing to do with the inprocessing effort. He was on our line, but without helping or hindering us. When he saw an individual he thought showed promise in another field, he would attach a note to the 201 file and send the man on. In many cases, this man would receive the suggested assignment from a combat MOS to something more suitable. Even I could see that we couldn't just reassign everybody out of a combat assignment, the MOS of 99 percent of the draftees. Besides Bill and myself, the re-up sergeant was promising the same thing, but for him a bonus came along with the promise. Someone had to fight the war, and those guys were the draftees.

During the miserable month of January 1970, one bright spot was my promotion to Spec-5. This was phenomenal because I had been in grade only two months and in the service only a year. The normal requirement was at least fifteen months' service and eight months' time in grade. The division had a lot of allocations. I don't know why, but we speculated that it had something to do with the departure of other units from Vietnam. There were thirty-five allocations for Spec-5, and fifty people went up before the board. I had heard that the board of three E-7s and three E-6s in the company would ask some basic questions about current events. This proved to be the case. They asked the name of the old imperial city that was once the capital of Vietnam. That was easy; we were quite near the city of Hue. I was asked how many troops had been pulled out of Vietnam by December 1969. I answered all the questions, and several weeks later Carpentier told me I had been promoted to Specialist E-5 with a date of rank of January 8, 1970, one year and two days after I had entered the United States Army. The promotion brought my pay up over $300 a month: $254 base pay, $65 combat pay, and $13 overseas pay, totaling $332. I would get an additional $105 if I were married plus another $30 if my wife did not live with either parent. The extra pay I could use for R&R that I had planned in March. I could survive on $40 to $50 per month because there was essentially nothing to spend it on. The books I was reading were free. Beer was 15¢ for a 12-ounce can and cigarettes were 15¢ cents a pack. My job remained essentially the same. The promotion relieved me of KP, at least that was the rule back in the states. In Phu Bai, mamma sans did the KP.

Pat Kelly also made Spec-5, which pleased him no end for the singular reason that he could fuck over Plummer when the latter returned from a thirty-day re-up leave in the States.

"I am so fuckin' happy," said Kelly. "I would have made two ranks while the motherfuckin' Plummer was on leave. I can't wait to see the look on his face when he sees my new rank." Actually, Kelly had made Spec-4 in mid-November, but he never received official orders for it, presumably because Plummer kept holding the action up. Kelly then got backdated orders for Spec-4, which Kelly pinned on only after Plummer had left for R&R. Kelly was right about Plummer's reaction. He wanted to know how Kelly could possibly be promoted that fast. As Pat gloated, Plummer cautioned that if you fuck up, your Spec-5 is mine, meaning that he would bust him. It wasn't long before Kelly was busted to Spec-4. He had mouthed off once more to Plummer, and the master sergeant kept his promise. Plummer further cautioned Kelly that if he kept insisting on fucking around, he would soon be a PFC.

Macfee worked a different angle with Plummer. He was not allowed before the board because he had an Article 15 for locking and loading on a fellow soldier. So when the rest of us or many of us sewed on our E-5 stripes, Macfee was peeved not with Kelly, but more with himself. I think he was motivated by Kelly making it. Macfee was not jealous of his hooch-mate Kelly. He just wanted that rank more than ever. Macfee's strategy was to work on Plummer. I would see him talking to Plummer every time he came by the inprocessing area. Macfee finally asked Plummer to promote him. Macfee admitted to Plummer that he had made a mistake and that he had served his penalty and that he deserved another chance. I could see that Macfee was sincere because he cut down the number of expletives he used in the conversation. In February, Plummer rewarded Macfee with a promotion to E-5. He did not have to go before a board. I don't know if Macfee got Kelly's E-5. It might have been Plummer's aim to make it look that way. Plummer knew that they bunked together. Maybe Plummer was trying to gain an ally against Kelly, or maybe Plummer wanted to show that if Kelly behaved he too could get his E-5 back. One just never knew the facts.

Anyhow, the promotion and demotion did not impinge upon Macfee and Kelly's friendship. They hung around together more than ever. In fact their hooch became the focal point for the alcoholics. There was always activity there. One could walk in with or without a six-pack and join in or listen to some conversation. I was always welcome there as were many others. One college graduate was there who had been in the class I taught at Bien Hoa. He asked me why I bothered to come. He said something about having a master's degree made me above these guys, and I didn't belong there. That hurt me more than anything, because I really enjoyed laughing with Macfee and Kelly. They were always busting on someone. It was very much like being with the guys in college and graduate school. I just loved to observe and listen and offer an opinion, but most of all to just sit down and sip beer. It was more like being at home in my big family and the easy humor that these guys represented. Macfee and Kelly were the center of more reality than even they knew. They dismissed the statement. The guy's a dip-shit anyway, they concluded.

One thing I observed with these two guys, besides their friendship, was their disdain of the potheads in the hooch about twenty-five yards from theirs. I don't know if it was blue collar versus the hippies, but the animosity was strong. I don't know whether Macfee and Kelly felt that it was more manly to get buzzed on booze rather than pot. They would holler crudities at the potter's hooch, telling them they had nothing between their ears but the fairy dust that was their brains. What really ticked off Macfee and Kelly was the location of the potheads' smoking room, dug deep into the ground under the hooch. A trap door under one bunk dropped down under the hooch to an underground room about seven feet by eight feet. In the middle of the room was a bowl with some pipe stems issuing forth from it. Five or six guys fit down there, and the smoke in the unventilated room could give everybody present a good secondary high. We were never quite sure whether the Seabees had built it for their own smoking or as a type of shelter. On several inspections of the hooch, several guys stayed concealed in the room blowing dew, and they were never found out. It was not a head count, just a goods check. Macfee and Kelly yelled over one day that we didn't have to go underground to do our thing, we are real Americans. This chance observation set them to another project involving the beer drinkers' own facility. The pair set out to build a screened-in porch in the front of their hooch so they could sit there and drink beer in a comfortable and reasonable fashion and, I am sure, harass the dew suckers from their strategic perch. They gathered the material, including lumber and screening, and had it lying outside their hooch. Every time they returned to the project, they would also start drinking. They never finished the porch. Of course, there really wasn't much free time, since the inprocessing and other areas were working almost every evening. I would start laughing every time I came upon them sitting on this pile of warped lumber and bent and torn screening, sipping brew and shouting insults at the dew suckers in the hooch across from them.

"Hey motherfuckers, got your lips pursed for a good snort? Why don't you suck this?" Most of it was done in jest. Of course, the other side learned to respond in kind.

"We see your porch is now rising above the dirt level! Oh no, excuse us, that's your pile of beer cans!" Or, better yet, "The war ends in 1990 . . . Do you think you will finish before that, or are you guys just going to sit and talk about it?" On and on it went, but the porch was never finished, nor was one pile driven into the ground. They would have been better off to have purchased a couple of chairs to sit outside instead of starting on the porch.

Despite the long hours, I managed to keep reading: Faulkner's *Rievers*, Hemingway's *Moveable Feast*, E. H. Carr's *October Revolution*, and *Boon Island* by Kenneth Roberts. I was also into an 800-page biography of Woodrow Wilson, but I didn't feel that my present efforts remotely matched the Wilsonian ideal of a war to make the world safe for democracy. The Roberts book reminded me of the Maine coast and places that were near my hometown of Portland. Beaches like Higgins, Ferry, Pine Point, Old Orchard, and Jordan all came to mind. I longed to be on one of those, although not in January or February. Winters could be tough in Maine, but less so along the coast, which was fed by the warmer Gulf stream currents, if tepid is ever possible with Maine waters.

Carr's book reminded me of World War I and the hazards of trench warfare. I had just put that book down when I got a letter from my dad's Uncle Charlie, a World War I veteran. He asked me about my outfit and whether I liked it or not. I realized that Vietnam was not World War I. While the airplane and the tank were new in that war, our enemy in Vietnam had neither of these at his disposal, at least in the area that I had been in. I had never seen an enemy plane or tank. Nor were there hoards of enemy a hundred yards from our bunker line. Our enemy was silent and stung you with quick blows when you least expected it. We had not experienced the horrors of suicidal attacks over no man's land, exposing ourselves to murderous fire and, if we remained standing a hundred yards later, descending upon enemy trenches. Our enemy was a sapper or a distant sniper. No one in Vietnam had experienced the daily horrors of World War I that Uncle Charlie had. He had seen all this and also had been seriously gassed twice and lived to tell about it. Uncle Charlie lied about his age in 1917 and joined the Army when he was fifteen. He was my grandfather's youngest brother. My dad was born in 1914 and Charlie was twelve years older. Grandpa died in 1926, when dad was twelve, and Uncle Charlie got a lot of respect from my father and my grandma because Charlie was the last link to his father. Uncle Charlie was a slight man and very sickly looking. Dad said he really never recovered from the gas attacks. Uncle Charlie married a young Parisian girl and brought her back to northern Maine, where the local French dialect was incomprehensible to this girl from Paris. We didn't see Charlie much because he lived with his son in northern Maine and later moved with them to New Jersey. Family lore had sort of beatified Charlie, and I was in awe of his legend. I felt honored receiving a note from him and wrote to him telling about the 101st Airmobile Division and the place where I was. I told him that I was not in a combat role but would be happy to come home.

I got a similar feeling when my grandmother (Dad's mother)

sent me a note. She was born in Canada in 1879 and came to the United States before the turn of the century. She had lived with us since 1945. She was ninety, yet she could write superb, legible, and comprehensible letters. I impressed many of my hooch-mates with these messages. Some of them had trouble communicating their ideas with a pen. She was born while the Indian wars were still going on, twenty years before the war with Spain, before the automobile, the airplane, the radio, and television. She had just recently witnessed the first man on the moon. The United States of America was fighting its fifth war and a myriad of other skirmishes in Central America since her birth. Her only medium was the written word, and she could communicate world events much more easily and clearly than many of the GIs.

During the first two months of 1970, a deck grew off the back end of our hooch. There was a door on both ends of the hooch and Freddie, the Puerto Rican kid from New York, suggested that we build a deck where there was only a stairway. He asked for volunteers, and with the indifferent showing in carpentry by Macfee and Kelly, some of the guys doubted that the project could be completed. I thought it would be a good idea, especially since we could anticipate regular sunny days in the next few months. Freddie knew what he was doing. He knew how to plant the pilings and level them, which I thought was tough because the area sloped downward about 30 degrees. We found a supply of lumber stored under the hooch, apparently left by the Seabees in anticipation of building a deck, but we needed more lumber and nails. Freddie wanted me to go to the engineers or the "Red-Faced Lifers" shop to plead for some materials. They had plenty of nails, but lumber was in short supply, and they offered me some short pieces. I surmised that if we had enough, they would be adequate for the deck floor. I brought some back to Freddie, and he said if that was all they had, then we had to use it. It just meant more cutting and nails. I must have given several hours for five evenings to the project. We finished a deck extending out about fifteen feet from the door, as wide as the hooch, with railings and stairs to the ground. In admiration, I asked Freddie where he had learned the trade. It turned out he had never built anything like this, but had worked with lumber in a high school shop course.

At the end of January, we had to beef up our defenses because of the threat of another Tet offensive. We had to assume blocking positions behind the bunker lines at night. This was in addition to our regular schedule of guard every five to six nights. To man the blocking positions, the whole company was roused at about 9:00 p.m. and double-timed it to the perimeter area to dig some small covering holes or sit behind some stones and communicate with other positions. We would stay out about two hours and then come back to the hooch and go back to bed.

By early February, our rumored intelligence claimed that a major portion of a Tet offensive, if it came, would occur in the Mekong Delta region where there were few U.S. troops. Truck traffic in Laos and Cambodia had reportedly increased considerably in the previous few months. The purpose of a Viet Cong campaign in that area was to disrupt President Nixon's Vietnamization policy. The U.S. had pulled out practically all of its troops from the Mekong Delta. I hoped that the South Vietnamese would be able to mount a solid defense and thwart any offensive. In our defensive system, we were too well fortified to worry much and had not received a rocket attack in nine months.

On February 4, I had my first daytime guard assignment. After being up all night on the line, we were allowed to return to the company area to eat and freshen up, and then returned to the bunker. About every third bunker had a guard. I was told that it used to be a more pleasant assignment with two men pulling the duty, one guy sleeping while the other one watched. The two would be relieved when the night shift came out in the evening. This was not the case now. One man was on guard in the morning while the other guy had a detail, and they would switch positions in the afternoon.

The morning shift left me alone with my thoughts. Vietnamese tended the rice fields and their buffalo moved at the same methodical pace established over the centuries. Two boys balanced themselves on the back of a water buffalo while the animal moseyed along the various paths, stopping here and there to bend down for a chew. The kids were fantastic, swaying barefoot just forward of the animal's hips and matching their stance to its movement. The buffalo took all this in stride, and the children stayed aboard through some quick turns. It seemed to be a game that both humans and animals had gotten used to and that the animals were babysitting the kids and entertaining them. I had seen plenty of American kids standing on the seat of a moving bicycle. It even looked like waterskiing.

On a summer day during high school long ago, a friend and I had hitchhiked to Sebago Lake in Maine to see some friends who had a boat and water skis. The boat was powerful enough to pull two skiers, so we hung in there for several minutes until my friend fell off. The driver of the boat stopped and turned to pick up my friend, so naturally I went into the water. When we started up again, the rope coiled unnoticed around my wrist and I was suddenly scudding along face down through the water. I knew I could hold my breath for nearly a minute, but I was using energy trying to escape the rope. I thought I was going to drown. Finally our boat driver slacked off when he realized my plight. I climbed into the boat, glad to be finished with skiing that day.

The people I was watching from the bunker seemed content. They would most likely be doing the same work under a communist regime, so they probably viewed us as a nuisance. I thought of our infantry troops. They must have found it difficult when going into a village to distinguish a Vietnamese farmer from a Viet Cong or a Viet Cong sympathizer. These Viet Cong were locals and thus had the home court advantage; they knew all the shortcuts and the best places to hide or ambush an American patrol. I remembered one episode from my teen years in which two of us ran through an industrial plant, crossed a few ditches in a construction site, headed down alleys and between houses to escape Portland police patrols checking on underage kids imbibing a few beers in the local parking lots. We just knew the terrain even better than did the local lawmen.

Later that day, I helped replace some old concertina wire between two bunkers. The section needing repair was about two feet underwater. A swamp separated the two bunkers, and I could easily see that a submerged sapper could sneak through that area much more easily than was possible at other bunkers. The forty-five-year-old sergeant first class who handled the detail had transferred to the 101st from another unit. He was an expert in demolition and camouflage. He was also a dog trainer and was doing some of that for the 101st. The area that needed new wire was virtually a unused rice paddy and the mamma sans on base refused to go into the water to replace the wire. As I waded in with the sergeant to replace the wire I soon discovered why the women felt that way. Leeches covered my legs when I came back out. The sergeant helped pluck four large ones from between my sock and pants. Before I waded back in, I pulled the bottom of my pants about halfway down my boots and tied them down with the shoelaces. That stopped the slimy critters.

The sergeant liked his job. He loved training dogs and wrestling with the vicissitudes of base defense. He was a good teacher, and he showed me how to lay the concertina wire. We tripled the number of strands in the water area just to make it more difficult for sappers. The best thing about that day was that it got me out of the routine of in-and-out-processing.

In early February, Carpentier presented me with a letter of appreciation from an American Red Cross field director who was attached to and stationed with Headquarters 101st Airborne Division. He thanked me and another guy for helping him locate a GI in a family emergency. We often got these calls seeking recently inprocessed troops who were still in transit to a unit. There might be a two-week period before an individual was assigned to his unit during which he had no fixed address. We could still track these people in the green book, the ledger we kept on every individual inprocessed. We got copies of assignment orders for everyone we inprocessed and recorded their unit in the book. So it was relatively easy to find his man when he gave me an approximate date that the individual inprocessed. The division's adjutant general and the division personnel officer, our boss, added their notices to the Red Cross kudos. Carpentier beamed when he handed me all this. "Damn good," he said; he'd like to have a couple of those in his records.

Carpentier set me up with one bit of a shit detail. He made me the sitting duck for a late-day appearance of a brigadier general from the an inspection team. I had to sit alertly at my table for the arrival of the general, who came in with the major, Master Sergeant Plummer, and Carpentier. He was the first general I had seen while in Vietnam and certainly about the oldest flag officer that I had ever seen, either in the newspaper or on television. He smoked like a furnace and looked like he couldn't run ten feet without collapsing. He asked the sergeants some questions and then queried me about how many people we had been inprocessing. I said in excess of a hundred daily for several months. He surveyed the inprocessing area, made spotless for his arrival. He mumbled a few words, sucked hard on his weed, and headed back to the records retention area. Carpentier came back a couple of minutes later and dismissed me. All this preparation for one man on a five-minute tour. If he had seen us under full operation, it might have looked chaotic, but he could have seen how inprocessing really worked.

Soon after we relocated north, the orientation briefing for the new guys also fell to me. I took over this chore before Jerry left for home. I stood on the lowest bleacher in the amphitheater and faced a hundred or more GIs in ascending rows in front of me. They got the usual forms, including the "dream sheet" on which they listed a choice of assignment once they returned to the world. They listened, uncomprehending as usual, to explanations of what inprocessing meant, the functions of personnel and finance, and the business of naming or changing their beneficiaries. More than once as I discussed the change of beneficiary, a medevac helicopter appeared overhead with stretcher cases on its landing skids, an awesome sight for any cherry. As they focused on this, I would tell them that those were wounded guys who were being transferred to a larger hospital, perhaps Da Nang, for further treatment. The U.S. Army had a real good system to transport wounded out of the battle area,

I added, and their chances of survival were real good with the excellent care that the Army had. This was nothing but truth: the helicopter and the medical evacuation system had saved thousands of lives.

To relieve the boredom of saying the same thing day after day, I took to delivering the speech in different accents, John F. Kennedy some days and a ripping good down-East Maine argot on others. Some of the Black Hats and other cadre used to sit in on the presentation, not to listen to my imitations but to see if there was information they required. A big white hayseed first lieutenant in the cadre came in to listen to the presentation. At six-feet and weighing over 200 pounds, he could have been a linemen on a college football team. He lurked around the company making people salute him at all times. He seemed to hate the faded uniforms of the guys who had been in country a long time, the very mark of the seasoned veteran he aspired to be. Macfee was on his second tour, and his bleached fatigues marked him as a real old timer. My pride was in my faded ball cap, something that had gone to a yellow-brownish color in time.

My hike to the amphitheater each morning at about eight o'clock was a reverie in itself. I diverted myself with thoughts of home and things like the great 1957 Ford Interceptor convertible my brother left for me when he went to Germany and that I had painted a red-orange. It had a 350-cubic-inch engine and flex pipes that made it sound like a husky eighteen-wheeler. With this thing I used to visit George's Gully, a sort of landfill consisting entirely of empty beer cans. The feature was so named by one of my friends who honored me with the notion that I had contributed much to the area's contents. One morning, I proceeded lost in thought to the briefing when this junior lieutenant brought me up short. I had neglected to salute him. Not only would this not do, he lit into me about my faded hat. It was Army issue, I told him, and I wasn't going to buy another out of my meager income. He told me not to get smart with him, he barked. I was just telling him the facts, I maintained. This blond "dumbshell" got on everyone's nerves.

Garbage truck duty entailed shouldering my M-16 and accompanying the Vietnamese garbage truck on its rounds in the compound. The rifle, which was empty, was more or less a status symbol. The real reason for the guard was to make sure that the Vietnamese didn't include things as garbage that weren't junk. In other words, we didn't want them taking furniture and other goods. I met the truck, a large covered vehicle between ten and twelve feet high, as it came through the front gate, and I stayed with it until it left the base. It was filled with junk and 55-gallon drums. Four men and one eighteen-year-old woman managed this enterprise. The honcho owned the truck and the other people who worked for him were family members. The honcho told me that he had fought with the French during the late 1940s and early 1950s against the communists. He spoke excellent English. I even helped push a barrel around, bought them Coca-Cola and offered them cigarettes. At the small exchange my offers revealed their preference for Salems. Selling cigarettes to the Vietnamese was forbidden, but giving them away was not. I bought a pack and presented some to the honcho and then one apiece to his assistants. Then I gave the rest of the pack to the head man. I enjoyed the duty for the same reason that I enjoyed day guard—it provided me with a change of pace.

Everything went fine until we got to a dump area that was full of barrels. The Vietnamese weren't supposed to take the barrels, but it was my understanding that everything else was there for the taking. Some pieces of lumber were lying there, so the crew picked them up immediately and placed the wood on top of the truck, out of view from the ground. I thought there was nothing wrong with this. I knew the Vietnamese would make good use of the materials. One piece would or could probably serve as a main roof beam. Most of their shanties were built of less substantial stuff. Some of the walls were made of flattened beer cans that had somehow been attached. This seemed ingenious though I wondered about the effects of lightning. They had placed several smaller pieces on the roof when the lieutenant yowled in his best command voice. "Hey, Specialist! Don't you know better than to let them have that lumber?" What in hell was he doing out in the dump? "I can report you for this."

By this time, I was so damned burned, but I kept my cool. This boob of a lieutenant would have to pay for chewing me out in front of these people whom I had befriended all day. The lumber was in the junk yard; it was theirs if they wanted it. He demanded that I make them throw the lumber down. I was just as determined to let them have the stuff. I used pidgin English to talk to the head honcho with whom I had spoken perfect English all day: "Take wood down," and adding, under my breath, "Only the big piece." The biggest piece overhung the truck so it was easily visible from below; the smaller pieces could not be seen. So the head honcho and another man made a show of struggling at length with the board that they had snapped up there in an instant. They knew whose side I was on. That seemed to satisfy the scumbag lieutenant. He headed off, tossing his last warning: "If I ever catch you doing that again, I am going to have your ass." I said nothing, but my eyes could have melted the bar on his hat. I had initially thought that this guy was just a big bluster fuck to be ignored, but after that performance I knew he was in need of a lesson. At the gate I told the guard there was nothing but junk aboard, and the Vietnamese got to keep the lumber. After all the graft and waste I had seen in Saigon and the tremendous cost of this whole fucking war, this asshole was blustering about pieces of lumber too thin even for use in our prized hooch deck.

I walked back up to lock up my M-16. Macfee and Kelly were already atop the pile in front of their hooch, sipping beer. They patiently listened to my tale of the lieutenant's performance. More people joined my impromptu audience and expressions of outrage ran around in a low rumble. At least I felt much better getting all this off my chest. Other guys repeated details of their own run-ins with our troublesome company officer. An opportunity soon presented itself for retribution.

One night when the lieutenant drew guard duty, it poured. We knew he was coming because one of the guys that I had helped get a clerical job was in charge of the duty roster. The weather just cooperated that night. Part of the officer's job was to periodically visit each bunker to check and see if everything was all right. At the same time, the occupants of any building in an Army compound had the obligation to require any approaching figure to stop and identify himself. As the asshole lieutenant made his rounds, every single bunker halted him at gunpoint and made him lie flat on the ground, low-crawl, and throw out his ID card. By the time he hit the last bunker, he was a soaking wet mudball. At each bunker, the guys saved up until just before the lieutenant arrived and then pissed themselves dry into the mud outside. The lights, though subdued, fairly well outlined a person's form, and we all knew the dirtbag's voice. Yet it was all perfectly legal. If he complained, it would be for naught. If he took names, it would be useless, because there were too many involved. And most important, he had to pull guard duty again as we all did. That boy was trapped. He got the message because he was much more pleasant to the GIs when he passed. He now had the nickname "Pig Pen Two," after our dirty pup. There was some debate over the insult to the dog, smarter than the lieutenant by a country mile.

The guys were a bit closer after this. Macfee and Kelly were even talking civilly with the "heads" about the incident. At parties or drink-ins, the incident frequently came up and entered the company lore. I was as happy as the next guy, but figured the guy got off easy. He was lucky he wasn't shot on guard duty. This was exactly the sort of character that made fragging an art form in the Nam. Had he gotten orders to a line unit, his fate would have been distinctly certain. I continued to pass him on my way to the orientation brief and saluted, but still refused to buy a new hat. Eventually I did that, but kept the old faded one to wear to the presentation on the chance I might meet him again.

Though the lieutenant's antics ran us ragged from January through March, my greater concern was the planned appointment in Hawaii on my R&R leave with Nancy. Her letters made my day, though she would write about robberies in the apartment house where she and another woman graduate student rented a flat. I conjured up all sorts of weird scenarios in which she possibly could be harmed. She most likely had similar thoughts about me. All was not easy in keeping the rendezvous, but we had cooked up my premier event of 1970.

Chapter 6

Rest and Recuperation

The long-awaited escape came in late March 1970. It was Holy Week—not a traditional time for marriage in the Catholic Church, but Nancy and I had coordinated everything in the way of baptismal certificates and the necessary blood tests. Everything was in place except for my nerves. We had been apart for ten months after the first fourteen whirlwind days following our first meeting in November 1968. We had gotten this far on correspondence alone.

Just before I left for Vietnam in June 1969, we had agreed to get married. Nothing had changed about that plan, but I wrote asking her thoughts about doing it on my upcoming R&R. "Anytime, anyplace," she wrote back. I was on Cloud Nine for weeks.

My tenth month in Vietnam earned me a trip to Hawaii. The more time in country, the more seniority and the more choice in an R&R. Hawaii was in any case more practical than Australia or Japan. Nancy would be on spring break from her Master of Arts program in social work at the University of Connecticut.

Then there was money. The Army paid a married man in my pay grade an extra hundred dollars a month. What the hell, if we were going to get married why not make a few bucks? I was sending

Nancy more than $160 a month to put away for us anyhow. That tidy little fund would now pay for Hawaii, too.

Then Nancy seemed to have second thoughts. On February 15 she asked if we should wait until I returned from Vietnam. That hit me in the stomach—and then panic set in. Why after all this time? Was this a variation on one of those heralded "Dear John" letters to come within a few days? I got on the Military Affiliated Radio System (MARS), a link to the states, but one with difficulties. The workings of the combined radio-telephone system generated a lag between a statement at one end and the reply coming from the other. You had to say "Over" after each phrase, then wait for a response. We faded in and out, but I had to find out if she was still planning to go to Hawaii. Finally I said, "Just be there, over." I was anxious, to say the least, but it was certainly better to get any bullshit out of the way before we committed to anything or anyone got hurt.

Nancy was the only child of two hardworking people who had managed to provide her with a very comfortable life. Nancy's mother had owned her own hairdressing business and had moved it to the basement of her own home shortly after Nancy was born. By the time I met Nancy, her mother had long since retired. Nancy's father Ken left a barber practice for work at the Bosch Company during the war, and then set himself up as an independent and successful realtor specializing in business properties. He also was a town committeeman for several years in Agawam, Massachusetts, a well-known and respected regular guy around town.

Nancy went to a private women's college, had a new Volkswagen during her junior year, and took trips with her college mates to Caribbean islands during semester breaks. She was her parents' most precious possession. I got a bit jealous at times, especially when she asked why I had never gone to an island during semester break. I had to tell her that was beyond me at the time and that I always had to work to pay for my tuition, books, clothes, and spending money. She herself had always worked summers during high school and college. For several years she was as a part-time waitress at Friendly's Ice Cream in Agawam. After college she worked as a social worker in Quincy, Massachusetts. But with me as one of six kids and her the one and only, we certainly saw the world differently. My hope was that we could get jobs after we both finished school and settled down somewhere. Some people liked to be told that their dreams can come true without much work. I figured that we were still in love, and something had changed her mind. Even now I knew she was more comfortable than I could immediately provide for, and she might have reason to doubt whether she was doing the right thing.

Macfee and Finney especially took my wedding plans to heart. It was one more excuse to throw a party. They got up the unheard-of sum of $65 on payday as a gift. I was touched, but now wondered if I would have to return the money if Nancy refused to get married. There were no stag flicks, no women, just a bunch of guys drinking beer and listening to Sonny Gatchell's stereo system. Finney listened to my troubles and told me not to worry. "If she goes, she wants you" was his argument.

After my "be there," I waited for three weeks for a letter. On March 8, her next note still talked about marrying me. Relief flooded my soul, but something was missing. She was coming, but I still wasn't certain about our marriage prospects. So we had both agreed to go, but we were not sure of our course of action. We would just try to get to know each other again, or perhaps more accurately, for the first time.

I got a suit made at the base Vietnamese tailor. The fit was good but my choice of material got something that could be classified only as "early modern ugly." The brownish color reflected the light in odd ways. Too long accustomed to olive drab uniforms, my tastes were way off, so anything looked fine. Never one to get excited about clothes, I thought it looked good, but not with the white socks my mom had sent me along with some casual shirts. If I had to choose between olive drab and white I would choose white or orange, anything besides olive drab. Mom's package also had some oxblood loafers, a white dress shirt, and a tie. The wardrobe was complete, and I bought a Samsonite suitcase at the post exchange to hold everything. I was ready.

I boarded a C-130 for Da Nang. There we herded into an R&R staging area operated by the Marines. From what I could see, the sprawling Da Nang base appeared to be quite safe, but it had a reputation as a target for Viet Cong rockets and mortars. To the west was a high ridge line that I presumed was controlled by our side; if not, then I could see how easily this place could be hit. The Marines were decent guys and did not try to hassle us. We were hustled through an R&R area and directed where to bunk for the night. I went to the enlisted club, had a few beers, and went back to the barracks. My upcoming meeting with Nancy got me anxious. Would we make love on the first night, or would we make love at all? Would we get married? We had really never gone all the way before. We had gotten close, but we really had known each other for only about two weeks. Were we crazy?

A siren ran like high voltage in the middle of the night. Rounds were indeed still incoming here. I shuddered to think that I would get hit while on my way to R&R. Why couldn't they have gotten us out of here without having to stay over on a strange base? This wasn't my home court! We rushed outside to the bunkers as the rockets landed somewhere on the base, but nowhere close. Soon the wail picked up again to signal the all-clear, and I went back to bed and eventually fell asleep. The next day after early chow we hauled luggage to the R&R center. There, our luggage was checked for drugs and firearms, but in general we were treated fairly and decently. After about three hours we were airborne. The majority of the GIs on the flight were going to Hawaii to meet wives, girl-friends, and family.

I only dozed at best during the nearly thirteen-hour flight. We stopped briefly in Guam and then droned through the night to Hawaii. A few hours before local sunrise, we took our first grateful look at the island of Ohau. A bus took us to Ft. DeRussy in downtown Honolulu. In the predawn darkness, the fort sure didn't look like any Army installation that I have been used to. But I had never seen an Army post in a non-war zone tropical area. It had little huts and palm trees, an oasis in the midst of giant high-rises. An Army major greeted us with "Welcome to Hawaii. You have been doing a magnificent job and now you are here for a well-deserved break. Some of you are here to meet your wives or girlfriends, and some of you are here to meet someone else's wife or girlfriend. Nevertheless, while you are here we want you to have a great time." We got a list of hotels, most with GI discounts. I looked for something with cooking and eating facilities. I wasn't planning to cook, and figured Nancy wouldn't either, but I wanted provisions for a late-night cup of coffee without having to go out.

I found an efficiency room, shared a cab with some other guys, and was at my hotel in twenty minutes. Three blocks from Waikiki Beach, the large room was on the eighth floor and sported a balcony overlooking the city, not the water. The small kitchen had a stove and a refrigerator. It was 8:00 a.m. and I had twenty-six hours to kill before Nancy was due. It had probably been a year since I soaked in a hot bath, and I nearly fell asleep in the tub after being awake and moving for the past twenty-four hours. There was even time for a short nap before I had to get a rental car and find out where the airport was. A GI in Vietnam filled me in on a rental deal that gave you a car for $50 plus gas for the whole week—less than ten bucks a day. I walked to the rental car office, paid my fifty bucks, and picked up a two-year-old Plymouth Valiant, hardly a sports car, but I was more concerned with reliability than image.

After getting directions to the airport, I made a trial run to find the terminal where Nancy would arrive. Running the drill twice made it clear that I had to allow about thirty minutes to park and get inside. Okay, now for the incidentals. I loaded up some beer, a bottle of vodka, since Nancy liked vodka collinses, and a few snacks. On the way back, I explored some side streets but did not travel outside the city, wanting to save that for the two of us together. Back in the room I sipped a couple of beers and was still munching chips when oblivion overtook me. I was out for twelve hours and fumbled awake at 2:00 a.m., my body clock still running on Vietnam time.

Sleep was futile, given my keyed-up state, and another bath didn't help. Coffee actually settled things, and I dozed off again, only to wake up consumed with wonder at whether Nancy's plane had left California. What would I say to her? Would I recognize her?

My mind was racing. Damn, why don't I just go back to Vietnam? She had to like me or, she wouldn't take her spring break from her master's program and go to Hawaii to meet just another Vietnam veteran. Maybe I'll do a third trial run to the airport just to see if I allowed myself enough time. Maybe I ought to leave a bit earlier because of traffic between 9 and 10 in the morning. Well, yeah, you know, I must be someone special to be able to talk a beautiful twenty-four-year-old woman into a trip to Hawaii to marry me. Oh shit, I had nearly forgotten that we were going to do that too. Did I look okay? I had lost a few pounds in Vietnam and lifted some weights the past few weeks.

She was scheduled to arrive at ten, so naturally I left for the airport about eight, and had an hour and a half to wait. Back and forth to the arrivals board to see if Nancy's flight was up there. The bottom of my third cup of coffee was staring up at me when her flight landed.

People walked down the steps of the plane in larger and smaller groups, then in ones and twos, to head across an open area in front of the terminal. The plane was packed. More faces kept filing out, but she wasn't among them. Maybe she didn't come.

Two women came down the ramp, one in sunglasses and a light dress. They chatted like old friends.

Oh God! That's Nancy! I hope she didn't bring a girlfriend.

Shut-up, George.

It all stood still. I couldn't see her eyes. The light dress was cut above the knees; her long hair went over her shoulders, and she looked beautiful. I reached for her, heart pounding, and an awkward New England hug followed—can't get too excited. But we sought each other's hands immediately. She casually sent a few words to another woman meeting her husband for R&R.

We were like two kids sharing a much too large secret and

unsure of what to say and do next. With her luggage, we walked to the car making small talk: How was your trip? Are you tired?

Driving back to the hotel, I was on automatic pilot—too hyped up. Nancy's legs twined ahead of her in the front seat. God, the hem of her dress hiked up enough to fill my head with her thighs. She smelled wonderful, her dark brown hair draped down her shoulders. I hoped my two baths made me presentable and erased the dirt and sweat of a theater of war.

Here she was sitting next to me in this studmobile, a Plymouth Valiant. I must have done something right besides taking all those trial runs. In all the chatter nothing came up about marriage, though. Upstairs, she unpacked her things.

"Why not the beach?" I ventured earnestly. Waikiki was down the street.

It was sunny, about 85 degrees. We waded into the water and swam around, still talking at each other. I had seen better beaches in Maine, much larger and longer. But I had never felt such warm water, especially in March. In Maine, the frigid water cramps your toes even in July and August.

"Do you think so?" she went on. "Get married, that is," and the subject was upon us.

"Sure, why not?" That was simple, I thought later, but the simplest things are always complicated. We decided to take a few days and get reacquainted.

I had bought a new camera. It had ten-second timer that let me focus on Nancy and run back to get in the frame with her. This got to be a silly game, and we still have the photographic record of all the horseplay. We spent a lot of time looking for stable horizontal surfaces to set the camera on for the "group" photos.

Back at the hotel we relaxed over drinks and then decided to go out to eat. We found a nice place. Nancy was interested in the finer things to be had on her Hawaiian vacation. I was more interested in crunching down on any American hamburger and other fast foods. I had not seen any for ten months and really had a craving.

It was dark when we got back to the hotel after having stopped for a few more drinks. Inhibition fled. I made us a vodka collins, and Nancy got into a silk nightgown. I hadn't thought about having the Vietnamese tailor make me some pajamas, so I just hung around in my skivvies. Luckily I did have some white underwear, having left the olive drab, military-issue green ones in Vietnam. We turned out the lights and grasped each other tightly. I was one horny son of a bitch, and with the alcohol I wasn't rating my performance or Nancy's. We were hungry, human, and cared a lot for each other. Nancy thought I was more gentle than she expected. She later told one of her friends who asked that her first night "hurt like hell." It really didn't hurt me a bit—I couldn't get enough, and, worse yet, we had only six more days. She was so beautiful. But would we get married?

The next day we did more beach and bedroom routines without waiting for nightfall. We rode around the island, not much of a jaunt, and stopped at roadside overlooks to talk again about getting married. I decided that I would let her make up her own mind. I was not going to pester or prod her about it anymore. I had convinced her to meet me in Hawaii, and I figured I had to mean something to Nancy.

On the third day we decided to go for it. We called a Catholic priest at Ft. Shafter and made arrangements to get married at his midday mass. Both of us called our parents to fill them in. My folks wished us the best. I left my mother as usual praying on the telephone, invoking the spirits to guide us.

"God be with you." Shit! We always said she would say that if a hydrogen bomb were descending on Portland in ten minutes. Nancy's parents wished us well and wanted us to call them back when we were man and wife.

Next morning we got in our best clothes, me in my shiny brown suit, loafers, and, thankfully, not the white socks. Nancy was a picture in a pink knee-length dress and half heels, but she also looked scared. I was nervous about how we were going to pull this off at the midday mass. We went to Shafter by cab, in case something went wrong with the car, or it didn't have the proper sticker to admit us to the fort. We were both giddy enough to want to do it this way, too. Our fears about a crowd at mass were for naught. It was a small chapel and only the priest was there. He talked to us briefly, looked at our papers, signed something, and told us we would receive our official notice in the mail. I did get a paper stating that we were married so that I could present it to finance immediately after I got back and attain the additional allotment for Nancy, my soon-to-be wife.

The church cleaning lady signed as the maid of honor, and a devout parishioner and base civil servant who served mass every day for the priest became the best man. We did the usual thing of "Do you" and "I do," and received communion at the abbreviated ten-minute mass. Afterwards, in his office, the priest asked if I were an officer and if was I in a combat zone. I said that I was not an officer and, yes, that I was in a combat zone, which encompassed all of Vietnam, but that I wasn't on the line, or wasn't an 11B10. I had an envelope with $20 for him, but he refused to take it. "Take some of your friends in Vietnam out for a drink." He never mentioned Holy Week. He most likely felt that we would be sleeping together whether we got married or not. So why not do it right?

The bride-to-be in her wedding dress, March 25, 1970.

After the tying the knot, the newlyweds returned to the hotel.

We took a cab driven by an older woman back to the hotel. I told her we had just gotten married. She studied Nancy and observed that she didn't look that happy. Nancy didn't look as frightened as before, but she was rather subdued. Her look seemed to spell "Oh God, what have I done?" At the door of the hotel room I picked her up and carried her across the threshold. We took a few more pictures of us doing that and then we went out to lunch. We called both parents again to tell them of our new status.

For the next few days we partied and stayed out late at various nightclubs. At one club Nancy saw the woman who was on the plane with her, and she asked us if we had gotten married. When we said yes, she asked us what we were doing out so late at a nightclub. I told her I couldn't find the proper manual. During the day we walked and went to the beach. I was constantly on the lookout for the perfect hamburger while Nancy searched for a restaurant with the best ambiance.

The weather was consistently warm, with no humidity. It was just plain wonderful. Even during the evenings we did not need sweaters because it was so balmy.

Hawaiian street scenes seemed strange, even startling, with the many white people or "round eyes" walking about the island. Even with one-third of the population of Asian birth, I had not seen as many Caucasians of both sexes in civilian clothes for ten months. While some of the women were nice to look at, I was definitely preoccupied with Nancy.

In Hawaii there seemed to be no awareness of the war in Vietnam. The couples on R&R were easy to spot. The guys' short haircuts were a dead giveaway amid all the civilians whose style was long hair. There was not much talk about the war. It was as if the people were oblivious to it. Maybe it was just me who every day over the past several years had to live with the possibilities of going to and then finally becoming a participant in the war.

VOICES FROM THE REAR

On the beach at Waikiki, walking distance from the hotel.

We did have our arguments, especially about politics. Nancy, being heavily steeped in liberal social-work traditions, believed the government should do more to help all people. I countered that people should do more for themselves and that there should not be free handouts for people capable of doing some type of work. She believed that all people should be allowed to have decent, respectable jobs. I believed that though I didn't particularly like my job in the army, I was serving my country in some fashion. I did not think the government owed me any particular job after my service. Every American should contribute something to the common good, whether it be in the Peace Corps or the military or whatever. I just didn't like the attitude of some people who wanted to receive 100 percent but gave nothing. So around and around we went—Nancy with government supports, and I with more reliance on self-reliance. I would argue that I didn't get to go to the best schools although I was qualified. I had to do what I could with what I had. Whether this was an age-old male-female discussion, I did not know. Or did our views diverge along party lines? Nancy was easily identified as a liberal Democrat, but I never considered myself a conservative. I was more of a Liberal conservative if that was possible. I believed that some people needed help, but not all did. Most people should help themselves. What I did know was that we came at things from two different angles.

I also gained some respect for people with what later became known as stress syndrome. On several occasions during our Hawaiian honeymoon, as I held Nancy in the middle of the night, street noise would cause in me wild reactions—sweat and adrenaline rushes. It wasn't lovemaking, it was instinctive fear. A siren sounding on any emergency vehicle outdoors sent me on a couple of occasions to the floor before I realized there were no incoming rockets. It took me a few seconds to grasp where I was and that I was okay. This bizarre bedtime business scared Nancy until I explained that the same sound warned us of a bombardment in Vietnam. "You have *got* to come home as soon as possible." This also set off our longest-running argument of the honeymoon, one that she won over time.

I wanted to extend my Vietnam tour for sixty days to allow me to ETS—get out of the Army—immediately upon returning to the states. After Nancy's letter in February, I decided I would extend, whether or not we got married. If I didn't, I would have to take a stateside assignment for an additional six months. So a two-month extension now would get me out of the Army four months earlier. Instead of going home on June 9th it would be around August 10th.

Nancy fought this logic. She felt that I was pressing my luck and that I should come home to her as soon as possible. She had come all the way there to marry me, and she wanted me back as soon as possible. It was time for me to make the sacrifice, she said. I kept repeating that 60 days was better than 180. In short, if I did not extend, my ETS would be January 5, 1971. At twenty-five years of age these months in the Army seemed like an eternity. Nancy said that if I extended I would be endangering our life together. Still I would not give in. I pointed out that I could be stationed in Texas and never even see her for that period. She said "at least you would be alive." I also told her that I didn't want her to see me humiliated at the hands of some lieutenant at some stateside base. It just wasn't good for my ego.

Finally, in the middle of a particularly passionate session one evening, she made me promise that I would come home and not extend, and in my weakened condition, I moaned Ye-e-e-sss! Y-e-ss! YES! Foiled again, she got me. What the hell! If it meant that much to her, I would stay in the Army an additional five months. But I was not done trying to convince her on this subject.

One day we visited Pearl Harbor, taking a launch trip around the harbor, and went to the memorial to the battleship *Arizona*, sunk on that infamous date of December 7, 1941. I hoped that I would make it back whole to the states and Nancy. My war and the one that started in this fleet anchorage were two different conflicts in my mind. World War II was necessary, and we fought with everything we had. Vietnam might have been necessary according to our ideology developed since World War II, but we certainly were not threatened as a nation by either the Viet Cong or the North Vietnamese. We certainly were not going all-out to win in Vietnam as we had done in World War II; rather we were politically hamstrung by Johnson, his government, and the Congress.

As we walked around the island we held hands tightly—time was growing short. Just a couple of days left, and we would part. That same rotten queasiness in my stomach returned, the same feeling that I had in Boston when I left Nancy for Vietnam. Nancy felt the same way.

Finally, the last day arrived. Neither of us could eat much that morning. Nancy had to leave about noon, and my plane would leave several hours later. We got to the airport. Nancy wanted ice cream, and pensively ate it. Behind her sunglasses, she suddenly burst into tears and reached for me. She begged me to be careful, and come back to her soon. Damn, I thought, this saying goodbye was getting old. We hugged and she sobbed and finally had to let go. It was awful as I watched her plane taxi and finally leave to go back to the world. I had several hours before my airplane left. I already missed her, and it would be another three months before I would see her again.

The return flight was easy, except for the pangs of regret reaching my gut the whole way. Now, though, I was a two-digit midget well under the hundred-day mark, especially since my new wife convinced me not to extend another sixty days.

No rockets on the way in and a swift return to Phu Bai—it was almost like an infantryman's prayer. The guys crowded around. Did I do it? "Get married, you mean? Yeah, I got married."

Finney was quietly triumphant. "See, I told you so." Yep, the ding-dong from Bell City, Missouri, was right all along. All I had to do now was wait for my next letter from my wife, Nancy.

I missed her too much.

Chapter 7

Goodbye, Vietnam

With the congratulations of my fellow sufferers loud around me, I went to ask Kelly about getting Nancy an ID that would let her into any PX or commissary on any base at home. Kelly forwarded the forms to Nancy with a note advising her of what a wise choice she had made. He told her to fill out the forms, have a twenty-five-cent photograph made of herself, and take everything to the nearest Army installation or the induction center in Hartford, Connecticut. I took the proof of marriage paper to finance to get Nancy on the monthly spousal allotment.

The only thing that I really wanted after returning from Hawaii was to get back to Nancy in one piece, the sooner the better. The guys reported a rumor that held a definite prospect of a thirty-day drop, meaning that for a specified time, people with thirty days or less remaining on their tours could be going home. This story persisted for several weeks and even developed into a forty-day drop. Soon the cutoff date was determined to be May 24, which left me out because my DEROS date was June 9. I don't know why the division had these drops. Perhaps there were slight aberrations in the numbers of people in the division. Conceivably the casualty rate in the 101st had not been as high as anticipated with the Vietnamization effort. If this were true, the division was actually over its allotted strength.

It was also rumored that the 101st Administration Company would be moving to Da Nang in July. I wouldn't be around for that if I didn't extend, but if I reconsidered, the bulk of my sixty-day extension would be consumed by the move and the adjustment to the new quarters. Da Nang was famous also for its numerous rocket attacks, though.

A few days after I got back Plummer asked me if I was going to extend. He added a plum that really brought me up short: if I extended for the sixty days, he would grant me immediate promotion to E-6. The job would be no different. I was practically in charge of the inprocessing section anyhow. The E-6 who was there was merely a cipher.

The re-up sergeant made some noise about the possible promotion. He didn't feel it was right. It took him five years to make it, and I would have made it in sixteen months. I had no intention of staying in the Army, so the E-6 allocation would be available again by the middle of August. I could see the re-up sergeant's point, but it was wartime, and promotions were much swifter now than in peacetime. This was the irony of the standard gag about the peacetime lifers: "Wow, you've been in the Army for eighteen years and you are already an E-6." Here I was, an E-5 in one year and possibly an E-6 in sixteen months if I extended for sixty days. I was flattered by the offer and thought I could see the reason he had ordered me to stay back from the Bob Hope show. He wanted to see whether I could follow an unpleasant order. I still would have liked to have gone. I thanked Plummer, but in a couple of days told him I had decided to go home at my normal DEROS date. I mentioned that I had just gotten married and the new bride wanted me to come home ASAP. I thanked him for considering me for the promotion. I think he understood.

The one thing that had changed at inprocessing during my absence was the relationship with the captain in the assignment and orders branch. I had a good rapport with this officer and his branch, although we barely spoke. I saw the new guys firsthand and screened their records. I was still culling out college graduates who showed some potential for clerical work or who wanted a change of MOS. Of course, the individual that I referred to was standing in front of me with an infantry MOS. So most assuredly he would welcome a change in his MOS. Usually he got a clerical position.

Before I left, I had showed Sonny what to do during my absence and how to write notes to effect these MOS changes. I told him never to write anything that sounded like an order. We had no authority for that and would be tampering with the ego of the captain who, as I reminded Sonny, was just one grade removed from some of those weird lieutenants we had been dealing with. I assumed that he got my point, but I was wrong. When I got back we had a directive from First Pig, as Plummer was now being called, to write no orders or directions into the 201 files. I asked Sonny about it and he told me he wrote something to the effect "ASSIGN THIS MAN TO 101ST ADMIN COMPANY." He had done exactly what I had told him *not* to do. I asked him why he had done that, and he said that he didn't know. I said, "Well, I should have known you would do something like that, because, after all, you did sign up for an extra year to get one month's leave to go home to see a girlfriend who was with someone else." I was a little pissed, because in one week Sonny had dismantled what rapport I had established with the captain and his branch. But then I looked at it philosophically: Hey, what do I care? I am going home in seventy days anyhow and will have nothing more to do with inprocessing. Someone else could do the job!

Before I left for R&R, SFC Carpentier had introduced a new Spec-5, Ralph Gable, who was going to work on our line. Carpentier asked me to show him around. I took him to get bed sheets, showed him his bunk, and introduced him to various people as we walked about. I walked with him to the PX and went with him to see a movie. I showed him the enlisted club and the igloo-sized hole that got us into the XXIV Corps area. Gable was a decent black guy over six feet tall and very slender, about 160 pounds, and about 23 years old. He told me he had signed up for four years to be a helicopter pilot. He was doing well and had passed all the written work and the flight portion, but then he decided to drop it. I kept pressuring him to tell me why, after he had put all that time and effort he decided to drop out. He was nearly a warrant officer, but since he decided to drop out he reverted back to a Spec-5. Ralph was never very clear with me about his decision. At the end of his year in Nam, he would ETS out because he would have only three months left on his four-year enlistment.

Ralph worked out superbly at first. He was a good team player. Then he started coming in late, missing a couple of hours in the morning, and working extra hard to catch up. He kept showing up late, and the E-6 warned him that he would have to send him to Master Sergeant Plummer, which he finally did. Plummer admonished him and threatened to bust him if it continued. The problem with Ralph was that he was on some type of upper. I never knew exactly what he was on, but he really couldn't seem to lick it. He would come to my hooch really high and thank me for befriending him and showing him around. I pleaded with him to get off whatever he was on and start showing up for work. He promised he would try. When I got back from R&R, Ralph was on his last legs at inprocessing. Plummer had busted him and had him right under his nose. I don't know if Ralph ever straightened out, since he never came around much after that. I felt bad for him, but I had other things on my mind.

One direct repercussion of Ralph's case was that it gave the E-6 a new sense power and how to use it. One morning shortly thereafter, I thought I had some type of flu. I wasn't feeling very well. The previous evening I had had three beers, hardly enough to make me feel this way. I had read some and had gone to bed early, about 11:00. By midmorning, I was feeling lousy and told Finney and Sonny that I was going to go on sick call. I would have told the E-6, but as usual he wasn't there. Instead, I went back to the hooch and caught some more sleep. At 1:30 I came back, feeling better. The E-

6 told me that since I hadn't gone on sick call, I was AWOL and had to go to report to Plummer. This was stupid: Ralph had missed six mornings before he heard any music. Nothing was done to a guy whom I saved from a beating when he kept greasing. He was removed and he wasn't busted because he was only an E-4 anyhow. I had missed no time since I had been in Phu Bai, and I missed only a half-day at Bien Hoa. Doesn't consistency stand for something? I didn't even argue much with the E-6. I just went to talk to Plummer, whom I believed to be reasonable. I told Plummer what had happened. He said go on sick call the next time, and don't let it happen again. He also told me that the E-6 just had Ralph removed and busted and that he was trying to show a tough hand, so I just became another example. Then Plummer asked me if I would reconsider extending and stay on with promotion to E-6. God, I thought, was this his ploy to get me to change my mind? I knew that the E-6 wanted another assignment, but did he have to go to these extremes? Can't they get someone to take the job? They were only going to get me for sixty days. But that was it, Plummer would DEROS in mid-August, which would make in-and-out-processing someone else's problem. Plummer wanted to finally resolve the E-6 assignment for the duration of his tour. Plus he had his problems with outprocessing too. Attitudes toward the war were changing. Guys who had spent a year on line were getting wind that they were not too well thought of back in the world. That pissed them off. Many were determined that they weren't going to take any shit anymore from anyone or anything, and that included the Army. Fergy, Bradley, Eddie Warbeck, and Charlton were still the mainstay of the outprocessing team. A group of 35 to 60 guys at a time would come in. Bradley would line them up for orientation and inform them what the procedure was. On several occasions, guys being outprocessed got a case of the "airborne ass," mouthing off and saying, "I ain't going to take no shit from you jerks after I just spent a year on line seeing my buddies getting blown away. I ain't going to take anybody's shit anymore." Some of them got into a confrontation with Bradley and Fergy, and a standoff followed. Our timid E-6 was no match for the

situation. He would go fetch Plummer, who had to cool down the situation without getting punched in the face.

Plummer calmed the waters by talking mild-mannered sense with the outprocessing veterans. They couldn't leave this unit without paperwork. They could go AWOL someplace in Nam, he allowed, but they needed orders to get on the freedom bird. "Let's play the game," Plummer would add, "and we'll get you home as soon as possible." Plummer perhaps was aware of the changing attitudes of the GIs, both those going home and those coming in-country.

There were other people-problems at Phu Bai that had not arisen at Bien Hoa. Several cherries who came to the division didn't inprocess for some time. They were actually AWOL within the admin company. These guys were aided by admin company people sympathetic to the cherries' fears by giving them a bunk and an area to hang out in. These guys would use the bunks of men on guard duty. They ran into problems when they couldn't get paid, but they usually lived off the charity of other GIs. They also couldn't get letters from home because they had no Army address. Some postal clerk would get excited if he could not find the person on some roster, so he could send the mail back or report the name to the company commander. Of course, if the postal clerk was in on the caper, he could take the mail and deliver it to the guy himself. These so-called "men without a unit" could use the chow line, because no one ever checked or asked for IDs or orders. So the guy could live free, and the other guys could buy him beer if he wanted. Most people stayed in that status for less than a month, opting to be sent to a unit somewhere rather than remain unconnected. One guy stayed in that limbo status for two-and-a-half months. Finally, he couldn't take it anymore and went through inprocessing after turning himself in to the first sergeant. This could not have happened at Bien Hoa because the entire personnel and finance in-and-out-processing function was a mile and a half away from the main admin company. Cherries inprocessing at Bien Hoa would never see members of the 101st Admin Company, except for us and the finance people. At Phu Bai the cherry hooches were within fifty yards of those of the admin troops, close enough for fraternization.

But if the 101st Admin cadre were helping to hide people, so were the Blacks Hats, specifically one master sergeant. This sergeant was a real old-timer, a black with enough time in that he had served in World War II and the Korean War in racially segregated units, and he knew his way around. He periodically came to hear my presentation. I liked him, but most of all I respected him. I would follow him in battle. He didn't kowtow to stupid lieutenants. Most lieutenants were smart enough to listen to this man, though there was always the exception. But he helped a couple of young black soldiers who didn't want to complete inprocessing. He would give them some job to do around his office. I knew who these guys were. I would occasionally have to see the master sergeant in his office for some personnel matter, and I would sometimes see these guys. The master sergeant looked at me, and I looked at him. I knew what he was doing, and he knew that I knew what he was doing. We said nothing about these guys. I just considered them as being in flux. The master sergeant had enough influence that when push came to shove, he would get these guys inprocessed without an AWOL penalty. It was all good time for these guys.

Many blacks who were processed into the division had been drafted and received a combat MOS. Many had had some high school or had graduated from high school, but their test scores, especially the scores of guys from big-city high schools, didn't show that they had picked up anything during their stay. Their GT scores, which combined verbal and math test results, were low compared with the scores of whites who had equivalent schooling in a similar environment. The scores of rural blacks and rural whites with comparable schooling tended to be higher than scores of inner city kids. Who knew? Maybe the guy had a bad day when he took the tests. I surely could have improved my score if I had gotten to take it with a full night's sleep.

A few black college graduates came through inprocessing, and their scores equaled those of any white college graduate. I got a couple black graduates with combat MOSs assigned as clerks within the division. However, some excellent candidates on whose 201 file I placed my little note did not get picked up for clerical positions. They had college degrees and great scores, and in the words of some blacks in the 101st Admin Company, they were not "jive-ass motherfuckers." It was my judgment that many black college graduates, one in particular, would fit in perfectly. I can't prove prejudice. I had no control of the situation. Many whites with similar credentials didn't get picked either. Perhaps there were no clerical spaces open at the time this one individual inprocessed. I will never know. Again, this would entail changing an individual's MOS from 11B10 (Infantry) to a 71H10 (Personnel Specialist). Whether black or white, if a person had signed up for a three-year clerical training position and had passed everything, he would get that MOS.

I didn't see much black-white animosity during my first few months. When I did see arguments, it usually stemmed from the type of music blaring out of jukeboxes in the enlisted clubs. The GIs favored rock 'n' roll, soul, hard rock, and country and western. I never heard a piece of classical music while I was in Vietnam. The blacks, especially those from the cities, favored soul and hard rock. Many of the white city-GIs liked rock, but they would also get into soul and hard rock. The white country boys who liked country and western made for friction. Usually, the guys would take turns and play three tunes either of rock and roll or of country and western. But as beer consumption rose, the rotation became less clear, and arguments and fistfights would ensue.

This was the time of black power, black militants, and black solidarity, Macfee had difficulty accepting the black handshake. There was a black E-5 who drove jeeps and trucks for the company who would often visit us. His major assignment was to assist the skin-headed reenlistment E-6. The E-5 would often meet and greet black guys who were inprocessing with the black-power handshake. Macfee, out of spite, jealously, or deliberate disrespect, said, "Damn it, I'm going to fuckin' invent a fuckin' white-power handshake." He would make one of the white cherries go through all types of hand gyrations. The blacks in the company or those who were inprocessing didn't say a word to Macfee, but one could easily see that they didn't like it. Like his screened-in porch, Macfee never really completed the plan for the handshake—it was different every time. The black E-5 would still come over to hassle Macfee, but he didn't like Macfee's antics. I think he knew where he stood with Macfee and what Macfee felt about blacks becoming too upwardly mobile. It would take a miracle to change Macfee. He would not only have to be knocked off his horse by lightning, but the lightning would also have to scorch away all the inbred prejudices in his head. He'd have to grow a new brain and try again. Yet Macfee possessed an inner sense of charity, and he went on helping the mamma sans with sick children. It was vintage Macfee, just demanding something for the underdog. I believe he had within him a passion for change.

Black troops often greeted each other with the handshake and the mantra: "It's not my war, man! It's not my war, brother." I knew they meant that it was the white man's war and that the blacks were being exploited by the white power structure into fighting and dying in this war. I wasn't black, but I felt the same way. I was being used by the system against my will! I could blame my plight on the white power structure, which my family roots were not connected to. But many sons of professional and blue-collar white families were in a similar situation. I knew that blacks had fought long to become integrated into the armed services and to become an integral part of the services. Now that this generation of blacks was given access to all the services and jobs, some didn't want any part of the system. Those blacks, like the whites, were the draftees who would be going into combat. I didn't believe the Vietnam war was a black or white issue. The blacks were not being exploited any more than the whites were. Maybe if I had a life-long image that the American power structure was controlled by blacks, and that whites were being used to pursue their economic benefit in this war, then I could feel as many blacks did, that they were being exploited by the white power structure. For the blacks who believed that, it was surely not their war. But, hell, we didn't even know the commander of the 101st

Airborne Division, much less who constituted the power structure in America. But for the black and white draftees in Vietnam, the real image of power in America was white. It mattered not that we didn't know who they were. When I saw blacks doing their greeting, I occasionally raised a clenched fist and said "Not my war either, brother." They usually met this with "Right on, man!"

Over one two-month period, I was charged with compiling statistics on the religious affiliations of the people we were inprocessing. I asked SFC Carpentier why I was assigned to do this. Was the Army looking for anything specific? Was it trying to prove something, or was this a local-level policy?

"Just do it," he grunted back at me. I reported back, surprised by several figures. By far the largest denomination represented was Roman Catholic, well over 50 percent of my totals. They came from all over the country but, as expected, mostly from the big cities like Boston and New York. Was my grandmother (born in 1879) correct? She had sprinkled holy water in the living room of our house after my sister dated a Protestant during college. She always feared Protestants. Were Catholics being unfairly used by the white Protestant establishment in this war? Her adamant stand for Catholic rights against Protestants always fascinated me. She was raised in Canada where a Protestant majority held power. I read of the anti-Catholicism of the Know-Nothing Party of the 1850s and the "Irish Need Not Apply" placards at employment offices in the nineteenth and early twentieth centuries. I thought that those issues died with the election of the nation's first Catholic president in 1960. It seemed that Catholics, once the bane of white Protestant society, were doing more than their part in the combat arms in the USARV, at least in our unit. I am sure they were also well-represented in the antiwar protests also.

The remaining 45 percent to 50 percent came from the various Protestant denominations. Just about every Protestant group was represented: Methodists, Southern Baptists, and a few Mormons. I didn't see any Episcopalians, nor did any Jews inprocess as E-6 or below during that two-month period. I never knew what was done with this information after I presented it. Maybe it settled a barroom bet amongst the senior enlisted. Did it have something so say about what classes were fighting this war? Perhaps it did. I already assumed that draftees were not sons of people with connections. Most of them would get out of the war or get a neat assignment in the National Guard or an Army Reserve unit. There were many more poorer blue-collar whites and blacks in the combat arms than there were Perry Puffins or Muffy Smith's older brothers. I knew that. In our company, we had a couple of guys whose fathers were officers in the Army, and one whose father was a two-star general. That alone would not confer membership in the upper class, but it did signify status within the Army. These guys were not "Gung Ho," and they were putting in their year without causing anyone much grief. The blue-collar types from the large cities of the Northeast and the Midwest with large Catholic populations perhaps did not fare as well on tests and therefore ended up in the infantry. This may have been the reason for the large number of Catholics in the 101st Airborne Division.

One episode that amplified the rising "I-don't-give-a-shit attitude" in the 101st Admin Company after coming to Phu Bai was the transfer of the remnants of the Big Red 1 into our division. The 1st Infantry Division was being pulled out in March 1970, and men who had fifty days or fewer remaining on their tours were allowed to go home. The rest were dispersed throughout other units in Vietnam. Perhaps this was one of the reasons the 101st had that thirty-day drop, to accommodate the influx of troopers from the Big Red 1. Those who had more than 120 days left were sent to various units within the 101st for the completion of their tour in Vietnam; those with less than 120 days but more than 50 were assigned as transients to our company. We had about forty-five of these guys from the Big Red 1. They did not work in personnel but did odd jobs that included guard duty. Their extra numbers among us sharing this duty meant that the interval between our stints of guard duty increased by nearly a week. Instead of every five to six days, as it was now, we drew guard duty more like once every twelve days.

But they weren't the most cooperative types, to say the least. Most were in the infantry or artillery in their former units. They were noisy, cocky, and, at the same time, confident, because they knew they were in a safe area and just had to wait out their time to go home. They had seen their last infantry duty, and now they could begin embellishing the memories of their experiences. They were in a halfway house, free of the anxieties of firefights and sudden death. They felt superior to us because they had been on line. These Big Red 1s had every reason to enjoy their last few months in Nam as best they could. They were spread around in our hooches with no more than two to any dwelling because there was simply not enough room to house them all in the single hooch they would have preferred. If they wanted to match up, they would have to wait until someone in their hooch DEROSed. They soon meshed into a normal routine of their jobs, mess hall, and the clubs. They neither fought more nor caused any more trouble than members of their new unit.

Guard duty was the area where their presence caused the most irritation. They did not take it seriously. On the bunker line they could get together in packs of at least four. They would often party and fall asleep, which pissed off the rest of us. "What are you going to do, send us to Vietnam?" they would yell. They made it their business on the bunker line to insult the admin personnel. When the bunkers checked with the command center, the former Big Red 1s begged to let us "clerks and jerks" know they were there. One evening I was on guard duty and was on the phone when a raucous Big Red 1 came on the line with his usual routine. Then Fergy fired one back up the line: "I got your motherfuckin' 201 file, asshole, and you ain't never motherfuckin' going home."

And it got better.

"How come you assholes are only supposed to be here for 120 days and you been here for 30 days and you still got 120 days left?"

More bunkers broke in. "Yeah, it must be because you assholes in the Big Red 1 can't count."

"Gee," came another voice. "You mean to say you guys have

already spent one month of the four you had left, and still have four left? How did you guys luck out?"

Inevitably Macfee chimed in: "Er . . .,how come the fuckin' Big Red 1 guys get to spend two fuckin' weeks in Cam Ranh Bay, then three fuckin' more weeks in fuckin' sunny Guam, after you leave beautiful downtown fuckin' Phu Bai? I'm goin' to fuckin' see my personnel fuckin' clerk to see if I can get the same fuckin' deal."

Another volunteer now warmed to the game. "Say, do you remember that E-6 who harassed us? Do you remember that he was the only guy who went back to the states through Thailand, India, Cairo, Italy, England, New York, then Ft. Lewis? Didn't he have to travel from India to Cairo by jeep and camel? I heard it took him nearly four months to DEROS, and when he got there they charged him with being AWOL and refused to pay him. Hell, I heard they were going to send him back to Nam to outprocess again to see if he could get it right. Shit, man, fuck, I heard they never found his 201 file or his finance records." The security lines were buzzing by now. If the enemy had ever chosen this moment to hit us, he would have walked into these verbal barrages. "I thought the Big Red 1 had already left Nam. I wonder what the clerks in Cam Ranh will think when they see these guys with no assigned unit for four months. Do you think they will charge them with being AWOL?"

The Big Red 1s got the point that evening, but they still needed to be reminded every once in while that they knew nothing about the mysteries and intricacies of personnel. They no longer had to fear the enemy; they now had anxiety about where, when, and how they would be going home. These guys on the whole were a rougher crew than we were. Fergy, Finney, Macfee, and Kelly were as tough as any of those characters, but I had the feeling that there was a higher caliber of talent and civilian training in the 101st Admin Company than among these transients of the Big Red 1.

This became more evident one day when a couple of representatives of Project Hope came to address our company. This program was supposed to help guys readjust to the world at home, help those without high school diplomas attain high school equivalency diplomas, and head them toward some type of college. The leader of this three-man team, a huge black man over six feet tall and about 280 pounds, spoke to us in the center aisle of the personnel warehouse building. He wore "cherry" green fatigues with no rank and appeared to be in his mid-twenties. I didn't know whether he was civilian or military. He couldn't have completed basic training recently at the size he was. I doubted whether he could trot a mile in twelve minutes, let alone run that distance in the 7½ minutes the Army required in basic.

He asked how many of the group had gone to college. It looked as if nearly 80 percent of the hands went up. Then he asked how many had degrees, and about 40 percent kept their hands up. He asked about graduate training; about 20 percent of the hands remained in the air. Graduate degrees accounted for 5 percent to 10 percent. The Project Hope guy was as amazed as I was at the statistical sampling he was getting here. I realized now that many of these guys were like me, caught by the draft before the lottery went into effect.

Between roughly 1965 and 1969, if you had dropped out of college for any reason—just to see what the rest of the world was like or to earn some money for your next year's tuition—your draft status changed. Not registering for school meant the loss of the 2-S, or student, deferment, and then an opportunity to spend a year in the tropics of Southeast Asia pondering what your life would have been had you not left school. My six-year deferment was considered enough by my draft board, even though a course of graduate study for the Ph.D. degree could take that amount of time and more if one were working to support oneself too. Those with families were all the more strapped and likely to take time out to earn enough money for another shot at the program. All of us were caught before the first lottery of December 1969. The lottery system produced random numbers assigned to draft-eligible men; the higher the number, the less likelihood of being inducted.

The Project Hope representative was more interested in people who had not completed high school or those who had had some college but planned not to return because they were now looking for some other type of training. He would find more customers in units where the education level was not quite as high.

Finney's time was up in April. He had been with us since late July 1969. Sonny and I walked up to the Black Hat hooch to see him off. Finney wore a cunning smirk as he stood there with his duffle bag and waiting for the truck to take him to the airport, where a C-130 would ferry him to Cam Ranh Bay and the freedom bird. We had sure shared some good times. I would never forget him at Bien Hoa standing over his M-16 late at night, drunker than shit and attempting to clean his weapon, and how he was so attached to Bitch and refused to go north without her. He kept up the party spirit in those last two weeks at Bien Hoa when we were the last company element to leave and scared about life in Phu Bai. His legendary barbecue sauces for the chicken that he and Bradley got from the 1st Calvary's cook made for memorable eating. I had an empty feeling as we shook hands and he boarded the half-ton. Sonny and I stared after him as the truck disappeared in the distance.

Finney's departure and my refusal to extend opened the door for Tate to assume the position as NCOIC (Noncommissioned Officer in Charge). Carpentier and Plummer had given up on the whiny E-6 and found him a less stressful job somewhere in the admin company. Tate had been in five years and decided to stay in. He was senior to everyone, and probably deserved the job. He was okay in the sense that he did his job along the line while at the same time was the designated NCOIC. He was not given the hard-five stripe as Finney had. He didn't boss us around too much and was slow enough not to cause any trouble. He would piss and moan at Macfee's antics, which Kelly spurred on.

Kelly visited often, and the two of them would bust each other and crack the place up. Macfee always registered his delight at Kelly's arrival. The banter ran on and on.

"Hey, Kelly, what the fuck are you selling today? Fuckin' ID cards, or what the fuck?"

Kelly would run it back: "Macfee, what the fuck do you care? You can't fuckin' read anyhow."

"Well, what the fuck have they got you taking motherfuckin' pictures for? If you could fuckin' read, the Army would give you a motherfuckin' better fuckin' job. All you fuckin' do is cut out fuckin' pictures, and shit, man, fuck, everyone here could fuckin' do that when they were fuckin' three fuckin' years old." The place was by now in an uproar, and Macfee entered the middle of the horseshoe of inprocessing tables, scratched his ass, and added, "Fuck, Kelly, if you had any fuckin' brains, the fuckin' Army, as fuckin' dumb as it fuckin' is, would give you a fuckin' better fuckin' job, like using your fuckin' mind like we are with this fuckin' pencil and fuckin' typewriter." His rhetoric, as usual, caught you with its growing meter and drive, and I was soon laughing at the thought of our mindless business. Kelly's own laughter rose as Macfee reached his finale: "But you, fuckin' Spec-4 Kelly, soon to be PFC, have reached your fuckin' potential by taking your fuckin' pictures and cutting them fuckin' up like we all did when we were fuckin' three."

Now swinging into a broad imitation of Tate's northern Alabama accent, Macfee brought it all home: "The fuckin' Army won't fuckin' do anything with you, Kelly, because you are fuckin' dumber than a fuckin' Government mule." This last line was the Macfee's signature ending. We were so used to it that we always heard it coming and chorused in perfect unison as Macfee raised his arms as if to direct the choir in the final Amen: "AND THAT IS FUCKIN' DUMB."

"Case closed."

Kelly inevitably blew Macfee a kiss and threw a simultaneous "bird" to inform MacFee it was his turn to buy beer. Unfazed, he executed a military about-face and returned to his job. We often wondered what these two would say if they didn't like each other.

Even the buttoned-up Tate would sometimes laugh at Macfee's antics. Tate was a hard guy to figure. He had a wife and four kids, responsibilities that made him different, far more serious than the rest of us. He never developed a sense of humor. What I didn't like was his budding "lifer" mentality. He stayed in the Army because he had nothing else to do. He had a job that paid little but provided a roof and medical care for his kids. He hadn't gone to college and had no interest in furthering his education. He did do his job, however slowly.

At a company going-away party, Tate and I got into it. It was one of Plummer's attempts to boost morale, so he held a party for someone's going away. It was an overcast day, which was fine because the temperature had been reaching 106 degrees, and it was even higher inside the warehouse. The beer and the food were plentiful. Most of the guys were sitting on the ground under some trees. I was sitting on the ground with Sonny, who was getting tanked. Tate was sitting there making some comment. A fight broke out in the distance, with loud and grievous threats, but it quickly died down. Tate and I began wrestling in jest, but we found ourselves in a more serious contest. Soon we were rolling on the ground. I lifted Tate's 6-foot, 210-pound frame on my shoulder and threw him down, but collapsed with him. He couldn't pin me, nor I him. After two minutes we were exhausted, and we both just fell apart and began to laugh. Tate had a cut on his lip, and I had a cut on a little finger and the side of my hand. We were also filthy. We both thought it wise to take a shower to clean off the sweat and dirt and clean the cuts. We were never mad at one another, but spontaneously began going for each other. Maybe it was the frustration and boredom about being in Vietnam. We had to release some energy. Tate and I got along fine, but we would never be in synch, as I was with my hoochmates. He never jumped on us at inprocessing; we knew the job so well. Macfee's antics at the inprocessing arena went unchallenged by Tate.

Tate even stood by without a word one Sunday when we left the inprocessing area for church. Macfee and Kelly pulled out a calendar and proved that it was in fact Sunday. Sonny, Macfee, and I got up on the pretense of going to church. We had been working seven days a week, and it was Macfee who decided that "Fuck it man, even in basic training they gave you time off on Sunday for spiritual matters." Kelly came by to join us in his Sunday best—he looked as though he had just gotten up after an hour's sleep. None of us had gone to church regularly, if at all, while in Vietnam. But the spirit moved us that Sunday. No one said a word, not even Carpenter who came by to view the depleted inprocessing line. Kelly and Macfee held services in their hooch by drinking a couple of beers and telling a few stories. Upon our return an hour later, the other guys got their turn. We tried to make a point, but in effect, we had just made our workday longer because we still had the same number of cherries to inprocess, whether we were there or not. We still had to work until we completed inprocessing the daily quota. There was no designated day of rest in Phu Bai.

Morale was poor because of the monotony of the daily routine. Because I was getting shorter, going home was something to look forward to, and it helped to keep me up. We welcomed any diversion. On another muggy evening, Macfee and I went to see a Vietnamese show at the amphitheater. A movie was slated to follow the show. I stayed for the show, but I told Macfee I was heading back to my hooch because I was not interested in the movie. About an hour later, as I lay on my bed reading a book, Macfee burst into the hooch. "You won't fuckin' believe what just happened in front of my eyes. I just saw a guy get shot. He was fuckin' sitting in front of me, and I heard this bang, and this guy keeled over." Macfee had leaned over the guy to see what had happened and saw a large head wound. He was dead. For a few moments chaos ensued, and finally the movie was shut off and the lights came on. Macfee was excited because the guy was sitting just to the right of him. MPs rushed in and some people were searched, but no one was implicated. No weapon was found. Hooches were searched for a recently fired pistol or weapon. No one saw anything and no witnesses came forward.

A company formation the next day generated a 100-man detail to comb the grounds in the compound. Squads searched the swamp area between the big enlisted club and the Air Force communications area, but nothing was found except an old rusty AK-47 and leeches on the legs of the guys who had to tromp through the marshes. The investigation, if it ever went past the level of the local MPs, never turned up any hard information as to where the shot came from or even the type of weapon used, or whether the death could be presumed accidental or not. We never heard anything during my remaining time at Phu Bai about charges or arrests. The dead guy was unknown to me, but I wondered how his death was officially recorded. No one ever talked to Macfee, who was there at the scene.

The rumor mills naturally ground on. Macfee came up with the best explanation. The dead man was an excellent card player. We now heard that he often played poker with some senior lifers—E-6s, E-7s, and master sergeants. The word was that these sergeants owed the deceased more than $5,000, so they blew him away. No one could prove anything. Some believed that the shot came from the marshes, which was why an intense search was conducted in there. No one ever attributed the shooting to an enemy sniper. Was it just a wild shot? We would never know.

The search for the weapon occasioned my first visit to the Air Force communication facility. Reaching that compound required a meandering, 500-yard walk on single width of PSP. It was quite a feat to balance on the metal strip, especially when walking back to our compound with a few beers in the evening. The consequence, if one fell, would be a dip into the marsh with its accompanying leeches, a most unpleasant experience, especially after dark.

One afternoon about five o'clock, Macfee, Sonny, Kelly, and I set out. The path ended on dry ground leading up towards the seven Air Force hooches arrayed like a little town situated on a hill. There were no trees in the area at all. The Air Force men actually had clotheslines from which their uniforms and sheets flapped and dried in the heat and the breeze. We entered the enlisted club, and it was another world. The floors were immaculately clean and shiny medium-blue linoleum. It was well lit, a vast contrast to the drabness of our clubs. The Air Force always had better quarters than the Army, but this was air-conditioned, too. It was almost too clean to sit down. For the first time in Vietnam, I checked my shoes for mud, and actually felt too dirty to go inside. About six tables filled in an open area and an L-shaped bar. On the back bar, a glittering row of liquor bottles reflected the light, but we, of course, wanted only beer. Three Air Force enlisted guys and the bartender eyed us on the way in. We must have looked like ragged remnants of some lost company. Kelly barked for some beers which they obligingly provided. I had the feeling that they were intimidated by us, because, after all as Kelly said, "They thought all of us are fuckin' crazy because we all jump out of fuckin' airplanes."

Most Air Force people signed up for three or four years, the real rationale for the better facilities. I guessed that a communications MOS meant a four-year enlistment. In order to attract a man for that long and to encourage him to reenlist after his first tour, it was wise to provide him with good accommodations and other amenities. The Army did not have to do that because the draft provided the bodies filling its infantry and combat slots. A boy or man learned fundamental infantry skills in a few months, and the Army did not have to compete with the outside world for that labor. Infantry experience was not transferable to civilian life, as communications or computers would be, so the Air Force made its people a whole lot more comfortable.

We drank several beers and basked in the air-conditioning. We got along fine with the Air Force guys. Macfee and Kelly were making wisecracks against each other, and when the Air Force enlisted men started laughing, Kelly and Macfee turned it on for their audience.

"Hey, Macfee, I'll bet you never been in such a place as clean as this. Shit I'll bet there ain't as nice a place as this in all of fuckin' Chicago!"

"Shit, Kelly, what the fuck would you know? You're from fuckin' Pittsburgh, the asshole of the world. Shit, man, fuck, the only bar you have ever been fuckin' in looks like a coal mine or a steel plant. You're fuckin' sitting here right now, fuckin' thinking that you were shot by a sniper and you are now in fuckin' heaven because you ain't never seen a place like this."

They milked it on and on, and with a few beers, it got funnier and more elaborate. The comforts of air-conditioning made it difficult for us to adjust to the heat on the return trip. Fortunately we left before dark and avoided the quagmire and its leeches. I didn't go back to the Air Force club again. I had seen it, and we had the same beer at the Army club. I did like to go to our large enlisted club and sit on the picnic tables and peer out towards the Air Force club at twilight, and on several occasions watch Macfee and Kelly struggling for balance on the PSP path. Guys took bets that one or both of them would hit the marsh before they made it back. I don't know if anyone could have made it back at night without a flashlight. If they low-crawled, they might make it by morning.

My beer drinking with Kelly and Macfee revealed both of them as real professionals at any sort of alcoholic refreshment. Both knew the E-6 head cook at our chow hall, a huge, better than six-foot guy who weighed in at 300 pounds. One night the three of us ventured over to his hooch. The cook produced a quart of Jack Daniels, and Macfee and Kelly proceeded to help him out with this. I stuck to beer. Kelly and Macfee downed the hard shots with a practiced adeptness that I had never seen. My stomach turned just watching them. When the cook found another bottle, I retired for the evening. Next day I asked Macfee and Kelly how long they had stayed. Not long after they had finished the second bottle of Jack Daniels, they told me nonchalantly. If I had stayed for that, a priest would have given me last rites. I had seen my share of drinkers over time, but these two guys were astounding.

At Phu Bai, the roll of events brought across my path another familiar figure from the past. Around my hometown the draft board had made a sweep of all eligible males, a fact made clear to me again on April 24, 1970, when I heard my name uttered as I climbed onto the last bleacher seat for my orientation for the new guys.

"George, George," came an unfamiliar voice, only because I hadn't heard it in a while. I looked down into the face of James Clifford Hobbins, a kid I'd known since high school. More of a bookworm, he was well-read in history and the classics, even in high school. He sure as shit didn't belong in an infantry unit in Vietnam. We were in the Young Democrats Club together, carrying banners for candidate John F. Kennedy when he came to Portland in 1959. In high school, Cliff idolized Teddy Roosevelt. He had my brother Ron drive his family's 1958 Ford Fairlane around Sebago Lake in near-zero winter temperatures with the heater off and the windows down. He took off his shirt and smoked a huge cigar while expounding on the true grit of his hero. I couldn't do this for long. He did it without the aid of alcohol.

We had a dance band for a time, with Cliff on the sax, my brother on trumpet, and I played the piano. He might have dropped out of the band by the time it played on a moving flatbed truck in the Nixon parade in 1960. Such a show for the Republicans was sacrilegious. For a time we also played together in pep band for the Cheverus High School basketball games. I pounded a huge bass drum only because we couldn't roll a piano onto the pulled-out bleachers at the Portland Exposition Building. We got into the games for free, so I didn't mind hauling around the drum. My brother Ron was really the star attraction, especially when he played a rocking "Sweet Georgia Brown." The crowd got into that.

Even though he had shaved the morning that I saw him on the bleachers, Cliff showed signs of a thick beard. His dark, swarthy face made him look all of his twenty-six years, and he contrasted starkly with the rest of the GIs. He smoked a pipe. Without the uniform he would look professorial. I was surprised to see him. We shook hands, and after my presentation we spoke briefly. Cliff had graduated from Marquette University in Milwaukee, Wisconsin, with a B.A. and an M.A. in American history in 1966 and 1968. He thought about pursuing a Ph.D., but he wanted to teach for a while and got a good teaching job at Fryeburg Academy, a prep school in a town in Maine by that name. In his previous life, he received a salary of $8500 a year with a five-room apartment and utilities thrown in, a fantastic deal in 1969. I concluded it was worth about $15,000 in a metro area. Fryeburg was right in the middle of ski country. The town was on the New Hampshire-Maine border, near Bridgeton, Maine, an excellent ski area and not far from the White Mountains and Mount Washington itself, the tallest peak on the East Coast. In the summer, there were the Maine lakes—Long Lake, Sebago, plus many smaller lakes—and the nearby town of Naples, Maine. New Hampshire had its summer beauty also. I was envious when I thought of this idyllic setting in which to teach. I couldn't wait to get back to academics.

The author and Cliff Hobbins, two who made it through.

But Cliffy might not get back to see this again if he went to the field as an infantryman. P-training would keep him busy for about eight days, and I told him that I would see what I could do to get him a clerical assignment in the rear. I made no promises. If successful, this would be by far my greatest coup. The captain wanted no more suggestions pinned to an individual's 201 personnel file since Sonny had ostentatiously issued his own orders and placed them in several individual files when I was on R&R. I had sent a few notices in with no repercussions. I went in to see Spec-4 DeWhitt personally with Cliff's 201 folder. DeWhitt was one of the guys who actually cut the orders and whom I had helped get assigned to his position. Holding Cliff's 201 file in my hand, I explained everything to DeWhitt, who allowed he might he able to do something. I took Cliff to finance, where a sergeant who knew me quietly asked if they were going to send that guy to the line. I hoped not.

It turned out that Cliff and I had similar experiences with the same draft board, and although we didn't wish they were eaten alive by ants or lobsters, we wouldn't have minded if they had suddenly lost their jobs. It was amazing how similarly we viewed our experiences, the feeling of being powerless against a group of people that we had little respect for. We agreed they certainly went about their jobs with little thought about whether their country's policy could be wrong or whether they themselves felt any guilt about sending young men to their deaths or a lifetime of disability. At the least, we shared this two-year imprisonment.

By this time in my short Army career, I could begin focusing more on the date of my departure from the service. The military's policy of keeping me another six months if I didn't extend for two more in the war zone had already caused a minor rift between me and Nancy during our idyll in Hawaii. The atmosphere at home didn't help either, I was to learn. Nancy had her own problems getting her relatives of the World War II generation to show any sympathy to protests against the war. As my DEROS date drew closer, she wrote to ask me if I was going to wear my uniform. She didn't want me to get hurt and thought I might encounter some trouble in Hartford if I wore it there. Returning World War II veterans never had to face that problem. They came home to roaring welcomes and never bought their own drinks at the local bar. Of course, they had the best GI bill known to man. They could go to any college of their choice, and the tuition and books would be paid for, plus they would receive an additional $75 per month for living expenses. Seventy-five dollars was a lot of money in 1945 and 1946. Benefits this generous did not await the Vietnam vet.

I got some great news about my stateside assignment. Instead of going to Ft. Leonard Wood, I was being assigned to Ft. Dix, where everything had started. A guy I knew in assignments initially told me there was nothing much he could do, but he quietly worked to get my orders changed to Ft Dix. Nancy would not have to give up her second year of graduate study, since Ft. Dix was only about 225 miles from her home. We could at least see each other on weekends, though even this separation would kill me. I immediately set to work to apply for an early-out for teaching starting in October 1970. Nancy sent me application forms for substitute teaching positions in various high schools. Before I went home, I had an appointment for an interview in the Springfield, Massachusetts, school system. Nancy was ecstatic. She and her mother began planning a reception to celebrate our marriage. Of course, all this running around looking for schools to teach at could have been avoided if I had just decided to extend for sixty days in Vietnam.

On the home front, events moved swiftly in reaction to Nixon's announcement of April 30 that 20,000 American and unspecified ARVN troops had attacked communist sanctuaries in Cambodia. This sparked protests on many college campuses, culminating in the Kent State incident when National Guardsmen shot and killed four students. When this news reached us, there were mixed emotions. Some thought that those in power would get this war over with and get us home. While I felt badly for the students and their families, I also felt badly for the Guardsmen, some of whom were the same age as the students, but who were in uniform and under military orders. From where I was sitting, this type of protest seemed exactly what the enemy wanted. The dissent against the war helped their cause.

From a tactical standpoint, Nixon was probably correct in attacking the enemy supply caches and routes in Cambodia, and perhaps our military should have gone in much sooner. In fact, we suspected elements of our division had been in that area much sooner than April 30th. In early March, our divisional casualty reports listed combat incidents far out of the 101st's operating area. The guys in the casualty branch passed on their conclusions to us.

The Nixon administration contributed to the stateside unrest ten days before the Cambodian invasion by disclosing a Vietnamization program. In turning over the war increasingly to our local allied army, Nixon had also announced that another 150,000 American troops would be pulled out of Vietnam by the end of the year. Male populations could assume the war was truly winding down and breathe easier. But ten days later, the White House embarked on another major campaign into uncharted territory, implying more casualties and more drafted replacements. It was no wonder that the campuses flared the way they did. If the withdrawal declaration engendered the hope that the war would soon end, the Cambodian incursion squelched that.

Some magazines reported that the war was over in I Corps, but suddenly in early May, the 101st was seeing a lot of action: from May 1 to 7 the division took 270 casualties. This made me jumpy. As a short-timer, I didn't want to be under some last-gasp enemy attack. I had been here too long. I went on another garbage truck detail and started talking with the Vietnamese people. I asked one guy how much time he had left before he went home.

With all this, Cliff Hobbins was still unassigned. The captain had pulled about thirty guys who had combat MOSs and told them they would be given rear-area assignments. I had asked DeWhitt to keep Cliff's record out of this group. He had never taken such a direct hand in things before, and I was suspicious, but I hesitated to open the subject of Cliff again with him. If the system was working, let it be, but the captain's behavior was just too out of the ordinary.

VOICES FROM THE REAR

When the division began taking all those casualties, the infantry needed replacements. Now DeWhitt told all thirty of the same guys they were going to infantry units. Some of theses cherries had even written the good news home and asked their families to ship their stereo equipment and other possessions. Even some of the Big Red 1 guys who had little more than a month left were sent to infantry units. Fergy wasn't around to tell them "I told you so," but this was a bum situation for these guys. With these guys gone, we also had more frequent guard duty, and the cycle reverted from once every twelve to fourteen days back to once every five or six days. Cliffy was not among those shipped out, but where the hell were his orders? He was already a couple of days overdue. DeWhitt confirmed that Hobbins was not among those whose orders were rescinded. He had assigned Hobbins to the 101st Admin Company, and that still stood. Maybe in the bustle of guys heading back out to the field, the orders were cut short. I told Cliff what I knew. I had done everything short of typing the orders myself. We were on tenterhooks until May 10, two days after all those guys had left, when the paperwork finally showed up confirming him to the 101st Admin Company. Cliff's background, like mine, made him different, but he still had that infantry MOS. Cliff credited me with saving his bacon. He later would even tell people in Portland I had saved his life. I pushed every button I was aware of, and I was glad I had. As to life-saving, the guys on the line did more of that in a day than I did in two years. But through all Clifford's apprehension, he never considered a three-year reenlistment on the spot to obtain a different MOS. Like most people, he had a lot invested and a good job to return to, but like most draftees, he wanted to get the Army over with as soon as possible. Maybe he owed me one, but Clifford had just as much guts as anyone else who went through Nam as a draftee.

The day Clifford got his orders, I had 30 days left in-country. I didn't invest in a short-timer's stick, a cane about 1½ feet long and used by short-timers to say they were so short they could use that cane. Some short-timers threw a dime on the ground and observed that "I am so short that, in a rocket attack, I could crawl under that dime and be totally safe." We still heard of guys getting killed just prior to their DEROS date. Hell, I was there in Bien Hoa when those guys got it after having spent 365 days in country. A fellow in my hooch got a letter and was shaken to learn that an old neighborhood friend was killed in Nam just prior to his DEROS. As the time drew near, I hoped like hell that I would come home in one piece to see Nancy.

The fact that elements of our division were in some heavy fighting did not help my nerves. In the evenings, guys on pot used to climb the roofs of a couple of hooches and watch the tracer rounds flow from the helicopters working out just beyond sight of our compound. The guys on the roofs reacted like they were at a fireworks show: "Woo-ooo, ah, wasn't that just wonderful." The pot made the red tracer light awesome, they told me. They stood on the roof to flap their arms like wings while jumping down. Pigeons, they said. Even with a surplus of beer, I had sense enough to know that flapping my arms would not help on the way down. Fortunately there were no broken bones.

The increased enemy activity multiplied the guard duty principally because the Big Red 1 troops were either DEROSing or going back to the line. One evening I got guard duty in another sector. The bunker reminded me more of Bien Hoa than Phu Bai. The bunker had large openings on three sides, which exposed us considerably more than any bunker that I had ever been in. The rickety roof supported a single layer of thinly filled sandbags and was not sturdy enough to mount an upper-level observation post. Bunk beds lined the back side of the bunker. The wire line ran about 50 yards in front of the bunker. On the other side of the wires were trees that partially covered or camouflaged a Vietnamese farmhouse some 100 feet distant. When nightfall came, we could see a light from the house. I had never been on guard duty where a village house sat so close to our wires. Why it just wasn't leveled was beyond me. It wouldn't take much for some bored or crazed GI to take a few shots at the place on the premise that there was enemy activity there. It could certainly serve as a vantage point for the enemy to watch our movements.

Three of us came out by jeep from the 101st Admin Company to join a fourth man who might have been a permanent guard. We soon came to know the ways of the fourth man. Huge rats infested the bunker, creatures larger than squirrels. Bold as pirates, they scurried all over the interior of the bunker and scampered along the windowline of the entire bunker. Our mysterious fourth man carried a huge knife. He said he could use it and could hit those rats if he wanted to. Just for the sport, we took him up on this, and he threw his knife a couple of dozen times at the beasts. He never came close to hitting anything in the herd. We had to put up with this asshole for the night, never quite sure whether he would let fly again.

The new sector didn't have the stadium lights that we had in our own area. Shadows presented themselves, especially in the vicinity of that farmhouse. Actually the frolicking rats helped keep me awake. I ended up feeding them some crackers I had brought along. Needless to say, I did not sleep well here. Unfamiliar noises kept me awake. I had been in Nam too long to see things, but the apprehension of something totally new and at the same time being extremely short made the night traumatic. The mosquitoes were rampant, so I could barely sleep. I was ecstatic to see the first light.

The next guard duty I drew put me in one of the towers for the first time. The 50-foot high structures had a closed room at the top. The one where I was assigned was actually clean and had bunk beds. Two of us ascended the ladder. Three sides of the tower room were sandbagged a couple of rows high. There were no mosquitoes because screened-in windows ran along the front and the sides of the tower. In the tower was the starlight scope, a large instrument designed to concentrate all the available luminescence from the moon, the stars, and the distant stadium lights to produce an image in the scope that was as bright as daylight. I could easily discern objects a thousand yards distant. Gravestones and all the shadows around them stood out in the device; no live humans were out there. I had to call in periodically from the tower to a central communications center and to our own sector. I felt really safe there, though a sniper could easily reach the occupant of the post. A mortar round would do some damage to the tower. I had to man only one 3-hour shift, 11:00 p.m. until 2:00 a.m., and for the first time on guard duty in Vietnam, I really fell sound asleep during my time off. The second man had to shake me awake at 6:00 a.m..

Rumor ran wild that Phu Bai was going to get hit. The lifers were really uptight, and from about the 17th to the 21st of May the company was on 100-percent alert. On Ho Chi Minh's birthday, we were all out near the perimeter serving as backup for the guys pulling regular guard duty. Our unit dug in behind some graves and slept on them that night. There was no enemy action, not even a sniper shot. Again, it was very difficult to sleep because of the mosquitoes. Fortunately, the lifers graciously gave us the morning off for sleep.

On the following night, we stayed in a warehouse with some bunks and all our gear. We could be instantly ready for the perimeter with helmets and flak jackets. We spent only four hours in the warehouse on a third night as backup. Again, no action. The fourth night the 100-percent alert was called off. The enemy would have been hard-pressed to overrun us even in full attack. If he had tanks, we were in trouble. I never knew how soon we could get air cover or how many 105-mm. artillery pieces would support us. Some artillery batteries were nearby, and they often boomed away at night. The artillery frequently moved around in our sector to prevent the enemy from getting a fix on its positions. Their noise changed from night to night, depending on their distance from us. The helicopter gunships were on-call too, and we could see their tracers every evening. If the Vietnamese came at us with infantry, they could be assured of some losses. The bunkers were loaded with armament, and we all had our M-16s with many extra clips. I passed out all the hand grenades in the footlocker. At first notice we would reinforce the bunker line and use the new foxholes that we had dug. If they shot out all the lights and somehow got behind us, we could be hurting, but we then had flares to light up the night. Our company would more than hold its own. So many people out there with me made me feel confident. We were on our home court, familiar with all the surroundings.

Toward the last of May, I got a report date for Ft. Dix of July 14, 1970. I was first due at the United States Army Returnee Detachment on June 5 and would probably leave Vietnam a couple of days later. I was informed that I would spend about two to four hours outprocessing at Ft. Lewis and would then be free to go home. Next would be thirty days' leave and assignment to HHC 5th Bde (WlMX) at Dix, whatever that unit was. I guessed I would report there and then be reassigned to some other unit.

We had large company assembly outside the warehouse in May, at which about sixty of us were awarded the Bronze Star Medal "For Meritorious Service In Connection With Ground Operations Against A Hostile Force." The language was impressive, but it was issued to all members of the 101st Airborne Division (Airmobile) who had kept their nose clean while serving in the Republic of Vietnam for at least ten months. The guys on line all got one of these, but they deserved more. Some infantrymen, but not all, received a Bronze Star with a "V" device for valor. The "V" required some extra work, though; someone had to write up a man for it, and that tended not to happen. The grunt could always proudly display his Combat Infantryman's Badge. That definitely made him different. I collected my medals and their cases from the awards branch and stuck them in my duffel bag.

About this same time I signed a circulating petition headed for the United States Senate supporting an initiative to block all funds for further operations in Cambodia. The thirty-one signatories had to be discreet because we were still soldiers in the United States Army, but I did figure I was short enough to avoid being sent to the field. By the time any debate over the issue got going, the Cambodian operation should be over. We went in to destroy caches and supply lines, and I should think this ought to have been done within five months.

I had first heard about Eagle Beach on January 22, 1970, when I was slated to go. But the demands of inprocessing and SFC Carpentier kept me on the job. Eagle Beach was the division's in-country R&R, or standdown, place for troopers who had been on line and who needed a break. Entire companies would either fly or truck down there to spend a couple of days just getting drunk and enjoying sports or simply lying on the beach. The place was open to all members of the division. The cadre of the 101st Admin Company used it to reward people who had done a good job. In fact, the captain had rewarded men who had served him well for a year with the bonus of serving as cadre at Eagle Beach for the remaining portion of their extension in Vietnam. In other words, if a man had ninety or more extra days to extend to ETS when his one-year tour was up, the captain could assign him as cadre to Eagle Beach. The job was similar to working for a resort hotel, except there were no tips.

The environs of Hue, on the way to Eagle Beach.

Wartime Vietnam was no cultural tour, but so much of the culture was still evident. My visit to the city of Hue on a special services tour fell through—no available transportation and just too much work to do. During the last few days of May I prevailed on Carpentier to let me out. The big perimeter alert had died down, and I was short and would never get another chance to go. Carpentier was almost apologetic, mumbling that he had never been able to spare me, although my work had certainly earned the break. I got a two-day in-country R&R to Eagle Beach. Another guy from the company and I boarded a small pickup truck with no cover on the back at about eight o'clock in the morning. Emerald green fields surrounded us. The Annam mountain chain rose from the fields. A white church, partially destroyed either by fire or by a bomb, rose from a small village closer by. The steeple was reminiscent of villages I had seen many times in the province of Quebec. Each village there, no matter how small, had a large church just like this one. This church seemed too big for the surrounding community, which consisted mainly of farms. A few miles later, another large church loomed, another vestige of French influence.

The truck skirted Hue, much to my disappointment, instead of going through the city. We were soon at the water's edge. From a distance we could see an island maybe a half-mile away. The driver dropped us off; he or someone from the admin company would pick us up in two days. At a small shack, a GI took care of one end of the landing craft shuttle. The vessel ran in and dropped its bow ramp while the engine shuddered in neutral. It carried medium-sized trucks and a number of personnel. About fifteen guys boarded the boat and stood in its hold. No one could see much unless he climbed up on the sides. Ten minutes later, we were on the hard-packed sand and a road leading inland. On both sides of the rise ahead were small houses and shops with Vietnamese milling about. I trudged along absorbing everything. It looked like a tiny fishing village in Maine, but the humidity and the absence of boulders in the sea ruined the illusion. The small porch of a cafe on my right had some tables and chairs where two very distinguished looking old men in colorful Vietnamese garb sat stoically. Their grayish white beards came to a point at their chins. They looked like pictures of old Chinese scholars. When their eyes finally met mine, I nodded my head respectfully. They solemnly nodded back and returned to their conversation and their drink. I would have liked to have asked them what they thought about the American Army in their country. What did they think of the South Vietnamese government? Did they think it could survive without U.S. help or intervention? Would the North Vietnamese eventually be the victors? Was the U.S. presence much different from that of the French? Did they fear China more than the North Vietnamese? I couldn't speak their language, and I assumed they spoke no English. Eagle Beach lay a half-mile ahead.

A crowd of children asked for money and tried to sell trinkets, cigarettes, and whatever. It was like Saigon, but there were not as many hawkers. They sort of mobbed the crowd when the ramp of the landing craft hit the sand. As I neared the top of the slope, one seven-year-old boy asked me if I wanted boom-boom, more specifically, did I want to boom-boom his sister.

"No boom-boom, thanks." None of the other guys bit, either. Out of curiosity, I later discovered the sister was only fourteen and learned, "She was good boom-boom because she has for long time do good boom-boom." Selling your sister's favors to the conquering army to make ends meet or just hold the family together was the common and desperate commerce of too many Vietnamese.

Outside the village, a heavily treed area began with cleared undergrowth to make a deeply shaded bower. Beyond this opened up the recreation compound of white buildings. A couple of GIs told us where to bunk down and they ran down the list of activities. A Vietnamese guide would take us fishing in the morning if we wished. The usual benign games like horseshoes and volleyball were available, and the beach was spectacular. Here, too, the crashing waves of a Maine beach were missing. Peeling off my boots and socks, I waded in to find the water as warm as a bathtub. Ten minutes later, I was into the gentle surf, then threw myself into one of the many beach chairs to stare at the water. From a bar off the beach I cadged a couple of bourbon and gingers and then fell back on the usual few beers.

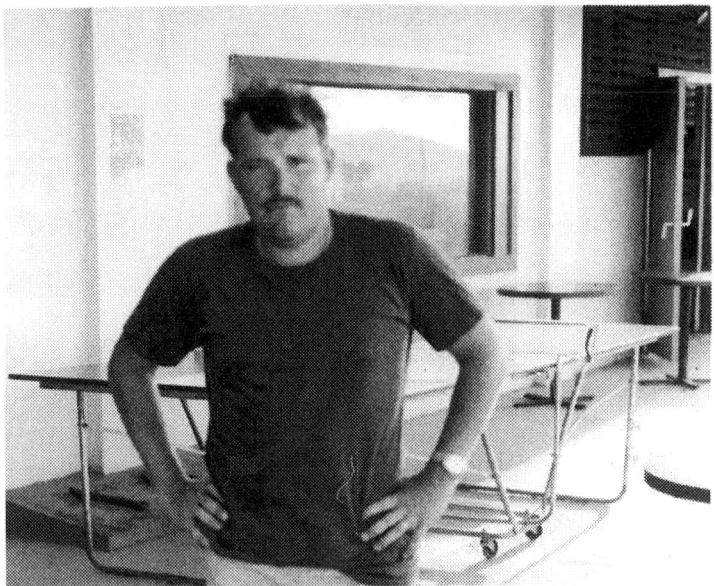

This GI enjoyed Eagle Beach.

In the afternoon, an infantry company pulled in ready to party. I recognized only one man in the company. He had been in my P-training class back at Bien Hoa, the redheaded guy the Black Hat made carry rocks in his sack because he had been screwing around. At least the guy had made it this far and should be winding up his tour. He would probably not head back to the boonies again because he was too short. The company hooted and howled through the night. There were no women in the camp, but it was only a half-mile to the village where the boy had offered up his sister.

That night, the local industry looked its most picturesque. All of the boats of this fishing community were out under the stars. A half-mile from shore, the boats all lined up against the horizon, their distinctive lanterns glowing in a line. They seemed to be maneuvering one huge net. I studied them for almost an hour before heading back to my bunk.

Vietnamese fishing vessels and their crews.

The next morning, two of us walked to a wharf where a Vietnamese fisherman picked us up to go fishing. He had the bait and rods. He took us around the waterway between the island and the mainland. We were out for about two hours, dropping lines where he thought it might be promising, but we caught nothing. If we had, we would most likely have thrown the fish back or given it to the fisherman. With only a bathing suit and a T-shirt on, I got sunburned but not badly enough to prevent me from going to the beach that afternoon to sip some beer, but with towels over my legs, head, and arms. The infantry left about midday, looking a little bedraggled. That night was quiet, and the fishermen's lanterns lit the horizon again. I thought of home and a new life with Nancy, less than two weeks away.

In the morning, we set out for the landing craft. In the village, a commotion began when an ARVN soldier dragged a huge snake, ten feet long and as thick as a truck tire in its middle, while a group of chattering teen-aged boys followed. The whole village started from their houses to view the spectacle. Within minutes the soldier had skinned the snake and had several big plastic bags of meat. He seemed very pleased, as did another Vietnamese who had the skin.

I wondered if he would make some article of clothing and sell it to a GI.

The return trip was uneventful, though we again bypassed Hue. I came away with thoughts about the future of Vietnam. I thought the beach could be developed into some type of resort area. People from all over the Pacific area could be potential tourists. They could combine a trip to the beach with one to the Imperial City. It certainly had possibilities.

I returned from this little interlude on May 30, five days short of my scheduled departure from the country. I got back to learn of one of the worst things that I can remember in Vietnam. Lonnie Hammond was a guy with a chip on his shoulder. I remembered him from Bien Hoa. He worked in the admin company back up the road. He used to come to see Johnny Bradley once in a while. Bradley was friendly with everyone, and I considered him a natural leader and a purveyor of a genuine good time. But Hammond was always getting into fights. He was shorter than average and maybe weighed 150 pounds. He had a mean streak, unlike Finney and Fergy who both liked to mix it up. Hammond always seemed a bit twisted, like he had something to prove. Once, in Bien Hoa, he appeared with a massive bandage around his face and nose. He told me that an MP had suckered him in a fight in the enlisted men's club. It was almost as if he was proud of his scuffle. He had signed up for three years and had returned for a second tour. He had applied for and had passed training for the Green Berets and was awaiting assignment to one of their units. I believe I had even seen him at Phu Bai with a Green Beret uniform. On guard duty one evening, he flat-out shot and killed a ten-year-old Vietnamese kid who came to the wire line during the twilight hours to sell the guys some pot. The kid always came and left the wire line much before dark. He was eventually a fixture known to everyone, even the dogs, which had ceased barking at him. The kid should have been warned off and threatened with arrest. I learned that he died instantly, but the sickening image of an unarmed and harmless ten-year-old dying like that never left me. This for me was an egregious act of cowardice, the worst thing I had heard about in Vietnam.

My intuitions about Hammond were well-grounded. He was no doubt trying to make himself a big man. More than likely he was bragging about his combat time while on leave at home between tours. No doubt, some of the people who knew him ragged him as usual and demanded to know how many gooks he had snuffed out, and he probably had to admit none. I later heard that nothing ever happened to him and that he got his assignment within the Green Berets. If that was true, I believed that he had got away with murder.

I had other things to think about. I was going home. I was done with work, and I started going around to say goodbye to some of the guys. I checked in to see Carpentier and thanked him for everything. I told Cliff Hobbins that I would call his folks to tell them that he was okay. He suggested that I stop in to see them, and I said that I would. I told Paul Vey, whom I had first met in the barracks at Bien Hoa, that I would call his wife to let her know that he was fine. Paul had extended for two months and was getting out in July.

I cleared the supply room on June 4, turning in, among other items, my M-16 rifle, bayonet with scabbard, helmet, helmet liner, flak jacket, poncho liner, gas mask, and rucksack. I also turned over to another guy in the hooch my key to the footlocker full of grenades. Sonny got the AK-47 rifle that Larry had given me. I wished I could have taken it home as a souvenir. Most of the guys of the Bien Hoa crew had left, including Larry, Jerry, Bradley, Eddie Warbeck, and Finney. Fergy had recently departed, but we had heard that he had not left Cam Ranh Bay. Rumor had it that he had been partying there for a week and had missed several flights home. He probably just wanted to get a lay of the land, among other things, before he returned. If he had a girlfriend at home, he had never mentioned her.

Macfee and Sonny were the only two remaining from the old gang. Charlton had extended, and he would be out in August, too. Kelly would also be leaving in late August. Macfee, Sonny, and Kelly came to say goodbye as I waited with my duffel bag and records for the truck to the airport. It was another scorching day. I shook hands with them and they wished me the best. Kelly said that he was trying for Ft. Dix or Ft. Monmouth, both in New Jersey, and he said that he would most likely get in touch with me. Macfee said he would try to stay in touch through Kelly if possible. We in the truck waved to them and traded insults as the truck pulled out of the area. My last glance at the Phu Bai compound at the gate gave me to know this was not a place I would miss, but these guys were my brothers forever. Knowing them had made it all so much more bearable.

Things moved after that. On June 5, a C-130 took me to Cam Ranh Bay and the final stage of my outprocessing from Vietnam. An hour and twenty minutes later I was in Cam Ranh, 175 miles from Phu Bai. Besides GIs, about twenty Vietnamese including women and children were on the flight. Wives and relatives of Vietnamese soldiers frequently flew standby on U.S. planes.

At Cam Ranh Bay, we were trucked to a compound near a beach. I turned in a set of orders and headed for a barracks and the chow hall. There would be several formations daily at which the names on the flight manifest would be read aloud. From there, we were to gather our belongings and proceed to a destination where we would be picked up and delivered to the airport and the freedom bird.

While there were no assigned duties at Cam Ranh Bay, there was some harassment. At the formations we had to spread out about arms length and help police the area. I guessed that several hundred guys were there. The guy at the speaker's stand preached at us that if we didn't pick up stuff, the patrolling sergeant would report this non-cooperation to the proper authority. The unspoken threat was that anyone could find his stay in Cam Ranh Bay extended. After 360 days in Nam, we had to put up with this shit again, heroes of the war bending down to pick up butts and anything else. No wonder so many GIs wanted to extend to get out of this harassment. I could see Fergy now saying, "Fuck this! I am going to find out more about this place, and I don't care if I am extended. What the fuck are you going to do to me anyhow, send me to Vietnam?"

The first evening formation was harrowing. During our departure roll call, the siren went off. Incoming! Everyone hit the dirt. My heart was in my mouth. Getting killed in the departure roll in Vietnam was at best unacceptable. Reaction was swift enough from the now prone masses. "Shit, I am too short for this shit. I don't need this anymore. Motherfuck, get off my fuckin' ass." I hadn't been under rocket fire since Bien Hoa, but the memory was fresh of those short-timers billeted across from my hooch at Bien Hoa who got nailed. We heard a couple of distant thumps, but soon our anxiety was relieved by the sirens ringing all clear. My name was not on the roster that time, but I found it on a couple of beers at the enlisted men's club.

At the next morning's roll call formation, I noticed a guy who looked familiar. As the group started policing the area I approached this guy, certain that I knew him from Niagara University. It was Bill Schwappacher, an undergraduate student who was on my floor for both his junior and senior years. I grabbed his shoulder from behind and he turned around with his fist cocked, expecting the sergeant patrolling the lines to be telling him to bend over and get to work. Fortunately, he recognized me before he let go.

"George! What the hell are you doing here?"

"Same to you, buddy!" I yelled. "What the hell are you doing here? He was a buck sergeant. He told me that his draft board starting getting on his case after he graduated in June 1968. He did not want to go immediately to graduate school and was drafted in the fall of 1968. He said that he had to extend about a month to ETS. He was in the infantry and in the Americal Division. The formation broke and we got together, conversed, ate, and drank a few beers for the duration of our time there. We talked about the people at Niagara whom we had seen in Vietnam. I told him that I had seen several of the lieutenants that had been commissioned at graduation in June 1968. He mentioned a few others whom he had seen. I was caught up with the coincidence of meeting Bill here in

Vietnam. At Niagara he would often come to my room to discuss the Vietnam war. We would question whether we would serve or not. Was the war right? Was Johnson a buffoon? Was Canada a viable option? And I recalled that we had both decided against that route. And here we were, the products of all that wasted thinking and energy. If we had known that we would both be sitting here waiting to go home from Vietnam, we could have gone on to another topic during those evenings at Niagara. No matter what we thought about the war, we had both done our time. Bill planned on law school when he returned. It was really great having him to talk to as we waited for our names to be called.

On the morning of the third day, as I stood beside Bill at formation, my name was called. He walked me back to the barracks where I had locked my duffel bag around my bed. There was a lot of thievery, mostly GIs stealing from other GIs, so if you had valuables like cameras, you had to carry them on you or suffer the consequences. In all my time in the barracks at Bien Hoa, Phu Bai, Ft. Dix, and Ft. Leonard Wood I had never had anything stolen. But I never gave anyone an easy opportunity and locked my things regularly in this transient area where people just didn't know one another. It was a marvelous opportunity for a guy who wanted to bring home a camera to find one sitting on a bunk with a duffel bag and just walk right out the door. That fellow could be gone on the next flight. Bill walked me to the transportation point.

It was a short trip to the airport where we waited for an hour or more. The freedom bird was already on the runway. The manifest was ready, and we filed out to the plane in an orderly fashion in an odd sort of introspective mood. We boarded the aircraft, a civilian contract plane that could tightly hold about two hundred people. The stewardesses were nice people in their mid-thirties or early forties, like the ones on the flight over a year ago. The cabin was hushed as the aircraft taxied and readied for takeoff. A rush down the runway and the bird vaulted upward to a roaring cheer from the homeward-bound troops. No matter how the people at home were treating Vietnam veterans, I could always say I was there and had survived. I had made it through an entire year and was coming home unscathed, more than enough to celebrate.

New anxiety unfolded in front of me. I was married to a woman I barely knew. I wondered how we would fare in our new life in the Army together. I was happy to be going home, but I would have been much happier if I were getting out of the service. Sleep eluded me over Guam, Hawaii, and Ft. Lewis, Washington. It was something like twenty hours, with short layovers allowing us to stretch our legs.

We landed about dawn on June 9, 1970, at Ft. Lewis, Washington, the continental United States. After balmy and humid Vietnam and the Pacific stopovers, the local temperature of 55 degrees shocked me from a sleepless daze. We couldn't believe how cold it was. The day finally delivered something in the low 70s. At the returnee center, we went through customs, with officials searching our duffel bags for pot and other contraband—like weapons. Then we went through various staging areas, where we were issued dress uniforms and other clothing that we had not seen in a year. The civilians waiting behind the different stages were nice enough, but they gave me a feeling of unease, as if they did not know whether to expect trouble from this crew. We were issued the ribbons we had earned in Vietnam. They had to explain how we were to put them on. I didn't even remember which side of the uniform they were supposed to go on, and asked for help. I didn't care if they were upside down, I just wanted to get home. ETS and DEROS people now split up. Naturally the ETS procedure would take longer, perhaps by several hours. But those of us being reassigned spent a bit less than two hours. We turned in a couple of copies of our orders and received some travel pay. We were permitted to eat, but I couldn't, with my mind fixed on the airport. Transportation didn't show for another twenty minutes.

An hour later, I was at the ticket reservation booth in the airport. I was able to get a one-stop flight to Bradley Field in Hartford, Connecticut. The stop was in Chicago. The plane was leaving right away, and as I entered the plane and neared my seat, I realized that

I had left my personnel and finance records at the ticket reservation counter. I asked the stewardess if I could race out and get my records, just as the door to the plane was closing. She told me that it was too late and that the records would be forwarded to the nearest Army installation. I thought, "yeah, right." I would be lucky to see those records in three months, if at all. I cursed myself privately. I was an adherent to the rule of "watch your things at all times in a public place." I had blown it. I could cut my own 201 file, but I didn't have my test scores. The finance records would be another problem. Without records, my pay wouldn't be straight until I got out of the service. I was exhausted. Maybe I had just hoped that I would be getting out of the Army anyhow.

I was the only GI on an uncrowded plane. These people had their own problems. If they knew there was a war on, it didn't seem to be their concern. Only hours before, I was somewhere else praying that a stray rocket wouldn't land near me. Now I was on a plane with people who were oblivious to the plight of so many young American men and women. This suddenly perturbed me: how a large element of the population was insensitive to the war; another part was antiwar, another segment anti-veteran, and the returning veteran was received either neutrally or looked upon as some foul tool of the administration's warmonger machine. A woman with a young baby a few rows up and across from me complained to the stewardess of a foul smell. She said it was if someone had chewed the end of a cigarette filter and let it burn. I lit another Winston and hardily bit down on the filter.

We landed in Chicago with nearly two hours to kill before the next plane. I anxiously called Nancy. I hadn't talked to her since leaving her at the airport in Hawaii two-and-a-half months before. She was so excited to hear from me. I told her I was in Chicago and would be in Hartford about 6:30 p.m. How great to hear her voice! We were about to start on a long journey together. I was coming back into her life and had no idea how we'd adjust to each other. We missed each other a lot, and that would help. As the plane taxied in at Bradley Field, I grew more anxious. A fleeting thought crossed my mind that I ought to go back to Vietnam to better prepare for this homecoming with my new wife. Maybe I could pick up my records along the way.

I walked off the plane eyeing all the window spaces in the terminal for a glimpse of her. We could spot each other now. The rest of the world disappeared, and we just stood there hugging each other. We couldn't let go while waiting for the baggage to roll in. We held hands all the way to the car. Nancy handed over the keys to her 1966 VW. The first thing we did was go to church to give thanks for our living through this and my coming home in one piece. She still worried about my being in uniform. We lit two candles, a strange bit of symbolism; I had not been inside a church since Hawaii, or for more than a year before that, yet it felt important to show my gratitude for making it through this ordeal.

We found a restaurant, but I don't remember eating. We just looked at each other and found ourselves again, chattering, laughing, and holding on. We rented a motel room somewhere near Hartford. I had survived Vietnam, I was home, and I was ecstatic with my beautiful wife. We were both marching to a new life, but that journey would take us through six more months of coping with the Army, a precarious enough beginning for a new marriage.

Chapter 8

The Final Challenge

That first night was memorable enough to conclude that I had made the correct decision to come home rather than to extend. The next morning Nancy and I shopped for a belt and a few shirts for me, and then we went to see her parents. They were welcoming and gracious. We were too much into ourselves to care about all the relatives prancing through the house. I was learning their names but couldn't keep them straight.

In a couple of days, we left on the four-hour trip to Portland, where my folks and older siblings were glad to see me. But there was no party to celebrate my return or our wedding. There was no tradition for such festivities in the family. After his three-year Army stint in Germany, my brother just wandered back in one day. Six hundred miles away at graduate school, I never heard of a celebration for him. He was now working in Florida. No one mentioned Vietnam. The war was still as unreal to my folks as it was for most Americans who didn't have to participate. I didn't see many of my school friends. I was just trying to adjust to coming home and to Nancy. I really didn't feel like seeing any of the guys, especially since I still had six more months to go before this curse was removed.

At Forest Gardens, the watering hole of my college days, Ralph Salmoni, the owner, lit up when he saw me in one piece, and ceremoniously set up a cold one on the bar. The haunt was still familiar, one of those places that had lived in my dreams over the last eighteen months, where I was free just to drink a beer and converse with someone on my own time.

After two days, we left for Agawam again where I had an appointment with an administrator in the Springfield school system. This decent fellow supported my attempt to shorten my stay in the Army by ninety days. He quizzed me about the war. It turned out that because of his age he had fallen between Korea and Vietnam. Probably in his early thirties, he was married and had two children. He had no full-time jobs then, but he wrote me a letter certifying that I was a fully qualified substitute teacher and that the Springfield school system would be glad to use me in that capacity. This testimonial became part of my application for an early-out.

When Nancy first wrote to me about her parents' intentions to have a reception for us, I thought that a few of her relatives would be invited to a modest buffet at their home. Her parents had in fact rented one of the finest places in the area, Chez Joseph, for a sit-down dinner. Nancy's mother, Helen, invited nearly two hundred people, including forty of my relatives and friends. While all this was in the works over the next two weeks, we headed for Canada, planning to return in time to help with the final arrangements.

Early one morning we headed north, but dropped off Route 91 in Vermont to enjoy some of the scenery. We stopped when the spirit moved us at roadside food stands and knickknack shops. Crossing the border, I waved my military ID. This was proof that I was not trying to escape the draft, though I still could have been going AWOL. I thought about the many opportunities I had had to make a run for it before and after I was drafted, but I was glad I had served most of my sentence and had survived. We were unable to find a room when we got to Montreal, so we backtracked to the outskirts of the city where we found a motel room. The next day, a travel agency found a room for us in a small but comfortable hotel in the city, convenient to many restaurants. Here we had a run-in with a uniformed parking attendant, who contrived to park Nancy's '66 VW too close to another car and bent the rear bumper brace, jamming the engine hatch shut. When I complained about this, the fellow admitted nothing, but managed to pull out the brace and straighten the bumper sufficiently so that I could open the hatch, though with difficulty. He probably wanted a tip for his efforts, but he got none from me. Hotel guests were not allowed to move their vehicles, and he was the only person moving the cars.

Montreal was chilly even in June. I was no doubt adjusting to northern temperatures. We went to "L'homme de Terre," or "Man and His World," an impressive remnant of Montreal's 1968 World's Fair exposition. When the wind was brisk, we needed jackets, but on nicer days, Nancy and I sipped wine at a sidewalk cafe and watched the people passing. What a difference from Vietnam. I savored it now.

In a few days, we stopped for Mass in Quebec City. Nancy nearly got the Spanish Inquisition after her. The still relatively new practice of placing the communion host in the recipient's hand instead of placing it directly on the tongue had not reached New England parishes, at least not the ones we knew. Having followed what everybody else was doing, Nancy extended her cupped hands for the host, but instead of placing it in her mouth, carried it back to her pew. I was behind her in the communion line, and the priest stopped everything to glare at this supposed desecration. The entire operation ceased as Nancy glided back to her seat and finally placed the host in her mouth. The priest's dumbstruck face made us think he feared Nancy was going to take the thing outside and stab it to death. Little things occupy little minds. I recalled how my Aunt Rita, a nun, gave me and my brothers and sisters unused but somehow flawed hosts to play with. This priest was so into his life as to be concerned whether or not someone properly consumed a flat bit of unleavened bread. Well, it was one way to keep his mind clear of important things in life. Inevitably, my thoughts turned again to Vietnam, where people were dying every day. This little issue seemed piddling by comparison. We left the church in one piece, without being drafted into the Canadian army.

We shortly reached Quebec and found a quaint motel a short distance from the old city. It looked quite the same as I had remembered it in the mid-1950s. The Chateau Frontenac, with its marvelous view of the St. Lawrence River, competed with the sight of the Plains of Abraham, where the British had defeated the French more than two hundred years ago. It all looked unchanged from the textbook drawing I had seen. For many of the French-speaking majority of Quebec Province, the war was not yet over. French President Charles de Gaulle visited Quebec in 1968 and stoked the smoldering local preoccupation with a separate, sovereign, all-French country. The old city was charming, and the food was excellent and inexpensive. On a buggy ride, the twenty-year-old French-speaking driver expressed his desire to live in America. America was the first country on the moon, so America is great. Why did I think that this guy was suckering me for a bigger tip? I told him that unless he wanted to go to Vietnam, he had better wait a couple of years until the war and the draft ended. If he went to America, he would be subject to the lottery and could end up in a country that was also formerly under French rule.

Back in Agawam for the reception, we found that Nancy's parents had really outdone themselves. Champagne flowed from fountains. My folks had come down from Maine, as did my aunts. Several of my friends from school had made it including Brud and Joyce Higgins. The best part about having gotten married in Hawaii was that we could stay for the entire reception and the party following it at Nancy's house. The party lasted until daybreak. My folks retired to a motel, and the younger crowd carried on until first light. My unattached brother Ron moved on the next door neighbor's unattached daughter. At dawn, Nancy's father, clad in his pajamas, got up for a drink of water and looked out the kitchen window to see Ron in fast embrace with the neighbor's daughter against a tree. I was alarmed about his reaction to my brother's creative activity, thinking he might be offended. Ken Foote turned to me with his usual wry smile, something I would often see again.

"Well, I see your brother is having a good time," he said. "And if we stay here long enough, we can watch him make his point." I had a pretty neat father-in-law.

We went to bed after sunup. My folks were coming over that morning for breakfast, but needless to say, we missed them. I think it was midafternoon before I remembered my name.

With the party over, we had to pack for my final assignment in the Army. I dreaded the thought of Ft. Dix less for myself, but more for Nancy. I could handle it and even finesse most of what the Army could throw at me now. But it would be a drab existence, and Nancy had no idea what she was getting into. She was a graduate of a private college accustomed to sojourns to the Caribbean islands. The Army sucked, and it sucked even worse for an enlisted man. I got back to arguing with myself over extending in Vietnam to end this curse. We were adjusting to married life. We had our disagreements in Montreal and Quebec. Nancy had a mind of her own. We weren't exactly basking in the delights of an extended honeymoon, but we loved each other, and Ft. Dix could do its worst.

Besides clothes, we packed as many small appliances as we could, including a toaster, an eggbeater, a hair drier, and so on, and a lot of the wedding gifts that we received. We crammed everything we could into the back seat and tiny trunk of Nancy's VW. We decided to leave a few days early, after my twenty-sixth birthday, not only to give us a chance to look around, but also to save the extra few days of leave for an extended weekend.

We arrived at Ft. Dix about noon, and after some driving around and asking for directions, located my reporting station, the Headquarters and Headquarters Company, 5th Brigade. In the orderly room, I told the clerk that I had my wife with me and wanted to get married quarters as quickly as possible.

Right there, the runaround started again. The Spec-4 estimated it would take about two weeks to meet my request. The Army ought to have informed me that it was better not to take your wife until you got quarters. Panic sets in at moments like these. All this meant we would have to live in a motel at my expense until I got quarters.

"Where's the housing office?" I demanded of the kid. The civilian running things there repeated the Spec-4's story, but he said he would try to get me quarters as soon as possible. I asked if there were temporary quarters for people awaiting housing. He gave me the number to a building and a slip of paper sanctioning my stay. We found the building and I went inside and asked a PFC for a room for myself and my wife. The rickety building was worse than any barracks I had ever seen in the stateside Army. I went upstairs to check out the room and was horrified. The door had no lock. Instead, on the inside of the doorjamb was a wooden swing catch that held the door shut, but the quarter-inch opening around the frame left no privacy at all. Two small bunks, three feet apart, sported the traditional Army "OD" (olive drab) blankets. The only facility was in the bathroom at the end of the hall, which I never bothered to look at. It would be criminal to subject Nancy to this. I wouldn't put a drunk in there overnight to sober up, though the place looked and smelled like it might have served that purpose.

Back in the car, I told Nancy we couldn't stay there. We went off base and rented a decent hotel room. Once inside, the tears ran. I wanted life to be better for us, but that first day, the impersonal Army treated us just like the usual shit. I was embarrassed to have Nancy see me dealt with like that. I just wanted so much more for us. The fact that I had been to Vietnam meant nothing to the Army. The place was full of returning veterans. Nancy was upbeat, convinced that we would get through this. I just wondered how long I would have to pay for a motel room out of my own funds on my Army shit wages. There was something wrong with the system. I knew that a Spec-5, no matter how many years in the Army, was authorized base housing.

The next day, I reported back to the company, and the staff sergeant tried to assign me to CQ. This onerous duty required a man to be up all night to take care of any eventuality, usually answering emergency phone calls. In the late 1960s, Ft. Dix had its share of antiwar protesters who would infiltrate barracks and cause a late-night ruckus. The CQ had to be alert to all this nonsense.

"No way!" I protested, "I have my wife outside, and we have no quarters. I'll take duties when I get settled." I felt like taking an M-16 and spraying this asshole, or just tying a Claymore to his head and make him beg for mercy. This shit was not unexpected in the Army, but the presence of my wife made me really jumpy. If the Army wanted me to do something now, it had better make damn sure that she had a roof over her head. I had earned *something* as a Spec-5 with Vietnam service. Also, I could see this guy had to be incompetent if he had to fill his duty roster with strays who happened by his office. His list ought to have been completed two or three weeks in advance, and I was the last guy in the door. I went to the billeting office again and saw the same civilian I had pleaded with earlier. A very decent fellow in contrast to the others so far, he treated me as if I were a customer in need. It was his job to find me housing, and he was concerned that I obtain it as soon as possible. Within two days he got me some on-base furnished quarters. It was a two-story, two-bedroom row house, with a large living room in front and a dining area towards the back and a small kitchen off of the dining area. The only bath was upstairs between the two bedrooms. The bedrooms were furnished with a large double bed and bureau. Downstairs was furnished with a couch and a couple of stuffed chairs and a table with four chairs. The entire row structure was a common, standardized construction style in the post-World War II Army when the need for a large standing force required that the services provide quarters for all its members, down to the lowest enlisted man. It wasn't the Hilton, but it wasn't a mosquito-infested bunker either. I know Nancy thought it could have been better, but it would do for six months. The rent and utilities for the place consumed my housing allotment. In my status as an E-5 with less than two years' service, the subtraction of the housing allotment would leave us $225 per month for living expenses. But at least I wasn't in the barracks and forced to endure inspections and other unpleasantries. Protocol also required that we get a phone. I really hadn't planned on that since I was going to be there for only six months and didn't want the additional expense. We could call home on a pay phone. The only other demand was to mow a certain small portion of the lawn in front of the house. For this I could borrow a lawn mower from the billeting supply office or warehouse.

The following day, I was assigned to Company A, Special Troops, a purely administrative assignment, but one that imposed on me additional duties such as guard duty and the CQ assignments. Every Wednesday we were obliged to check the company duty roster. I was told that about every third Saturday there would be a battalion assembly at which we were required to wear our dress greens and be subject to inspection.

My real job for the duration of my Army career was in the troop records of four basic training companies. These companies were staggered so that every three or four weeks the troops of one company would complete basic training and outprocess to other units. My office was in one of several long brick buildings with painted cement-block interior walls. The inner rooms were sparsely furnished with desks and file cabinets. There were no pictures. A loading dock ran the entire outside length of the building. It was as if these offices were meant to be warehouses, since they were shaped and modeled after the old, long wooden single-story buildings that had served the Army for forty or more years.

The last building in the row was the same one I had outprocessed from seventeen months earlier. It gave me a jolt to recall my outprocessing experience that followed basic training, my raging fever, the week I spent in the hospital, and missing goodbyes to my comrades in basic training. I soon found out why my shot records were lost. It was just sheer incompetence shot through with a willful and ever-present "I don't give a shit" attitude among the troops, especially the short-timers like me. It was part of my job to hand-carry records to this building when one of my companies completed basic training.

My boss was a ROTC second lieutenant about twenty-three years old. He was a nice guy, smart enough to keep out of the way of things and sensible enough not to harass the Vietnam returnees. When I got the lay of the land, I wasn't about to let a cherry-ass lieutenant screw with me anyhow. Walking around with that 101st Airborne patch, especially in a basic training area, gave me a semblance of respect. I wasn't cocky, but I knew they couldn't send me to Vietnam.

The lieutenant had not been overseas and still had about two years left on his sentence, so he was anticipating a Vietnam or some other overseas assignment. He was never very clear with me about whether he planned a military career, but I rather suspected that he would not. Later that autumn, he got an assignment to Vietnam, but he had his orders rescinded when he broke his ankle in a base touch-football game. He was out of work with his foot in a cast nearly eight weeks. After one week, he could have gotten around on a walking heel and crutches to serve in his simple desk job. But the Army believes that every soldier is an infantryman, so you are not fit for duty until you are able to double-time it for three miles with all your gear on. In contrast, the Army always used enlisted guys during their sick spells. At the end of my one-week stint in the hospital, I had to mop the floor and empty wastebaskets. This guy was home watching TV during his recovery.

My immediate boss was a short, heavy Spec-5. He had served three years without an overseas duty assignment, an amazing achievement in the 1967-1970 period, and he couldn't wait to get out. He showed me my job, which took about twenty minutes to digest. He was actually filling an E-6 position because he was supervising five other record clerks like me. He and his wife had everyone over to their back yard for a cookout one Saturday afternoon in July for a sort of farewell party for himself. I was disappointed to see him go.

In the adjoining office bay there was an E-6, Don Spiller. He was a beefy, twenty-seven-year-old Midwesterner with a college degree and now in the last few months of his four-year enlistment. Another rare E-6 without a Vietnam tour, he had worked for a couple of years at the Ralston Purina Company where he planned to return after his Army stint. Married with two children, Don often played with his young kids on the front lawn outside their three-bedroom place in our Army housing complex. His wife's parents lived in Longmeadow, Massachusetts, across the Connecticut River from Nancy's home in Agawam. We once rode to Massachusetts and back with Don and his wife and kids for a three-day weekend. He was a straight guy. He had signed up for four years in an intelligence MOS, but had backed out. He still owed the Army the enlistment time. He was lucky he wasn't assigned to the infantry instead of personnel.

Other guys worked with me for at least a few months. One, a good-looking young Italian kid from New York City, looked like Paul Anka and had a very cute wife. He had a year left and was trying desperately to avoid going to Nam. His desperation gave him a reputation among the rest of us. He tried to get assigned to the overseas replacement unit, which stayed stateside. He importuned people to write letters for him and harangued anyone who would listen to him about his case. It was perpetual whining about his assignment; he was just too frightened to go to Nam. Whenever he got orders, something dire would come up: a close family member died, then his cute wife had to have a serious operation, from which she recovered just fine. His orders would be rescinded. Then as he awaited a possible new assignment, we would have to listen to him all over again. When I got out of the Army, he had about ten months left and was still whining and writing letters.

If there was ever a guy who epitomized the attitude of the troops at Ft. Dix during the summer and fall of 1970, it was the Spec-4 who worked across from the whiner. This guy did everything he could to screw the system. At once a wiseass and an asshole, he was the antithesis of honest work, another three-year man who had not gone to Vietnam. He had signed up for clerical work and had been at Ft. Dix for the duration, a fairly good feat in itself. Of average height, he had a wide butt, much too big for a guy of twenty-two, and was supposedly in some kind of shape. He was always out of the office. How did he do this? He was in some type of Army band that had to practice several times a week, usually in the afternoon for a couple of hours. This meant he had to take off at about 11:30 in the morning to have his full lunch hour, or two, before band practice started at 2:00 p.m. Of course, it was impractical for him to return to work, which got out at five, because it would take twenty minutes to get there and he would therefore be able to work less than half an hour. So he just didn't bother to return to work. The nights that he had guard duty, he would leave an hour early so he could get home in plenty of time to get the proper nourishment before defending his nation. He would most often line up guard duty the night before he had band practice, so that besides the morning off for sleep allotted for guard duty, he would add the afternoon for band practice, even if that activity was canceled. He sometimes volunteered for special work around Company A Special Troops area. He would show up, report in, work for a few minutes, and then just disappear, only to return two hours later after the detail was completed. He would talk the lieutenant into allowing special emergency leave because his favorite grandmother had just died. If he could have gotten away with it, he would have claimed the death of his pet weasel to get time off. This guy was constantly at the dentist or some other medical appointment. He conveniently stretched a 10:00 a.m. appointment into a 2:00 o'clock one, or would sometimes not show up until the following morning. If asked, he would plead that the doctor was late, which delayed the appointment.

No one ever bothered to check on him. The officers knew that morale was poor. It wasn't a nice time to be in the military. The place was full of Vietnam returnees and other short-timers. The soldiers were not appreciated by society. Most would not be here and would never have joined the Army if they had had a choice. Even this asshole enlisted for three years so that he could keep his large butt out of the infantry and Vietnam. The same attitude infected even the officers, most of whom were in for a short time and looking toward their next, or final, assignment. They made a conscious effort to keep a low profile and avoid controversy. After all, many of them had recently been on a college campus. I personally didn't care about this guy's act, but his "greasing" affected our work.

We often bailed him out and just did his work. On several occasions, he would have a whole company of basic trainees outprocessing, and not only had he not prepared the records, he was gone. The whole company formed a line in front of his desk, trailing out the door and extending all the way down the loading dock. The records ought to have been at the outprocessing building the day before. Then outprocessing sent the whole company up to this guy's desk to get their individual records. I could have done nothing, but, as usual, I felt bad for all the trainees. For some of them it was their last day in basic training. They had estimated their time of departure and had already made plans about bus, train, and airplane transportation. They had perhaps even called someone about their arrival time. I had been in their position a few months ago. Why should they have to wait because of this scumbag? Indeed, this hurt the trainees, but it also damaged the already fragile morale of the working troops who took up the slack. We would have to go through the scumbag's files to find company records that were supposedly in alphabetical order and hand each trainee his records as he gave us his name. Sometimes we would grab a bunch of records and just call off individual names, and the men would come forward, take their records, and head for outprocessing. We could do the entire task in less than an hour, providing there was a record for everybody. Often we couldn't find a person's records, which meant the guy would be held over a day or two to while the search for them went on, or, if need be, we made a new set.

Sometimes, our recalcitrant would show up in the middle of our efforts and remained unapologetic. The Paul Anka-whiner would bitch to the asshole about doing his work for him, and the asshole would counter with a wiseass answer. Finally, after about the third time, listening to this, I mentioned that we were getting tired of doing his job for him. He started a tirade: "I don't give a goddamn. I don't give a shit about this place or this job. You ain't my boss, so I don't give a shit. I have a legitimate excuse, so you all can stick it." I was taken aback by his attitude, but not surprised. He was yelling at us for covering his ass. "We're *not* putting up with your shit anymore," I said in a low tone. The asshole started coming at me, but I stood my ground as he began pushing me. I knew I could take him, though he was bigger than I. I went for him, and he turned away and started to run. I grabbed him from behind and flung him to the floor, where he curled up with his arms over his head, whimpering, "Don't hit me, don't hit me." I decided not to hit the little pussy, so I let him up and I walked away. He was like a little kid who wanted to be stopped from doing something bad, but no one would oblige him. From then on, he was never late when one of his companies was outprocessing. I guess he got the message, and I wound up with a reputation for punching out the asshole. Spiller later told me the guy deserved everything he got. He was getting too pushy. When the incident happened, Don was only twelve feet away in the next bay. He didn't see anything, but the story grew as it spread. I never put my fist to any part of the guy's body.

There was no doubt that discipline was breaking down. Other short-timers would just take off from their jobs to do nothing but sit outside on the grass to catch a few rays. Some would feign sickness, go to their barracks, sleep a bit, and then come back. If no one missed them or said anything, they raised the ante and did it more often. Usually no one in authority spoke up for fear of rocking the boat. The negative attitude towards the Army and its oppressive system appeared worse at Ft. Dix than in Vietnam.

With the breakdown of morale came an underlying tension. Everyone that I knew hated the Army and just couldn't wait to get out. If there were some potential lifers or if someone possessed those tendencies, they were reluctant to come out of the closet—it was just too dangerous for them. Ft. Dix itself had been besieged by civilian protesters over the previous few months. The troops were constantly anxious that they might be called in to forcibly put down a protest that had gone too far. No one really wanted to be part of another Kent State affair, especially those returning from Vietnam. I certainly didn't want to have to shoot the same people whose interests and rights my government claimed I had just spent a year in Vietnam defending. This would be just too confusing.

There were moments when that underlying tension exploded. Perhaps the worst case I witnessed at Dix was between a white lieutenant and a black enlisted man. The incident took place near a parking lot. I don't know what the officer said to this man, since I was about twelve yards away, but something set him off. This skinny black guy ripped off his hat and wildly pummeled the lieutenant with both fists. I was silently cheering for the enlisted guy. I hated being harassed by anyone, especially a cherry-ass second lieutenant. I had despised these shit-for-brains second lieutenants parading around Newark airport telling the new trainees that their ribbons or nametags were out of place or upside down. It was a real true-life example of big brother watching you. The episode was over in seconds, with other guys intervening and yelling for a halt to it. I disappeared just to avoid being called as a witness; I didn't want to hurt the enlisted guy's case because clearly he was wrong for beating up the lieutenant. I never learned why the fight started or what the outcome was for the trooper. For me, the event showed where morale and discipline were in the U.S. Army during the summer of 1970. Luckily, not all the guys were stressed enough to take a swing at a second lieutenant.

Vietnam bred some real heroes, and I met one of these at Dix. One day a Spec-4 came to work in our bay for a brief period. I helped show him the ropes. He was a short, slight, twenty-one-year-old kid with blond hair who looked younger than his age. A quiet, good worker, he also had a story attached to him that gradually made the rounds. We learned one day that he had been put in for the Medal of Honor. It was like pulling rusty nails to get him to talk about it. He eventually related his tale, which absorbed me completely. With his twelve-man infantry squad, he slogged around for a whole day with no enemy contact. At dusk, they set up an ambush across a small clearing. Dug in, they waited for activity. About midnight they opened fire on a gaggle of figures in the dark, and they killed several outright. What they didn't know was that this wasn't a small foraging party. In seconds, all shit broke loose, seemingly from all sides. It was a big unit. Heavy mortar, machine-gun, and rifle rounds took their toll among the friendly troops. They fired wildly all around them. A massive enemy rush failed to break them. Bodies were all around him, including many of his own guys. In two hours, his unit was down to three. He was manning the machine gun and trying to work the radio when they repelled another attack that left him the only one unharmed. He radioed coordinates, but no help came. In the silence, he heard the enemy talking not far from his position. He had four hours until daylight. He was alone and scared, and yet he hung on to the M-60, awaiting one more assault amid bandoliers of M-60 ammunition. He had a couple of M-16s locked and loaded, and he had some hand grenades. The voices in the dark grew silent. The fatigue and tension took him to near unconsciousness even as first light broke. Bodies of his fellow soldiers and a few enemy dead lay around him. In the gathering dawn, a voice screamed out in English, "Holy shit! Look at this place." Several other squads from his company had finally come to the rescue of the ambushed team. Weak with relief, he stood up. Bodies littered the terrain. The gooks had moved many of their own comrades, but they couldn't possibly get them all. His company commander put him in for the nation's highest military honor. I don't think he ever got it, but he should have gotten at least a Silver Star.

He felt lucky to be alive. He told me how frightened he was and how he prayed for survival. Why hadn't the enemy found him, I asked. They had made a quick search for fallen comrades, but he had remained silent. They never made it to his position and must have thought that everyone was wiped out. They knew other American units would be in the area soon. To me this quiet young kid was a hero.

This was my first Army assignment with civilian employees, some of whom were better workers than others. In the last bay of my building was a thirty-five-year-old woman, the wife of a lieutenant colonel. This pleasant laborer in our vineyard, a graceful conversationalist, handled lost records and searched for a person to match the records when files were left over from outprocessing. She reconnected lost personnel files with their owners, but she still had two cabinets full of orphaned stuff while I was there. In contrast, a retired master sergeant handled AR and NG trainee records. Here was a man who knew how to play the system. He was not quite as bad as the asshole we had in our bay, but he came fairly close. He was a big man, but not a tough one. He was like a scared weasel, as if he knew you knew he was goofing off but he knew no one would do anything about it, perhaps because of his age. He didn't have extra duties to pull as a civilian, but he was always out for a doctor's appointment or some luncheon. Almost laughable were his stints on jury duty. I think he was a professional juror. He pulled six weeks of jury duty in the summer and another three weeks in the fall, and the possibility was good that he would be called back that winter for another session. In other words, he wasn't at work that much. He was getting the minimal jury pay per diem plus his regular pay. All the time he was on jury duty, he was accruing benefits on his regular civilian job: annual and sick leave, plus the time spent on jury counted towards his retirement. He was also receiving a retirement check for twenty-five years' service as a master sergeant. I have nothing against jury duty, but perhaps one several-day session every couple of years would be adequate. The state of New Jersey was sufficiently populated to allow more people a chance to serve in the process.

This left the Vietnam veterans and other short-timers cold. They had to pull extra duties like guard, CQ, and other menial details, including policing up the outside of buildings, while this guy was getting paid for his job while he was working another. Someone else had to do his job when he was absent. Finally the enlisted guys just refused. They just flat out told the lieutenant they were not going to do it. The lieutenant ended up doing it himself. If the system consistently treated you unfairly, then why not take advantage of it every chance you get? Why not grease off? Why not disappear? It did not make for an amiable working situation.

Even though this was not joy, our lives were not total drudgery. Nancy and I managed to have some fun during the summer. We went to the nearby beaches at Cape May, Wildwood, and Atlantic

City almost every weekend. The New Jersey beaches were fine but always crowded; nevertheless, we enjoyed ourselves. We would leave early in the morning, get to the beach about midmorning, and then head home in the afternoon. We went to Philadelphia for a play, "Jacques Brel Is Alive and Well and Living In Paris," at a theater in the round. We also visited the Liberty Bell and Independence Hall and wandered about other parts of the city. We ate at some restaurants and frequented a couple of bars near Trenton. Nancy's folks came for a few days, and we drove to Amish country in Lancaster, Pennsylvania. My folks came on another weekend. My dad told my brother how much I complained about the Army. Maybe after all this time, he figured out that I didn't like it. All these events were welcome interludes that made the stay at Ft. Dix more civilized and bearable. It wasn't like Vietnam, where practically every day was the same.

The local economy was typical of what grows up around a military base. It was just neat to get out of the area, especially away from the typical ugly towns of Wrightstown and New Egypt. Wrightstown had the bars, cleaners, pawnshop, and jewelers—everything to service the needs of transient and lonely GIs. Nancy really didn't like the place. She was alone during the days, although she had the car most of the time or whenever she wanted. If I had guard duty on a Friday night, Nancy would have everything packed, including coffee, to keep me from sleeping while we drove to the beach on Saturday morning. She just couldn't wait to get out of the house and off Ft. Dix.

Nancy was not the typical Army wife, either. Company A, Special Troops pulled police call at regular intervals. About thirty of us would line up at arm's length from one other and move out across an open field or a parking lot to pick up any trash or cigarette butts. One time as I policed a parking lot with a line of troops, Nancy waited for me in her car. For some reason, she thought it appropriate to empty her ashtray onto the parking lot. Why not use your time with something important? When we were released, I told her what I had been doing. I asked her if the pile of butts on the ground was her handiwork, and she said yes. We both just laughed. "I'll be out here tomorrow doing the same thing. Thanks a lot."

We had the usual family crises, things that seem hilarious years later. Nancy's mother Helen kept in close touch with her daughter. One day I received a call from Helen at work. She was clearly upset; she couldn't find her Nancy. Nancy had called home and happened to mention to her father that she wasn't feeling particularly well, and then she had gone to talk with the woman next door. Helen called back an hour or so later and couldn't reach Nancy. She was positive Nancy had passed out or that something drastic had happened to her. Helen called the base locator and hounded them until they found me. Without knowing anything about anything, I fell under the spell of the rolling situation. When I couldn't reach Nancy after several tries on the phone, I raced home to find her whole and healthy just coming out of the neighbor's house after having a cup of coffee. I asked Nancy to call her mother to let her know that she was all right. These were just some of the things I now had to endure because I was married.

One evening I came home to find a crowd of thirty people, including the military police, and an ambulance on our front lawn. I was happy to see that the focus of their attention was at another townhouse in the complex, and not mine. I got Nancy and we went outside. A foreign-born service wife had gotten furious at her husband and had actually stabbed him. Apparently the guy had been fooling around on her, and she crossed their difficult language barrier with a vengeance, about forty stitches' worth. He went back to his wife in a couple of days after some intimate discourse with some Army social workers. Fortunately, that was the only incident like that in my six-month stay there.

In mid-August, another disturbing phone call at work nearly launched me toward the base hospital. Nancy had been in an accident. My stomach hit the throat-line again as I managed to contain my lunch. A second call, this one from Nancy, revealed that she was being released from the hospital but that she had a headache from hitting her head on the windshield. Nancy was quite nauseous for a several days, but all X-rays indicated that there was no damage to her head. It wasn't Nancy's fault. An officer's wife forgot to look as she left the commissary for the street. She struck Nancy's car on the driver's side front-end.

The usual comedy for a serviceman ensued when I tried to settle on the damages. We contacted our insurance company and negotiated with a local body shop to fix the car in a week. My insurance company in Massachusetts asked if I would take some pictures of the car and the scene of the accident and try to get the accident report. This latter task I found unbelievable, so much so that I actually took notes on the ordeal.

I went to the MP office and asked for the report. I was told I couldn't see anything and was sent to the Staff Judge Advocate's Office. The SJA's Office had no record of the MP accident reports. An E-5 told me that the SJA Office handled only military vehicle reports, but he told me he would send for the report. I left my name and address with the E-5, who told me to expect a copy of the accident report in three to four days. Ten days later, with no report in hand, I called the SJA Office again; they had no record of having sent for the DA 19-68 traffic accident report. A Staff Sergeant Martinez asked me to call back in the afternoon because he had been there only two days. I called back in the afternoon, and Martinez really didn't know, so he turned me over to a Private Hughes, the guy I wanted to speak to in the first place. Hughes checked his files and found he had no record of having received the report. He told me that his files were only fragmentary at best. He reiterated what the E-5 had told me earlier, that the SJA Office handled reports for military vehicles. He suggested that I call the Provost Marshal to obtain the MP traffic accident report. I called a Sergeant Singer who referred me to the SJA Office again, even though I told him that office handles only military vehicle claims. I called Private Hughes at the SJA Office again, who checked again on procedure and kept me waiting for thirty minutes. Hughes told me to call a master sergeant at the Provost Marshal Office. This sergeant told me to come over to his office to see the operations sergeant and look at the military blotter. I drove to the Provost Marshal Office and saw the sergeant first class who was able to locate the blotter. The blotter stated very little, only that the accident had occurred; it had no indication as to who was at fault. He said I could have my insurance company or lawyer write to the SJA Office to obtain the official traffic accident report. He told me to send a copy to the Safety Office and one to the Provost Marshal Office. I told him that the SJA Office had searched several times for the elusive traffic report, but no one there could find it. I asked him, if a traffic accident report did exist, would it contain more information than the blotter? He of course didn't know. I memorized what the blotter had said and reported it to our insurance agent in Massachusetts. This was "Catch 22" revisited. After all my efforts, I had gotten nowhere, with the exception of having looked at the blotter. I got a helpless feeling. I kept reminding myself I was getting out soon.

I had run the gauntlet with this case and come up empty. Fear of the next step drove me on. Nancy was next to report to a local magistrate with the officer's wife or her representative. Our tentative plans were that Nancy would be back in school in Connecticut by the time the case was heard, and it would be inconvenient for her to appear. I basically feared a setup because it was a case between an enlisted man's wife and an officer's wife. Even though it was a civilian court, I was leery of the local court, located in an area for which the military provided many jobs and much sustenance. I called the judge and asked that Nancy be excused and that the insurance companies hash out the payments as to who was at fault. The judge excused us, and the matter was dropped.

In the meantime, an insurance agent from the officer's company came to our door telling us that his company would pay for all damages to the car and asked us to sign a paper affirming that there were no physical damages to report. Nancy was definitely not feeling well after the accident, so I would not sign any paper, and I told the guy to check with our insurance company. He was trying to get out quick and easy. They were worried about Nancy's injury. I wondered how many other GIs were treated this way. The insurance company figured that an enlisted guy couldn't be too bright and that he would sign off on anything. Our insurance company finally paid for our car repairs, which took another week. Presumably our company collected from the officer's company.

This business with the insurance hustle seemed to follow a pattern. Before Nancy and I had lived at Ft. Dix for two months, we must have had five salesmen at our door pushing various products. One guy was selling smoke detectors, a good idea, but I thought the Army ought to install them in all base housing at government expense, not the soldiers'. This salesman brought another E-5 along to help with the demonstration. That way he could get on base easier, or perhaps it was a gimmick to get me and everyone else to buy something that a fellow GI had bought. The E-5 lit a cigarette and blew smoke into the detector to make it sound off. I didn't buy it or anything else from anybody. One salesman wanted us to buy a membership in a nearby discount warehouse for $25. When I asked if it was nationwide or limited to New Jersey, the guy admitted it was only in New Jersey, but its one huge warehouse there would let me order by mail. I would be leaving in several weeks, so I didn't need it, and I wouldn't even think of throwing away that amount of money. The guy was insistent, and when he left with no sale, he referred to me as a hard man to deal with. I often wondered how many GIs he had signed up.

By late August, the time of reckoning for Nancy and me was drawing near. Would she or wouldn't she go back to school? She said she would stay with me if I wanted her to. I wanted her to stay, but not at the expense of her master's degree. Why should the draft ruin the plans of two people? I wanted her to get her degree because it would certainly be helpful to us in the future, when I went back to school. So there was no debate, she was going.

Before Nancy left, we ran through another ritual. One Sunday morning she took my picture throwing the "bird" in front of the re-up sign near the main gate at Ft. Dix. Sunday morning offered the best opportunity because there was just not that much traffic. We had to gauge the traffic flow so as not to be spotted and reported to the military police at the gate. The photo-op was by then standard with short-timers, and it was definitely representative of the time and of the sheer hatred of the Army and the system that put us there. My brother had done the same in Germany prior to getting out. Patriotism runs in our family. We were two brothers who as Americans supported their country as soldiers but never liked giving up their freedoms in the process. My "bird" was the mere gesture of what I thought of the oppressive system I was forced to join. Even that wouldn't have been too hard to swallow if all American men had an equal opportunity to relinquish their freedoms for two years.

One man's opinion.

At the end of August, the personnel records I had left in the Seattle airport showed up at the personnel center at Ft. Dix. I received a couple hundred dollars in back pay and was even more relieved now that no unfinished business would interfere with outprocessing for my early-out in October. I raced back and presented the money to Nancy for back-to-school clothes. "Is that all? What do you expect me to buy with that?" she said, incredulous.

For a good portion of the summer she had made her own clothes, and I really thought she would be happy with the money. Her comment was a stinging putdown for someone who had just felt that he was a hero. But there ain't no heroes in a marriage, as I was finding out. Shit, I could have taken the money and bought some cowboy boots and exotic beer.

On that cool note, we packed her things for the final trip home. She was happy to leave the place, but my male ego detected a certain exuberance at leaving me. When I left her on a Monday morning in early September 1970 to head back to Ft. Dix, she was crying and holding on to me because she didn't want me to go. Somehow, this made me feel good. But I still found it difficult to figure out her moods. There was no logic to them, and I direly needed logic. I told Nancy that I would come back on weekends and the present situation wouldn't last for too long because I was hopeful that my early-out would come through for 14 October.

I made so many 450-mile round trips from Ft. Dix to Agawam that I could practically do the journey in my sleep. From Ft. Dix to the New Jersey turnpike, to the Garden State Parkway to the Tappan Zee bridge, to the Saw Mill River Parkway to Route 684, to Interstate 84, to Danbury and Hartford, Connecticut, to Route 91 north at Hartford to Springfield, Massachusetts, and then Route 57 to Agawam. It took about a five hours, no matter how you cut it. The real trick was to time a departure from Dix to get through Hartford before the evening rush hour. In that neighborhood, two stoplights separated the connection between Interstate 84 and Route 91. Hit it wrong, and you were in traffic for more than half an hour. That short stretch of highway had to be the most archaic on the entire East Coast. A cloverleaf was finally added in the 1980s.

Two days after I left Nancy at Agawam, the horrible news hit announcing that my application for an early-out had been refused. A Major K. E. Donohue, whom I had never laid eyes on but who was supposedly my boss, disapproved the action by avowing that I was considered "essential to the mission of his assigned unit, therefore application is in direct contravention with paragraph 5-10, AR

301

635-200." "I cannot complete mission requirements without a replacement for Sp5 Watson from 14 October 70 to 5 January 71 despite the worthy basis for his request," the justification went on. It was nice to feel wanted like this, but there was no way I was indispensably essential to the mission. Was it because I was the only one working? There were enough greasers around that building to do my job twelve times over. I had already watched others released for the same reason. My case appeared to be one in which the Army tried to stop the hemorrhaging of manpower from a stateside activity. It took a lot of effort to get the required letters and paperwork completed for an early-out, and not many wanted to go through the motions, opting for a bored existence until their date came up by the impenetrable workings of Army policy. I couldn't make up the time. Any one of my colleagues of the moment just arrived from Vietnam could have replaced me.

Not wanting to cry in my beer, I was royally pissed, partly because it was my own fault. If I had really wanted to be out of the U.S. Army, I should have extended in Vietnam for sixty days. I would have been out in August. I wrote to Senators Margaret Chase Smith and Edmund Muskie from Maine and Senator Ted Kennedy from Massachusetts, pleading my case. I had been inducted into the Army in Maine, but I now claimed my residence in Massachusetts, so I thought I would cover all bases by contacting both states.

All three senators responded immediately with promises that they would contact the Army immediately and look into my situation. My hopes rose. About three weeks later, letters arrived from all three senators. It seemed they had turned the crank in Washington. Indeed, the Army still concluded I was "essential to the mission" and that my conduct to that point had been excellent. Each reply included a copy of a letter sent to them from A. F. Zoda, Chief, Congressional Affairs Division. Around the second week of October, I gave up on obtaining the early-out.

My next hope was for a Christmas drop. In the past, the Army had given people who were getting out of the Army around

Christmastime a fifteen- to twenty-day drop. Since my last day was January 5, I thought I just might qualify.

The Army never showed any vindictiveness for my letter-writing campaign. My new boss, a tall black E-6 operator who had been in for ten years and was a good guy, in fact, was interested in the letters and wanted a copy so he could use some of the language in the future. He merely wished me luck. He took his time off during the day, but not at crucial times. He was there when we needed him. He was there only about a month, and no one really replaced him. We just sort of floundered on our own.

I told Nancy of our misfortune, and she asked if I wanted her to leave school. I said absolutely not. I would work something out for us. I arranged to cover for the E-6 during the week, and he would let me leave at noon on Friday and not return until noon on Monday. This gave me a full weekend with Nancy. During the week, I even worked until 9:00 in the evening, when there was a big push to clean up all the excess records in coordination with the outprocessing center.

Throughout this time I hung on to the military housing. Technically, when Nancy went back to school I should have moved into the barracks, in order to let some married couple have the house. I kept the quarters against the possibility that Nancy would come down for a long weekend in the fall. The downside to this was that I lost my quarters allowance that would have been sent to Nancy, but she was living at home, so her expenses were few. She also had a Department of Veteran Affairs fellowship for her internship at the VA hospital in North Hampton, Massachusetts, which paid for her tuition, plus a stipend.

I earned yet another extended weekend with Nancy at considerable pain to myself. A routine checkup revealed that my wisdom teeth were impacted. Though they didn't bother me then, the military dentists had a special on that fall, and they had to come out eventually. Why not let the Army pay for that? I scheduled an appointment for a Thursday afternoon, and with the allotted twenty-four-hour bed rest, I could get a three-day weekend.

The doctor was from Jamaica and had a lilting British-Caribbean island accent. The human jaw was shrinking, he intoned, and the number of teeth we needed millennia ago for crunching our food was no longer as essential. Then he had a jackhammer inside my head. Fortunately the procedure didn't hurt, but he was covered in blood before I got out of the chair. His cheerful recitation about the evolution of the human jaw slackened and his brow broke out in sweat as he labored over the upper and lower teeth on one side. He stitched up the hole in my gums and handed me some pills. You must not drive when you take these, he warned. Outside, I hopped into the car and drove five hours to Agawam, without benefit of painkillers. One side of my face blew up like a baseball, and it hurt for days afterwards. Nancy's mom fed me her great tortellini soup, about all I could eat. What a deal! On another weekend I got the last two wisdom teeth removed.

At Dix I kept running into old friends and acquaintances. John Gorham was two years behind me in high school, a star basketball player and former caddie at the Portland Country Club. Jimmy Murphy, also a couple of years younger than I, was a star quarterback for Bates College. Jimmy was training as a military policeman and worried about his assignment to Vietnam. From my own experience, I could tell him that if he retained his MOS, he would not be humping the boonies; instead, he would be guarding a gate at a base camp or pulling some similar duty at a larger installation. He seemed relieved at my theory on his assignment. One day in mid-September, I got a call from Anthony Anglissano, a sometime contact in Vietnam. He was in the 101st Admin Company, but not with the in-and-out-processing team. We shared guard duty a couple of times, and he left Vietnam about a month after I did. He lost about seventy pounds there. I actually didn't recognize him once when I hadn't seen him for about five months. We exchanged a lot of news, and he told me that nothing had happened to Lonnie Hammond, who had blown away the kid at the wire in Vietnam. While I was talking to Anthony, I sat on the edge of an empty desk in front of his and remained there while we conversed. An E-6 in charge of that office came by and ordered me off the desk. "This isn't a barn," he declared. Anthony and I just looked at each other and shook our heads. I climbed down and asked Anthony when he was getting out. "February, and not soon enough," he said.

One evening, Anthony invited me for dinner with his wife. She was nice, and it was great to get out of my home for an evening. His big decision was whether or not he should go back to college to get his degree. He needed another year. His wife wanted him to go back, but he wasn't interested. He would take over his father's company someday and figured he didn't need the degree. I thought that it would be handy to have the degree, especially if the company ever went under. He would have something to fall back on, or at least he would have one-upmanship over someone who didn't have a degree. I thought his job would still be there in a year, but it would be difficult to go back to school after starting full-time work and perhaps a family. Hell, what was one more year of school? By the time I left Ft. Dix, he still hadn't made up his mind.

In mid-October, I picked up a ringing phone when a caller demanded, "Hey, you need an ID card, man?" Pat Kelly was stateside and stationed at Ft. Monmouth, thirty miles north of Dix, off the New Jersey turnpike. He was in touch with Macfee, also out of the Army since August. He said they were going to get together. Kelly had about ten months left in the Army. He wanted me to come up on a weekend.

On a rainy, dismal, but warm Sunday afternoon in late October, I got to Monmouth. It looked like monsoon season in Vietnam. At 2:00 in the afternoon I found Kelly just getting up in his barracks room. He looked like he had just gone to bed hungover and about to toss his cookies. Very slowly he revived enough to walk to the club. He wore his slippers. "Fuck it," he said. "Who gives a shit? What are they going to do, send me to Vietnam?" This was vintage Kelly. A few beers and some food seemed to wake him up. He had been there only six weeks, yet, like in Nam, everyone knew him. Everyone shouted his name as he went by, seeking his acknowledgment, like a godfather. Kelly was now a Vietnam vet and he had a lot of stories to tell. And he had an audience. He was already playing the maverick role. He talked about taking on the lifers, just like he did Plummer in Nam. We talked about Nam and some of the guys. He didn't know what he was going to do when he got out. We really couldn't get that close because there were too many guys sitting around the table talking with Kelly. I stayed for about three hours, then headed out. We called each other a couple of more times before I got out. I was glad I made the trip.

On other slow evenings, I hung around with some of the guys I worked with. Mel Merrill was from Maine. He had reenlisted once, but he saw his mistake and planned to get out when his second tour ended in two years. He was married but often caroused in the evenings with the guys. Once he and I and a couple of other guys went out for a lunch that ended around 9:00 in the evening. I carried him up to his apartment, knocked at his door, and handed him over to his wife, who was not delighted, to say the least. My head wasn't too fresh the next morning, either. Mel and I put on a comedy routine with Maine Down East accents for anyone listening. He knew his way around the base. He knew guys in supply and helped me trade in my two-year-old coat for a new one just before I got out. I worried about the stability of his marriage. His wife would periodically leave him to stay with her mother, and I really couldn't blame her. He was a treat to have around, especially when I was living alone. After his wife had left him and took his car, I gave Mel a ride to the Massachusetts Pike on several occasions when he went home to Maine. He hitchhiked from there.

Some of the guys got wind of my extra room and asked me if they could use it for a couple of nights while they waited to process out and after they had cleared their own housing and sent their families home. I was very agreeable and glad to provide the service. I had the room, so why not? Don Spiller was greatly appreciative, and I was happy to help him.

As a Spec-5, I pulled guard duty, but I did not actually have to stand outside and guard anything. I took guys to their posts in a truck and picked them up after their shifts. Otherwise, I stayed up with the officer on duty back at the guard quarters. We were usually up for two hours and down for two, but we never felt very rested. We also had special duty in support of the MPs. Two of us armed only with billy clubs sat in the back seat of a military car (not a police car) while the driver slowly maneuvered through specific base areas, but not including family housing. I just hoped I would never have to get out to break up a fight at a club. Our major job appeared to be looking for protesters sneaking onto the base and confronting military people. The Army feared riots on and off the base that might involve civilians and soldiers. The paranoia kept us all on edge, but it helped expedite the details. Most of the serious incidents occurred on the weekends, and fortunately, my three stints on duty came during the week.

Spec-5s didn't pull KP, either. Spec-4s and lower did that. But the way to get out of all duties was to pay someone to take your slot. One guy named Stanley Dancer constantly bought his way out of KP and guard duties. He was the son of the famous horse owner and trainer who produced one horse that I remembered, Dancer's Image. I saw Stanley pay someone $80 to assume his KP and guard duty. We had one married guy who looked forward to the easy money. I saw nothing wrong with it; at least he was doing his time. So many others didn't have to do anything for the war effort.

On Thanksgiving Eve, I drew guard duty, though I had planned to be in Massachusetts with Nancy. Mel took my car and would pick me up in the morning, Massachusetts-bound. The lieutenant in charge was a big black man over six feet tall, a really decent guy who did a lot of listening. That night, he spent untold hours listening to one of the three E-5s who was a West Point dropout. After three years at the Point, he left, but then he owed the Army three years as an enlisted man. He talked like an officer. It was as if he knew more than the ROTC lieutenant about being commissioned. Most of the time on guard detail was spent hearing this guy out. I wanted to gun him down with a reality check, but our tall ROTC lieutenant quietly listened to all he had to say. Merrill picked me up on the fly at six in the morning. I slept while he drove. At home with

Nancy for the holiday, I recalled my last Thanksgiving, when my family was the guys at Bien Hoa, all sweating the transfer to Phu Bai. Living without Nancy during the fall of 1970 was something I didn't want to do. I started running to stay in shape and shed pounds. I also kept reading in full anticipation of going back to my Ph.D. program for the fall semester of 1971.

If there was any pleasure in the Dix job, it was in helping out a new enlisted guy. Some guys who had spent eight weeks in basic training had barely two orders in their 201 files. Their company records showed they had completed training and then had orders to leave, but little else. Somehow they fell through cracks. A couple of times, guys came to me in tears because they just wanted to go home for a weekend before they shipped out to a new assignment. Their girlfriends and mothers were waiting for them. I did everything I could to get them out of there the same day. For one guy, I cut new records, drove him to his company to sign out, and dropped him off at the bus depot. Another eighteen-year-old kid from Chicopee, Massachusetts, really lucked out. He had no records and wanted to catch a five o'clock bus. I cut his records and asked him how much his bus was going to cost. The $17 bus ride would get him only to Springfield, Massachusetts, around midnight. If he could be ready by three o'clock, I told him, for ten bucks I'd take him right to his house about 8:00 o'clock that evening. Chicopee was about fifteen miles from Agawam. The kid's eyes really lit up. He would get more time with his girlfriend. He thanked me all the way to Chicopee.

In early December, I was talking so much about an early-out that I got stung by the local wise guys. An enlisted man handed me orders one day that listed my name with about four others. I was awarded a twenty-day early-out as part of the Army selective policy for a Christmas drop program. I would be getting out on December 15. I couldn't believe it! Quickly I scanned the bottom of the sheet only to discover lines to the effect that I had just received Christmas early-out hoax orders. Some of the guys in the orders branch had drawn them up. They looked authentic, and had I not read the hoax statement, I would have started packing. This little teaser made me all the more anxious to be out of uniform.

About three weeks before Christmas, I found out I drew guard duty on Christmas Eve, though I had carried it on Thanksgiving eve. With all the people in the company, I felt like holiday duties could be shared. No one person should have to work both holidays. I knew the E–6 would have trouble filling that date, though, with everyone trying to scramble home for Christmas. At this point, the situation could be turned to advantage. I told the E-6 I didn't think it was fair that I had guard duty on the eve of two successive major holidays. Without giving him a chance to interrupt, I hastened to add, "I realize your position, so let's make a deal. I will take this duty without complaint, but since I'm getting out on January 5th, you take me off the duty roster as of now." He bought it immediately, leaving me one more duty during my last thirty days in the Army. My plan was to have everything cleared by Christmas Eve so I could take off on Christmas Day and not show up until January 5, 1971, to outprocess. My house had to withstand inspection. It was clean, but forty bucks hired a company to guarantee that. It passed inspection on the twenty-second, and the next day I turned in the keys. I spent one night in a trailer owned by a friend of Merrill's.

In the meantime, Mel helped me clear the base and made sure that my 201 file and finance records would be at the outprocessing office on January 5. In the previous weeks I gradually transferred our household goods back to Nancy's place. In November, I had taken my final physical, including pissing into a jar to test for the presence of drugs. I stopped working about December 20 and spent some time in the PX looking for bargains and Christmas presents. The place was decorated for Christmas, and for the first time in two or three years I was getting into the spirit. I bought some things and had them gift wrapped by some officers' wives in a trailer outside. So on the evening of December 24, 1970, I performed my last official duty as a member of United States Army. Guard duty over, I drove Mel to Massachusetts and was home for Christmas dinner with Nancy. I had the next nine days off as uncharged leave. I had given myself an early-out.

There was still outprocessing. Nancy wanted to come with me for that, and I wanted her there to watch. She stood by me through the entire two-year ordeal. We left on January 4 and planned to stay in the same motel we stayed in when we arrived at Ft. Dix in July. January 4 was stormy—wet snow and sleet all the way to New Jersey. I started to get paranoid and wondered what I would do if I didn't make it to Dix the next day. At least they couldn't send me to Vietnam. The drive took about six hours. We ate at a restaurant. I was more nervous about the next day than I was about getting married. I had a lot of "what if's" going through my mind. I didn't sleep well and was up early. A quick breakfast, and I was back in the room to put my dress uniform on.

It stopped snowing by the time we went through the main gate. Even in the overcast I knew the way to the center, a mere block away from where I first arrived at Dix 729 days ago. Voices from the red speaker stand still echoed. "God, am I actually getting out?" I gave Nancy the keys so she could keep warm while she waited in the car for me to outprocess. My knees were weak as I got out of the car, and I was queasy. In the long, one-story building, I entered a large room where ten of us gathered. I had expected more. A captain thanked us for our service to our country. We were told to go to our VA representatives if we needed help. Some guy gave us a sales pitch offering ten copies of our DD Form 214 plus a small wallet-size laminated covered copy for $2. I bit on this, thinking it was a good price, especially the wallet copy.

Next, our names were called out to enter a smaller room. A couple of clerks sat next to several wheeled bins containing 201 files. I sat down. The clerk made some entries in my 201 file from the bin. Another clerk announced he couldn't find my finance records. Now what? I knew personnel had my once-lost finance records. I had seen them. The second clerk departed and returned in five harrowing minutes. He sat down to make a few more entries. About $700 in back salary and leave pay was coming. With my DD Form

214 in hand, I stopped at the cashier's cage for the money. I walked out the side door with a cluster of cab drivers asking if I wanted a ride to the airport. Other people were hawking things, but I paid no attention. In the parking lot, I hugged Nancy. Ralph Salmoni, from Forest Gardens, told me that on his first day in the Army, he saw other guys getting out. He cried. Well, I had just got out of the United States Army, and tears were blurring my vision.

EPILOGUE

In 1974 I earned a Ph.D. in Modern European History from The Catholic University of America in Washington, D.C., fulfilling my own promise not to let my two-year involuntary service interfere with my plans. I still had nightmares of the draft board snaring me again. In dreams, I would reach for my wallet-sized DD Form 214 and discover it gone. I could never find the ten extra copies of the form in my house. No one would listen to my pleas that I served my time. Huge, faceless people came to my house, and I struggled and attempted to pull away while yelling that I had already been drafted. They never spoke, but hauled me off kicking and screaming. I woke several times in a sweat, fumbling for my wallet and the laminated copy of the DD Form 214. The tensions coming with some deadline or the written comprehensive examinations for the doctoral degree were enough to bring this on. Gradually, this phenomenon left me, though I have no idea what to do with the more than 400 copies of my DD 214. I still carry my wallet copy, but as I get older the fine print becomes more difficult to read.

Vietnam syndrome is real. For a while, nights also brought irrational fears of sappers and ground fire. When I came back to live with Nancy and her folks for about six months following my release, I had this nagging feeling of being in an exposed position. I wanted to know who was pulling guard duty. Her folks' place was 350 feet from a main road with a wooded area behind it. I truly was nervous about being that much in the open. For two years in Vietnam, I felt safe, with the exception of the random rocket attack. I felt much safer living in an apartment that was on the second floor. I had a fear of outsiders when Nancy and I went camping, which we did very frequently in the early 1970s. I just couldn't sleep until almost first light. Sounds spooked me in a tent. Nancy slept soundly, since she knew I would be up. Once I heard bells ringing all night, and it nearly drove me crazy. I woke Nancy up to ask her if she heard them. She didn't hear a thing because she has poor hearing and often had ringing in her ears. After I spent a sleepless night, a park ranger next day remarked that the sounds of cowbells from a farm a few miles distant echoed off the mountains at night.

My fears of something out in the dark were borne out in the Great Smoky National Park. A huge black bear had broken out a window of a small Asian-made car in a neighboring campsite. Rangers chased the bear off and promised that after being driven out once, the animal wouldn't return the same night. We moved from the tent to my 1973 Chevrolet Impala station wagon anyway. The wagon was the last of the great American behemoths. I felt quite safe. Two hours later, the bear put his weight on the windows, rocking the car ominously. He couldn't get in, but left some paw prints as an autograph. There was no M-16 to comfort me. We left our tent and headed for a motel. Next morning we gathered our things. Ranger promises and the appearance of the bears reminded me of the many cadre warnings of the crack North Vietnamese Army units roaming the jungles near our position. The rangers did wear those funny Smokey the Bear hats, just as our drill instructors did. For a time, the sound of a siren sent chills through me. As I had on R&R in Hawaii, I woke up several times from a sound sleep before realizing where I was. All this died off within three years.

Strangely enough, I never dreamed about the rocket attacks, the bad nights on the berm line, and the misguided intelligence reports. They were clear and memorable in my conscious, mind but they never came to me in my dreams. I had long ago concluded that there were no real rear areas in Vietnam. The Viet Cong and the

North Vietnamese regulars could attack on any given night. At Bien Hoa, the path of a Viet Cong rocket was a matter of chance. We all lived with that.

I kept another promise to myself. I would never again count the days left before any event. If I was ever tempted to do so, I would leave the situation. The memory of those times, my efforts at getting an early-out for teaching or for Christmas, really make vivid how much I wanted to get out of the Army. The period from Columbus Day to Christmas 1971 now seems to flash by in an instant. Living it then was another matter.

As time passed, I thought more about the guys I served with and wondered what they were doing. Sometimes I would laugh spontaneously at the recollection of Macfee and Kelly or Bradley bantering back and forth in front of the inprocessing line: Fergy replays in my mind's eye throwing a rock on our tin roof hooch at Bien Hoa and yelling "Incoming!" The frantic Jerry hits the floor to whine at Larry, "Has the attack stopped yet?" Larry answers, "If I knew that I wouldn't be here." The memory continues of Bradley and me heading down the road wearing officers' insignia to cadge some extra food from the cook Bradley had befriended. Macfee and Kelly still sit on the jumble of material collected for the deck and screened porch, drinking beer and harassing the pot heads. I missed them. But those feelings were never as strong as the relief at making it back in good health.

At the time of the dedication of the Vietnam Memorial in Washington, D.C., Nancy and I headed for the hotels where I hoped to find someone I knew in the 101st Admin Company. Several hours of searching and visiting the packed suite of the 101st Airborne Division yielded no one I knew. The 101st Admin Company was such a small part of the whole airborne division. There were so many good men. Nancy and I often visit the Vietnam Memorial, although less now that we have three young children.

Indeed, many Americans were affected by that war. It was a time of turmoil for so many of us: assassinations, protests, sit-down strikes, people hating cops, and the police taking out their frustrations on youthful protesters. The violence of battlefields repeated itself at home. Even my father, who didn't know quite what to think of the antiwar movement, eventually refined a definite opinion. He flatly stated that his third son would not be going into the service, no matter what he had to do to prevent it. The silent majority had spoken. When my dad, about as patriotic as most Americans, said something as assertive as that, you can be sure that others felt that way, too. The war lasted too long to sustain the support of a democratic nation. When South Vietnam fell in 1975, there was not one iota of support for sending troops or money back into the morass to retrieve the situation. For any officeholder to propose that would have meant political suicide. The generation that fought the war has aged, and memories of it have dimmed. But the same feelings that characterized that period could again be resurrected by a new generation faced with a similar challenge. A volunteer force could not sustain a five- to ten-year war like the one in Vietnam. The draft would have to be reinstituted and there would be protests against it. "No more Vietnams" became the American political mantra of the late twentieth century.

This account describes what it was to be involved in the events of that time. I was one of those swallowed by the system and spit back out again two years later. Young Americans with an imperfect notion of what they have might well endure the Army's basic training. Eight weeks there would provide them with a clearer view of the freedoms they give up, but at the same time those they might be called on to fight for. Peoples' lives were disrupted and lost, veterans maimed for life both physically and mentally, and families forever changed. Many who evaded service by flight to Canada now struggle with their decisions. This memoir is a small contribution to preserving a bit of that era.

I will never forget it.

Glossary

Abn—Airborne
Admin—Administration
AG—Adjutant General
Airborne—Personnel and equipment air-dropped by parachute
Airmobile—Personnel and equipment landed by helicopter
AIT—Advanced Individual Training
AK-47—Russian- or Chinese-manufactured automatic weapon, the standard small arm of the Viet Cong or North Vietnamese forces.
Article 15—A portion of the Uniform Code of Military Justice; also a form of nonjudicial punishment
A-O—Area of Operations
APC—Armored Personnel Carrier
APO—Army Post Office
AR—U.S. Army Reserve
ARVN—The South Vietnamese Army or Army of the Republic of Vietnam
ASAP—As soon as possible
ASA—Army Security Agency
AWOL—Away without leave
Bde—Brigade
Berm or Berm line—A dirt mound of earth around fortifications—in this case, bunkers
Big Red 1—Nickname for the 1st Cavalry Division

Black Hats—Cadre that trained or reoriented new troops coming into the 101st Airborne Division

Boonies, Boondocks, Bush—The expressions used for the jungle and areas away from base camps or inhabited areas

C-7—Twin-engine Army and later Air Force cargo airplane built by de Havilland and named Caribou

C-130—Four-engine Air Force cargo aircraft built by Lockheed and named Hercules

Cav—Cavalry

Charlie—American designation for the enemy. The term derived from the military alphabet letters for Viet Cong—Victor Charlie.

Cherry—A term of reference designating any newly arrived person

CH-47—A large, twin-rotor cargo helicopter built by the Vertol Division of Boeing Aircraft and named Chinook.

Chopper—Any helicopter

Claymore—An antipersonnel mine

CO—Company

C.O.—Commanding Officer

Conex—A large metal container used for storing supplies. We used them as the inner linings of bunkers.

Cobra—The AH-1G attack helicopter

Cong—Shorthand reference to the Viet Cong; *see also* Charlie

CONUS—Continental United States

CQ—Charge of Quarters

DEROS—Date eligible for return from overseas. The estimated date when a person's tour would terminate

DI—Drill instructor

Div—Division

DMZ—Demilitarized Zone

Doughnut dollies—Red Cross girls

Dust-off—Nickname for medical evacuation helicopters

ER—Enlisted Reserve

ETS—Estimated time of separation (from the Armed Forces)

Fire base—Artillery firing position often secured by infantry

Firefight—Combat between opposing units or troop elements

VOICES FROM THE REAR

FNG—fuckin' new guy–a newly arrived person

Fougasse—Jerry-built defenses constructed of drums filled with any handy material or jellied gasoline and fitted with an explosive charge used defensively as a fixed fire weapon. Also spelled foggas.

Frag—To kill or attempt to kill persons in leadership positions, usually by a grenade

Free fire zone—Any area in which permission was not required prior to fire on targets

Freedom bird—A generic designation for any aircraft taking soldiers from Vietnam back to the United States.

Ghost—Taking off; doing nothing; greasing; or just plain fucking off.

GI—Army enlisted man; the term dates from World War II when it meant government issue.

Glad Bag—The man-size plastic bag used to contain dead bodies.

Gook—A term used for the Vietnamese enemy. Sometimes used as slang for any Vietnamese.

Gooney Bird—Nickname for the C-47 aircraft, a World War II vintage transport.

Greasing—Goofing off; taking off; doing nothing; or just plain fucking off.

Grunt—Term used to describe the infantryman in Vietnam. Ground pounder was another term for the infantryman

GT—General Test

Gunship—An armed helicopter

HQ—Headquarters

Hooch—Living quarters

Huey—Nickname for the UH-series helicopters

ID—Identification card

Incoming—Enemy mortar or rocket fire arriving in friendly positions.

Infusion—The transfer of personnel within or between commands to reduce the effects of the simultaneous departure of contingents of troops whose enlistment term was over in a unit.

In the field—In any forward combat area or in any area outside of a town or base camp.

Klick—GI term for kilometer.

KP—Kitchen police. Being assigned to kitchen duty.

LERP—Long-Range Reconnaissance Patrol; a LERP ration was freeze-dried food reconstituted in boiling in water.

Lifer—Career soldier

LP—Listening Post forward of the defensive perimeter

MACV—Military Assistance Command, Vietnam; pronounced Mac-Vee. The senior U.S. military headquarters in Vietnam.

MARS—Military Affiliate Radio System. Radio transmissions linking civilians in the United States with soldiers calling from Vietnam through use of Army Signal Corps apparatus and volunteer amateur radio operators in the states.

Medevac—Medical evacuation by helicopter.

MI—Military Intelligence

MOS—Military occupational specialty

MP—Military Police

NCO—Noncommissioned officer

NCOIC—Noncommissioned Officer in Charge

NG—National Guard

NVA—The North Vietnamese Army

OCS—Officer Candidate School

P's—Piasters, the Vietnamese currency unit.

P-38—Can opener for canned C-rations.

PCS—Permanent change of station

PFC—Private First Class

PRB—Personnel Records Branch

PSP—Pierced steel plank

Puff the Magic Dragon—A C-47 multi-gunned Air Force support aircraft.

Puking Buzzards—Slang term for the 101st Airborne Division derived from the design of its Screaming Eagle shoulder patch. *See also* Screaming Chickens.

Punji stake—A bamboo stake with a sharpened end placed in large numbers under water, along trails, at ambush sites where American troops might encounter them. Sometimes coated with animal dung to produce infection.

PT—Physical Training

PX—Post exchange

R&R—Rest and recuperation. Vacation taken during one's one-year tour in Vietnam.

RA—Regular Army

Recon—Reconnaissance

REMF—Rear Echelon Mother-Fucker

Rock 'n' roll—To put an M-16 rifle on full automatic fire.

ROKs (Rocks)—Republic of Korea soldiers and marines

ROTC—Reserve Officers Training Corps

RVN—Republic of Vietnam

Saigon tea—An "alcoholic" beverage consisting primarily of Coca-Cola.

Sappers—North Vietnamese Army or Viet Cong demolition assault troops.

Screaming Chickens—Nickname for the 101st Airborne Division taken from the eagle emblem of the divisional shoulder patch as well as a disparagement of the division motto, Screaming Eagles.

Seabees—Term for the U.S. Navy's Construction Battalions.

SFC—Sergeant First Class

Shake 'n' Bake—Sergeant who earned his rank quickly through NCO schools with little time in service.

Short or Short-timer—Individual with little time remaining in Vietnam.

Spec-4—Specialist 4th Class, an enlisted rank equivalent to a Corporal E-4

Spec-5—Specialist 5th Class, an enlisted rank equivalent to a Sergeant E-5

Stand-down—Period of rest and refitting in which a unit goes back to the rear to rest.

Starlight Scope—An image intensifier using reflected light from the stars or moon to identify targets.

Tet—Vietnamese Lunar New Year holiday period. The enemy's Tet offensives of 1968 and 1969 were the most prominent because of the enemy attacks.

USARV—United States Army in the Republic of Vietnam; pronounced You-Sar-Vee.

USO—United Service Organizations, the organization that provides a home away from home for enlisted persons in the armed services.

Yards—Montagnard soldiers usually trained, equipped, and led by the U.S. Army Special Forces with CIA assistance